CREATING EQUAL

CREATING EQUAL
My Fight Against Race Preferences

WARD CONNERLY

ENCOUNTER BOOKS

San Francisco

Published by Encounter Books, an activity of Encounter for Culture and Education, Inc., a nonprofit tax exempt corporation.

Encounter Books website address: www. encounterbooks.com

Manufactured in the United States of America

The paper used in this publication meets the minimum requirements of ANSI/NISO Z39.48-1992 (R 1997) *(Permanence of Paper)*.

Library of Congress Cataloging-in-Publication Data

Connerly, Ward, 1939–
    Creating equal : my fight against race preferences / Ward Connerly
    p. cm.
    Includes index.
    ISBN 1-8903554-04-X
    1. Connerly, Ward, 1939– 2. Afro-American political activists—Biography. 3. Political activists—United States—Biography. 4. University of California (system), Regents—Biography. 5. California—Race relations. 6. Race discrimination—California. 7. California—Politics and government—1951– 8. United States—Race relations. 9. Race discrimination—United States. 10. United States—Politics and government—1989– I. Title.

E185.97 C74 2000
305.896073'0092—dc21
[B]   99-088627

10 9 8 7 6 5 4 3 2 1

To my grandchildren, Brittany, Ryan and Katherine,
who will inherit the fruits of this struggle.

ONE

WAITING TO BE CHECKED through the White House security area on the afternoon of December 19, 1997, I thought about distances. Even though I am black and he is white, for instance, in many respects I felt quite close to the president I would soon be meeting. Both of us are from the South and from the generation that finally escaped the burdens of Southern history. Both of us are from painfully broken homes, and both were saved by powerful maternal figures who had, in their desperate struggles to keep from slipping further down in class, somehow managed to set us each on a course of achievement. And yet we were also very far apart, not because we were from different races, but because of our different views on race. And here the vast distance between us was filled with irony: Bill Clinton's views had led him to be praised by people such as novelist Toni Morrison as "our first black president," while mine had led people of Morrison's political outlook to attack me as "a white man with black skin."

I also had a sense of the distance we have traveled as a nation, of what a long and tortured road we have walked in our search for racial fairness and how, in recent times, we seemed to have doubled back again on our own tracks. A generation ago, when Martin

Luther King, Jr. stood in roughly the same spot I was standing in, waiting to be ushered into the Oval Office, he brought with him a simple and eloquent plea for equal treatment under the law for all Americans, black and white. The presidents he spoke with—John Kennedy and Lyndon Johnson, men who until reaching high office never really questioned the malicious racial myths of their day— agreed with him and committed the government to King's great cause. But now, after almost forty years of national introspection and determined civic and political action had made America a different country from what it had been, the situation was reversed. I had come to Washington to reaffirm King's message, but I knew I would be opposed by a president who, although he claimed that his views had been formed by the moral urgencies of the civil rights movement, nonetheless insisted that race mattered even more today than it did in the distant past, and that equality under the law was no longer enough.

I knew that I was here on this Friday afternoon, moreover, not because members of the Clinton administration had any particular enthusiasm for me or my ideas, but because I was potential political damage to be controlled. Indeed, if pushed, they probably would have agreed with black Florida Congresswoman Corinne Brown, who called me "a freak of nature," or with Jesse Jackson, who called me "strange fruit." They had certainly accepted the line being pushed by Jackson and other civil rights professionals—that in trying to destroy the legal and social monstrosity that went by the name of affirmative action, I was merely a black puppet representing the interests of reactionary whites. They wanted to believe that I was David Duke in black-face, and that in helping to pass California's Proposition 209 I had built a regressive and racist movement aiming to "resegregate" society.

I didn't think I could change their view of me, and I knew they couldn't change my view of the problem at hand. As I see it, the generation of black people before my own would do anything to get ahead—dig ditches, clean houses, whatever. No job was too small and no day too long. In a brief thirty years, programs such as welfare had changed all this, replacing these heroic efforts at self-betterment with a culture of dependency. And affirmative action was the kissing cousin of welfare, a seemingly humane social gesture that was actually quite diabolical in its consequences—not only causing racial conflict because of its inequities, but also validating blacks' fears of inferiority and reinforcing racial stereotypes. As the brilliant writer Shelby Steele once noted, affirmative action is *a white man's notion of what a black man wants*—at its best, a Tammany of grievances; at its worst, a form of racial racketeering.

Proposition 209 was anathema to the Clintonites precisely because it unmasked affirmative action for what it had become over the last quarter century: not a "subtle plus" that imperceptibly affirmed black ambition, but a regime of systematic race preferences that put the government back in the same discrimination business it had been in when Thurgood Marshall, as lead attorney in *Brown vs. Board of Education* in 1954, wrote, "Distinctions by race are so evil, so arbitrary and insidious that a state bound to defend the equal protection of the laws must not allow them in any public sphere."

By winning in California, we had shown that the people of this country now accepted these once-controversial sentiments as simple common sense; that they were right to say they smelled the rat of sophistry in formulations such as "we must take race into account to get beyond race"; and that they were ready once and for all to get beyond the numbers games and the obsession with group identity and make the vision once articulated by Martin Luther King and Thurgood Marshall and others a reality.

The Clintonites may have seen themselves as "progressives," but they were actually fighting a rearguard action. In an effort to placate the civil rights professionals who had staked their future on keeping this country color-conscious rather than color-blind, the president announced the formation of his Advisory Council on Race six months earlier, in June 1997, when he traveled to San Diego to give the graduation speech at the University of California campus there. The victory of Proposition 209 was still resonating in state and national politics at this time, and shortly before his trip was announced, I was informed that presidential aide Ann Lewis called the University of California to ask if I would be attending the ceremony in my capacity as a regent, and if so, where I would be sitting on the stage. Thinking of how often I'd been identified in the papers as the "black regent," I had to laugh: "Believe me, wherever it is, you won't have any trouble locating me." In fact, the president gave me a nod upon arriving at the ceremony, and just before he announced his new initiative—"a national dialogue on race"—he gave me a look that was either triumphant or concilia-tory, I wasn't sure which.

But the so-called "race panel" that the President named to coor-dinate this dialogue represented only one view: that America was racially more divided than it had ever been. American heroes like Michael Jordan, Colin Powell, and Oprah Winfrey might have almost iconic stature in our nation, and blacks might feel, as *Newsweek* recently pointed out after a massive sampling of black opinion, more confident and better positioned to succeed in America than ever before, but the president's men and women on the panel wouldn't take yes for an answer. They were still looking for—perhaps at some unconscious level hoping for—the fire next time.

Leaks that surfaced from the race panel's closed-door meetings in 1997 suggested that its deliberations had sometimes broken down into the bickering that might be expected from people who believe that group identification is everything. The eminent black historian John Hope Franklin, chairman of the panel, said that the group's work should focus exclusively on race, for instance, while Asian representative Angela Oh insisted that the issue wasn't just race, but ethnicity as well, an opinion seconded by Latino and American Indian groups. There was also the fate of affirmative action, of course, looming portentously in the background. Some members wanted to keep this inflammatory issue quiet because they knew that the majority of Americans opposed preferences, while others said that heading off the movement to kill affirmative action was exactly the reason the commission had been set up in the first place.

But the panel had become a problem for the administration less because of reports of infighting than because what was supposed to be a "national dialogue" when Clinton announced it in San Diego had never been more than a monologue, as the media had begun to point out with increasing insistence. Presidential Press Secretary Mike McCurry had inadvertently stoked the fires by saying that alternative points of view had not been represented because they would merely "frustrate" the panel's work. Then, during one of the panel's carefully choreographed town hall meetings in November, John Hope Franklin was asked if I was going to be invited to join the discussion. He responded unequivocally that I would have nothing to contribute.

Comments such as these had increased the murmuring in the press about whether the race cards this panel was dealing came from a stacked deck. This was no doubt why I was here, waiting to be ushered into the Oval Office. A couple of weeks earlier, I received a call from Deputy White House Chief of Staff Maria

Echaveste, asking if I'd be willing to meet with the president, along with others who had "different points of view" about race. I immediately said I would. I didn't know all the other participants, but those I did know were distinguished figures, as distinguished certainly as most of those appointed to the official race panel. Stephan and Abigail Thernstrom had recently published an important book, *America in Black and White*, which argued that despite the trendy gloom among some black intellectuals and activists, the prospects for black people had improved dramatically in the last thirty years and that the upswing had been caused by the 1964 Civil Rights Act and the opening of opportunity, not the later creation of a preference regime.* Linda Chavez had served as one of the nation's first female Hispanic cabinet officers during the Reagan administration. Congressman Charles Canady had co-authored the Dole-Canady bill, an effort to ban race preferences on a national level that fell victim to Presidential politics in 1996. Lynn Martin had served in the Bush administration, and Elaine Chao had been an outspoken critic of the way affirmative action programs penalized high-achieving Asian students. Thaddeus Garrett, former Chairman of the Howard University Board of Trustees, had made a reputation for himself as a "black Republican." Former New Jersey Governor Thomas Kean was attending as a representative of the race panel.

Jack Kemp and Congressman J.C. Watts had been invited but declined. Kemp, I was told, felt that being submerged in a group would diminish his reputation as a racial "healer," a reputation he

---

* This assertion, criticized at the time the Thernstroms published their book, was later confirmed by *Newsweek's* extensive polling data. When asked what they thought had caused the black economic and cultural renaissance in America, 46 percent of black respondents said black churches and another 41 percent credited black self-help. Affirmative action was well down on the list.

believed had survived the electoral debacle of 1996. Watts was genuinely conflicted about affirmative action, which he knew would be the central theme of the meeting with the president. I'd had long talks with J.C. and knew that his ambivalence about the issue came from negative personal experiences, which, he readily admitted, all the affirmative action in the world couldn't have prevented. For example, shortly after winning his first election to the Congress, J.C. was pulled over for "driving while black." On another occasion, one of his best white friends, in the course of a disturbingly candid discussion about race, blurted out that he doubted he would want a child of his to marry a child of J.C.'s. In Watts's fuzzy logic, the personal was political. "You're right morally," he had told me during one of our discussions, "but we're just not there yet."

＿ ＿

When we had all gathered at the security kiosk, a White House aide came out at precisely one o'clock to guide us to the Oval Office. On the way, Communications Director Ann Lewis popped out of an office to shake our hands. She was bubbly and pleasant, and seeing her for the first time in person, I was surprised by how much she resembled her brother, Congressman Barney Frank.

We waited in the outer office for a short time. Then, as we were about to go in, I saw the daughter of George Skelton, one of the *Los Angeles Times'* chief political writers. She told me she was now a White House employee, and I stopped to exchange a few words with her, which put me a few steps behind the others entering the Oval Office.

Al Gore greeted me impassively as I entered. The president was so genial, by contrast, that it occurred to me that they might be doing a bad cop/good cop act. "Ward, it's good to see you," he said, shaking my hand and clapping me on the shoulder at the same time. He eyed my tie, a new one with Christmas lights which my wife Ilene had bought for the occasion. "And I like your tie."

Clinton was a larger man than I expected. I was also struck by how at ease he was in the face of what could have been seen as an adversarial situation. He seemed to be quite happy, as if he were hosting a pleasant afternoon get-together of close friends. (His relaxation seemed all the more amazing to me months later when I found out that it was earlier on this very day that Vernon Jordan called with the news that almost unraveled his presidency—that Monica Lewinsky was going to be deposed by Paula Jones's lawyers.)

Clinton introduced Christopher Edley, the black legal scholar from Harvard who'd been assigned the task of writing the report eventually to be issued by the race panel, and Judith Winston, former White House aide now serving as executive director of the panel, who was seated with Edley near the rear wall. Members of our group sat on two facing sofas. At the head of this formation, the president and vice president sat next to each other in a pair of armchairs. Before I could choose a spot, the president patted the sofa and said, "Ward, sit right here next to me."

For the next hour I watched him out of the corner of my eye. He was like an accomplished actor, every gesture both entirely spontaneous and at the same time entirely artful. For example, when one or another of our group tangled with Al Gore, he chuckled and held his hands up like a friendly traffic cop, as if to say: *Hold it now, let's remember we're just having a friendly little discussion here.* Or on another occasion, he leaned forward, propped his elbows on his knees and rested his chin in his hands to concentrate on a new twist in the conversation, making his body language into a declarative sentence: *What you all are saying is so interesting that it has caused me to become pensive.*

The president didn't tell us that the meeting was being taped, or that the tape would later be transcribed into a rambling text filled with incomplete sentences and lost words marked as "inaudible." He started the meeting in his best town hall manner by saying that he looked forward to hearing from us on the question of whether race still mattered and was "still a problem." Then he looked my way and said, "And if you want to talk about affirmative action, I'm happy to do that," leaving the implication that this policy which his administration had pursued so fiercely was somehow a small issue I had chosen to make into a big deal.

I saw this posture for what it was: an almost mischievous challenge on the part of someone who, when he was helping found the Democratic Leadership Council, the centrist group that carried him to the White House, had strongly opposed quotas, and then, once in office, had embraced the affirmative action bureaucracy with the absolute seamlessness that marked his other radical shifts in opinion.

"We can't get to the problem of moving this nation forward," I replied, "unless we deal with the perception that there are preferences being given to people simply because they check a box and that benefits are being conferred on the basis of checking that box.... You said in June of this year that we need to have an honest dialogue. Well, up to this point, frankly, many of us think that the dialogue has been less than honest."

Then I stepped into an area I knew the President regarded as not open to discussion. "I think that choice, school choice, is one way to respond to it." I spoke about the desperate need for changes in testing, class size, and teacher quality, and about how those factors could affect minority students who are presently not qualifying for college and often not even finishing high school. "But even if we don't make these changes," I summed up, "there is never, in my view, a rationale for discriminating against someone on the basis of skin color, regardless of what we want the outcome to be. That's my perspective and I think it's a perspective that our nation has to hold true to."

Thaddeus Garrett spoke up immediately, trying to disagree without appearing to be contentious. Noting that he had worked "in this house under three Republican presidents," Garrett insisted that race still mattered greatly in America because of white "attitudes" and that we should ignore the subject of affirmative action and concentrate on prejudice. It was clear, less from what he said than from how he said it, that Garrett had been invited to the meeting as a sign that even black "conservatives" disagreed with my position.

Linda Chavez tried to bring the discussion back to the central question. "Affirmative action preferences," she told the president after Garrett had finished, "are part of this debate because there's a whole world of people out there who believe that they're wrong and that they send the wrong signal from government."

Clinton heard her out and then launched into a rambling speech about how the U.S. was now a multi-ethnic country that would have a "non-European" majority in the next fifty years. He ended by tenuously defending the "economic side" of affirmative action as a "sort of networking thing."

Then Abigail Thernstrom spoke up to disagree with Garrett's notion that white "attitudes" were causing a host of new racial problems. "A generation ago," she pointed out, "only one-fifth of white people said they had any black friends, and today 87 percent do… The rate of interracial dating has gone up spectacularly. The rate of interracial marriage, though low, has gone up dramatically. So I do think there is much more positive change than is generally thought." Abigail's calm demeanor was particularly impressive given the fact that Clinton had personally bushwhacked her with an unfair question on affirmative action when they appeared together in Akron at one of the race panel's town hall meetings earlier in the month.

As members of our group spoke in turn, the president continued to act as moderator, keeping the meeting going, smoothing the edges of potentially sharp points of contention. In his own commentary, he kept talking about race as if it were the perdurable fact of American life, the universal solvent that made all other important elements in our social life disappear. I had to check myself to keep from interrupting to tell him that if racism—however he chose to define it—were to disappear tomorrow, black students would still be getting poor test scores and black families would still be in crisis. I wanted to say that all his facile talk about "racism" was really less a description of a pathology than a form of sign language letting everyone know that he, like all right thinking individuals, felt bad about black misfortune. And that while this show-guilt might make people like him feel good about themselves, it always involved a bad bargain for black people. Whites who express such sentiments get to let themselves off the hook by tossing blacks a bone in the form of some entitlement—welfare, affirmative action, etc.—that blacks embrace not because it changes their lives for the better but because it symbolizes the righteousness of their suffering. But, as Shelby Steele and others have argued, nothing has really changed after this deal has been struck: blacks are still subordinate, their success determined not by their own independence and autonomy, but by their ability to manipulate white guilt. And these guilty whites are still the keepers of the souls of black folk.

As the meeting progressed, I tried to be alert for details, knowing that my wife Ilene, my kids, and others back home would be interested in hearing what had happened. One thing I noticed immediately was that the president seemed to be a Diet Coke junkie. Every few minutes an orderly would come in with a fresh can, taking away the previous one, which he had hardly touched. I also saw that Clinton genuinely relished intellectual combat and liked tossing abstractions around.

While the president seemed to be enjoying himself, Vice President Gore had sat stiff as his stereotype, his mouth compressed into a disapproving slit and his eyes boring holes into those of us whose ideas he found most distasteful. After remaining silent during the first part of the meeting, he finally spoke up, posing a loaded question to Congressman Canady about whether a community that was half black but with an all white police force wasn't in clear need of affirmative action in hiring.

Canady gave a thoughtful answer about how a community with a problem of this nature probably needed to consider a more creative solution than simply counting by numbers—community policing, for instance, or a requirement that police officers live where they worked.

Gore shook his head and made it clear that he strongly disagreed: "To say that there's nothing to the idea that a police force with black representatives would have an easier time relating to the black community is to deny the obvious."

Canady answered that hiring policemen of a certain race to appeal to the racial sensibilities of a part of the citizenry reminded him of the South during Jim Crow. Stephan Thernstrom added that the community he lived in outside Boston was almost all white. Did this mean that the city government should tell qualified blacks applying for the police force to "go back to Roxbury" and police their own? To Gore's assertion that affirmative action should be credited for much of the progress in integrating big city police forces, Lynn Martin countered that it was actually the end of formal and informal policies of discrimination in the 1960s that had accomplished this.

As Clinton continued to preside over the meandering discussion, it seemed to me that while he took pleasure in the words and in the personalities, it was the vice president who was more invested in the subject of race. I got the impression that Gore was waiting for another opening so that he could *testify* in the manner of so many liberals, and assert a vision of moral purity in front of those of us whose opinions he regarded as benighted. It always amazes me how easily well meaning liberals like the vice president work themselves into a lather defending a morally incoherent policy like affirmative action that benefits a handful of middle class blacks, but draw a blank when it comes to addressing the real racial problem in America: the underclass seething helplessly in the inner cities. This is a group of real people confronting real daily tragedies that won't be helped by rigging the entrance requirements at a few elite universities.

I was about ready to ask Gore about this when he suddenly kicked up the rhetoric another notch. Referring to my earlier statement, he said that he believed it was "naïve in the extreme to assert that there is no persistent vulnerability to prejudice rooted in human nature, prejudice based on race and ethnicity and other characteristics as well." When others in the room began to disagree, he demanded that they let him finish, and then he made it clear what he was driving at when he said, "I think that evil lies coiled in the human soul." The implication was clear: It is the solemn duty of government to root out that evil.

I found this view of human nature, of *American* human nature, truly shocking. After Lynn Martin and Congressman Canady finished disagreeing with Gore, I told him I found his comment "frightening." I looked at him squarely and said, "The presumption of our nation is that we're good people, that we can be fair, and that we will do the right thing."

Gore gave me a cold smile that didn't involve the eyes. I got the impression that he pitied me.

I noticed that staffers Christopher Edley and Judith Winston, both of whom had listened to Clinton with a polite but somewhat bored look on their faces, had snapped to attention when Gore spoke and were giving each other surreptitious looks of triumph. I half-expected them to pump their fists in a gesture of solidarity with the vice president as he spoke.

At this point, the president glanced at his watch and began to wrap things up by recounting some of his own political accomplishments, both in Arkansas and in Washington D.C. It was one of those squaring-the-circle semantic exercises with something for everybody for which Bill Clinton is justly famous. ("The reason I have consistently supported affirmative action programs—but I really have tried to change them and make them work—is not because—I basically think all that stuff you said is right. I am sick and tired of people telling me poor minority kids who live in desperate circumstances, they can't make it.")

After that, Thomas Kean spoke up to defend the work of the race panel and to assure all of us that our opinions would always be valued in its deliberations. The president then slowly rose, a signal that the meeting was finally over, although he gave the impression that if not for a heavy schedule he'd like to continue talking for hours. As the rest of us stood too, he said to me in a lowered voice: "Ward, you seem to be a student of public policy. I'd appreciate it if you would write me a memo about how you think we can keep the whole spectrum of opinion included in our race dialogue."

He seemed so absolutely sincere that I thought that maybe, just maybe, we had made a breakthrough after all—Abby Thernstrom had expressed such a hope at the end of the meeting—and that now there might actually be a genuine conversation about race after all. The president held my arm warmly with his left hand as we shook. Then, as I was going out the door, the strangest moment of the entire meeting occurred. Al Gore grabbed my hand too, but instead of shaking it, he ground my palm and fingers in his grip as hard as he could. I felt the cartilage compress and almost cried out in pain. I looked at the vice president and he stared back at me with a slight smile as we walked out.

When I got home, I immediately wrote the president the memo he'd asked for. I told him that if he could get past the divisive politics of affirmative action and put America on the road to color blindness instead of color consciousness, this would stand as his great legacy. I sent this memo to the White House by Federal Express. In the weeks to come, I waited for an answer. But I never heard from Bill Clinton again.

TWO

NOT LONG AGO, after I'd given a speech in Hartford, Connecticut, at a meeting sponsored by the National Conference on Christians and Jews, I saw a black man with a determined look on his face working his way toward me through the crowd. I steeled myself for another abrasive encounter of the kind I've come to expect over the past few years. But once this man reached me he stuck out his hand and said thoughtfully, "You know, I was thinking about some of the things you said tonight. It occurred to me that black people have just got to learn to lay down the burden. It's like we grew up carrying a bag filled with heavy weights on our shoulders. We just have to stop totin' that bag."

I agreed with him, of course, and I knew as well as he did exactly what was in this bag: weakness and guilt, anger, and self hatred. But laying down these burdens isn't easy, as I was reminded once again not long after this Connecticut meeting. I had just checked into the St. Francis hotel in San Francisco for the California Building Industry Association's annual Hall of Fame dinner, an event I was attending as master of ceremonies. After getting to my room, I realized that I'd left my briefcase in the car and started to go back to the hotel parking garage for it. As I was getting off the basement elevator, I ran into a couple of elderly white men who seemed a little disoriented. When they saw me, one of them said, "Excuse me, are you the man who unlocks the meeting room?"

I did an intellectual double-take and then, with my racial hackles rising, answered with as much irritation as I could pack into my voice: "No, I'm *not* the man who unlocks the rooms."

The two men shrank back and I walked on, fuming to myself about how racial profiling is practiced every day in subtle forms by people who would otherwise piously condemn it in state troopers working the New Jersey Turnpike. As I stalked toward the garage, it seemed that almost everything I had achieved in my life had been jeopardized by the comment that had just been made. But I didn't feel uplifted by my righteous anger. On the contrary, I felt crushed by it. It was a heavy burden, so heavy, in fact, that I stopped and stood there for a minute, sagging under its weight. Then I tried to see myself through the eyes of the two old men I'd just run into: someone who was black, yes, but more importantly, someone without luggage, striding purposefully out of the elevator as if on a mission, dressed in a semi-uniform of blazer and gray slacks.

I turned around and retraced my steps.

"What made you think I was the guy who unlocks the meeting rooms?" I asked when I caught up with them.

"You were dressed a little like a hotel employee, sir," the one who had spoken earlier said in a genuinely deferential way. "Believe me, I meant no insult."

"Well, I hope you'll forgive me for being abrupt," I said, and after a quick handshake I headed back to the garage, feeling immensely relieved.

I have made a commitment not to tote that bag of racial grievances, and I've made it more frequently than I'd like to admit because the status of victim is so seductive and so available to anyone with certain facial features or a certain cast to his skin. If we are to lay this burden down for good, it seems to me that we must be committed to letting go of racial classifications—not getting beyond race by taking race more into account, as Supreme Court Justice Harry Blackmun famously (and disastrously) advised, but just getting beyond race period, and realizing how absurd it is to use an outmoded nineteenth century concept, which never had any scientific basis, as a foundation for public policy in the twenty-first century.*

Yet, I also know that race is a scar in America. I first saw this scar at the beginning of my life in the segregated South. And now, over fifty years later as we enter the new millennium, I know it is still there—prominent, disfiguring, often inflamed—evidence of the terrible injuries of the past. Black people should not deny that this mark exists: it is part of our connection to America. But we should also resist all of those, black and white, who want to rip open that scar and make race a raw and angry wound that continues to define and divide us.

Left to their own devices, I believe, Americans will merge and melt into each other. This is as it should be. They crossed seemingly insurmountable racial barriers during slavery. (The saga of Thomas Jefferson and Sally Hemmings certainly demonstrates something more profound and human than a slave owner's sexual appetite.) Throughout our history, there has been a constant intermingling of people—even during the long apartheid of segregation and Jim Crow. Since they first set foot on the shores of the New World, blacks and whites haven't been able to keep their hands off

* In fact I was tempted to put quotation marks around the terms "black" and "white" every time I used them in this book, to indicate how imprecise I believe they are in defining those to whom they are applied.

each other. Usually the touch has been violent and hurtful, but sometimes it has been compassionate and even loving. It is malicious as well as unreasonable not to acknowledge that in our own time the conditions for anger have diminished and the conditions for connection have improved.

We all know the compelling statistics about the improvements in black life: increased social and vocational mobility, increased personal prestige and political power. But of all the positive data that have accumulated since the Civil Rights Act of 1964—that landmark moment when America finally decided to leave its racial past behind—the finding that gives me most hope is the recent survey showing that nearly 90 percent of all teenagers in America report having at least one close personal friend of another race. By any token, this is amazing progress, especially given the fact that less than a generation ago young blacks and whites were staring uncomprehendingly at each other through the invisible barbed wire of forced separation.

We still have much ground to cover before the scar of race fades from the face of America. But it seems to me that in the last few years we have finally reached a clearing after struggling through the tangled undergrowth of racial hostility for three centuries, and at last we can hope to one day see each other as individuals rather than categories.

This should be a cause for jubilation. But there are those who won't take yes for an answer; those who seem to find this good news disturbing and who claim, against all the evidence of history and reason, that racism is "worse than ever." These people seem to have a perverse stake in the continuation of what the Asian writer Eric Liu aptly terms "ethnosclerosis," a hardening of the walls between racial and ethnic groups. For some reason, they need to believe that Rosa Parks is still stuck in the back of the bus, even though we live in a time when Oprah is on a billboard on the side of the bus.

We have always had such rejectionists among us, of course. A generation ago they would most likely have been whites fighting a desperate and despicable rearguard action against individual rights. Today, however, it is often blacks—especially the civil rights professionals—who insist on the primacy of group membership and the irrelevance of individual achievement and aspiration.

I use this term "civil rights professionals" intentionally, for that's what they are now—an establishment, not a movement; a franchise that is more anxious to maintain its power than to take the risks that true leadership demands. These professionals never hesitate to mention Martin Luther King's name, but in my opinion they have defiled his legacy by suggesting that if he had lived this visionary leader would have stood with them at the racial pork barrel, ladling out preferences based on race and ethnic membership; that he, who wanted only that black children should be allowed to come to the starting line with whites, would have acquiesced in policies that place black children in a racial version of the Special Olympics.

In place of King's vision of black people competing successfully in the race of life if just given the chance, these professionals substituted the notion of blacks as hobbled runners, in Lyndon Johnson's unfortunate metaphor, who must be given a running start. They have fashioned a philosophy and worldview out of the notion first advanced by LBJ back in 1965: that in order to help blacks out of the ravine of history it is necessary to treat them not only equally but differently.

Of course what began as a temporary and provisional idea soon became a permanent demand. Special advantages were required, according to the civil rights professionals, not only because of the injustices of the past but because of the "institutional" racism of the present. The rationale for affirmative action continued to change over the years—from remedying the consequences of past discrimination to promoting "diversity"; to preemptively preventing future discrimination; and, most recently, to helping whites who require exposure to other racial and ethnic groups for their psychic well being. Clearly, affirmative action has hardened into an ideology in search of a justification.*

If the civil rights movement of Martin Luther King was clear about one thing, it was this: the person who was denied a job, admission to college, or the winning bid—because of his or her race—suffered a fundamental amputation of his rights and personhood. King saw us all as God's children and wanted the walls between us to come down. But the professionals who have appropriated his legacy are threatened by intermarriage, integration, and intimate contact between the races, knowing that such developments could put them out of business some day. They favor the little boxes on bureaucratic forms that indicate race, but they are against a box for "mixed race" because they realize that so many of us would check it and thus administer a setback to the racial spoils system they have created.

They want more race in American life rather than less. They want race to be a simple choice—a black or white choice—with none of the ambiguities that make identity such a complex reality. They have stripped their black followers of their autonomy and

* And also an ideology caught up in the laws of unintended consequences. In *Ending Affirmative Action,* Terry Eastland points out that the 1970 census listed 9 million Hispanics and 1.5 million Asians in the U.S., while by 1990 the figures had grown, because of immigration, to 20 million Hispanics and 7.2 million Asians. Since some fifty percent of these groups is now composed of immigrants and their children, and since both Hispanics and Asians are prime beneficiaries of affirmative action, this means that a program begun to remedy the past effects of U.S. history on one group now disproportionately benefits groups not disenfranchised by American history but whose history in America is just beginning.

made them dependent on whites to "level the playing field" for them. Far worse, they have made "racism" into the catch-all explanation that is invoked the minute this black dependency fails, as it inevitably must. These civil rights professionals don't want a single standard, a single set of qualifications, a single curriculum for all. Why? They dare not say it but it can only be because they believe deep down that blacks can't compete.

My wife Ilene is white. I have two racially mixed children and three grandchildren, two of whose bloodlines are even more mixed as a result of my son's marriage to a woman of half-Asian descent. So, my own personal experience tells me that the passageway to that place where all racial division ends goes directly through the human heart. This strikes me as an obvious fact, but racial consciousness has been burned so deeply into our worldview that some regard it as a debatable proposition. Not long ago, for instance, Mike Wallace came to California to interview Ilene and me for a segment of *60 Minutes*. During the interview, Wallace asked me if we had ever talked about our marriage with our children. He seemed shocked when I told him that race wasn't a big topic in our family. He implied that we were somehow disadvantaging the kids by not having such a discussion. But Ilene and I decided a long time ago to let our kids find their way in this world without toting the bag of race. They are lucky, of course, to have grown after the great achievements of the civil rights movement, which changed America's heart as much as its laws. But we have made sure that the central question for our children, since the moment they came into this world, has always been *who* are you, not *what* are you.

My life experiences tell me that this question—*who are you?*—is the most important one we can ask. And when we ignore the appeals to group identity and focus instead on individuals and their individual humanity, we are *creating equal*, and thereby inviting those principles present since the American founding to come inside our contemporary American home.

— —

Most people call me a black man. (My enemies deny this, of course: for them I'm an "Oreo"—black on the outside and white within.) In fact, I'm black in the same way that Tiger Woods and so many other Americans are black—by the "one-drop" rule used by yesterday's segregationists and today's racial ideologues. In my case, the formula has more or less equal elements of French Canadian, Choctaw, African, and Irish American. But just reciting the fractions doesn't tell who you are. It provides no insight about the richness of the life produced by the sum of the parts. Nor does it predict the fears you will have to face, the obstacles you will have to overcome, and the strengths you will discover along your journey. Nor does it remind you that your "race," whatever it may be, is the least interesting thing about you.

A journalist for the *New York Times* once described this bloodline of mine as being right out of a Faulkner novel. He was right. And with all these pigments swirling around in its background, my family, like the Compsons and all the other residents of Yoknapatapha County, was always trying to understand how the strands of DNA dangling down through history had created them, their individual selves. They had their share of guilty secrets and agonized over the consequences of bad blood, whatever its racial origin. But in their actions, they, like Faulkner's characters, treated race and other presumed borders between people as being far more permeable than the borders between counties or states or nations.

For reasons I'll indicate shortly, I don't know much about my father's family. I grew up with my mother's people and was part of their world. My maternal grandfather was Eli Soniea, a mixed-blood Cajun born in the tiny Louisiana town of Sulphur. As a young man, he moved to Lake Charles, and then, finally, settled in Leesville, not far from the Texas border. When he arrived in Leesville, it was a sleepy town that just sat there on an inert plane stretching up gradually into hazy foothills that looked like a movie backdrop.

Eli died in 1929. This was ten years before I was born, so I never knew him. But his photographs have always intrigued me. He was light skinned and had straight black hair; while far from severe, the face in these old snapshots usually had a serious look. I've been told that he spoke a pidgin French and English and was an ambitious man. By the time he married, he owned property and worked as a carpenter. He sometimes ran a construction gang and amassed enough money to buy some land and build a restaurant and bar in Leesville. He was evidently a no-nonsense type who didn't like anyone, especially his own kin, putting on airs.

According to one family story, Eli once had to leave his crew of carpenters to attend an appointment and put his son, my Uncle William, in charge while he was gone. When a worker who had prearranged with Eli to go to some church function started to leave, William, anxious to prove his authority, fired him on the spot. After Eli came back, he asked where the worker was.

"I fired the son of a bitch," Uncle Bill said.

"Well, then, you're fired too," Eli said, making him leave the job site as payment for his impertinence.

Eli's wife, my grandmother Mary Smith—or "Mom," as I always called her—came from a marriage between an Irish woman named Lula Orton and a Choctaw Indian named Smith. Lula Orton Smith, family rumor has it, didn't like dark-skinned people and treated her darker children differently from her lighter-skinned children. I'm not sure where Mom would have fit in this emotional scheme. Her Choctaw heritage was clearly evident in her high cheekbones and broad features, and in the bloom of her young womanhood she was sometimes referred to as an "Indian Princess." Mom was born and raised in Texas. She married Eli Soniea as a result of an "arrangement" brokered by her parents, after which he brought her to Louisiana.

In their early life together, the two of them lived in that part of Leesville known as "Dago Quarters" because of the large number of Italian immigrants. After Eli's early death—when I was growing up you didn't ask why or how someone died; the mere fact of it ended all discussion—Mary's only income was from the restaurant and bar he had built, which she leased to people who did good business with the servicemen from nearby Camp Polk Army Base. Because money was tight, she moved the family to a less expensive neighborhood, the predominantly black "Bartley Quarters."

The complexions of Mom's own six children ranged from light to dark. (William, for instance, was always known as "Red," because of his Indian look and coloring.) But whatever their exact coloration or facial characteristics, they all had "colored" on their birth certificates. In Louisiana in those days, being "colored" was not just a matter of blood; it was also a question of what neighborhood you lived in and what people you associated with. The word "colored" is on my own birth certificate.

The Sonieas' race problem came not only from whites but from blacks too. Leesville's social boundaries were reasonably porous, but if you were falling down through the cracks rather than moving up, as the Sonieas were doing after Eli died, you attracted notice. My grandmother often recalled how her new neighbors in Bartley Quarters called her and her children "high yellers," a term coined by white Southern racists but used with equal venom by blacks too. In fact, Mom's kids had so much trouble that officials tried to convince them to transfer out of the school to escape the racial animosity. This experience left some of my relatives with hard feelings that never really went away. During the campaign for California's Proposition 209, for instance, when I was being accused of selling out "my people," my Aunt Bert got annoyed one day and said, "When we lived back in Leesville, they didn't want to be our 'brothers and sisters' then. They didn't own us as 'their people' then, so why do they think we owe them something now because of skin color?"

My mother Grace, Bert's little sister, was the youngest of Mom's children. I wish I had more memories of her to describe. I can almost remember her sitting with my stepfather, William Parker, a smile of contentment on both their faces. But maybe that's an image I've stolen from the family photo album. In truth, there is only one image of her in the back of my mind: a face resting in satin in a casket. Old photographs show my mother as a beautiful woman with a full, exotic face. But she wasn't beautiful lying there with a waxy, preserved look, certainly not to a terrified four-year-old dragged up to the front of the church to pay his last respects. I still remember standing there looking at her with my cousin Ora holding my hand to keep me from bolting as the pandemonium of a Southern black funeral—women yelling, crying, fainting, and lying palsied on the floor—rose to a crescendo all around me. Because my mother was all dressed up in the casket, I asked Ora where she was going. Ora just said, "She's going away for a while." My mother's dead face haunted my dreams for years to come.

According to family legend, she died of a stroke. But I suspect that this claim was really just my family's way of explaining away something infinitely more complex. Two other facts about my mother's life may have had something to do with her early passing. First, she had been in a serious car accident that left her with a steel plate in her head. And secondly, she had been physically abused by my father.

I didn't find this out until I was in my fifties. The information accidentally escaped during a conversation with my Aunt Bert, who said, when the subject of my father came up, "You know, your Uncle Arthur once said, excuse the expression, 'That son of a bitch once took out a gun and shot at me!'"

I asked her why.

"Because Arthur told your father that if he ever beat your mother again he'd kill him, and your father got out a gun."

I guess Roy Connerly was what they called a "fancy man" back then. Judging from his photos, he was quite handsome, with light skin and a wicked smile, and a reputation as a gambler, a drinker, and a womanizer. He worked odd jobs, but from what I've been told, it seems that his real profession was chasing women. I have no image of him. But I've been told so many times about the day he got tired of me and my mother and turned us in at my grandmother's house that it has come to feel like my own legitimate memory.

He arrived there one afternoon with the two of us and with his girlfriend of the moment, a woman named Lucy. My Aunt Bert was watering the lawn when he walked into the yard.

"Is Miss Mary here?" my father asked.

Bert said yes.

"Go get her," he ordered.

Bert went in to get Mom, who appeared on the porch wiping her hands on her apron.

"I'm giving them back to you, Miss Mary," Roy said, gesturing at my sobbing mother and at me, the miserable child in her arms. "I want to be with Lucy."

Always composed in a crisis, Mom looked at him without visible emotion and said, "Thank you for bringing them."

A few days later he brought my red wagon over. Then Roy Connerly vanished from my life, and my mother married William Parker, who treated her decently for the year or so that they were together before her death.

Later on I learned that Roy Connerly eventually got rid of Lucy and, at the age of thirty-nine, entered a relationship with a fifteen-year-old girl named Clementine and had a couple of kids by her. But I heard nothing more than that for over fifty years. Then, just a couple of years ago, a writer doing a profile on me for the *New York Times* called one day.

"Are you sitting down?" he asked melodramatically.

I asked him what was up. He said that in his research about my background he had discovered that my father was still alive, eighty-four years old, and living in Leesville. The writer gave me his phone number.

I didn't do anything about it for a long time. Then, in the fall of 1998, I was invited to debate former Congressman William Gray at Tulane University in New Orleans. One of the things that made me accept was how close it was to Leesville. But I didn't actually decide to go there until after the speech. I came back to the hotel, rented a car and got directions from the concierge.

It was a four-hour drive in a dreary rain. It felt like a portentous moment: going to meet your maker. I warned myself not to surrender to counterfeit sentiment that would make a fool of both me and my father.

I stopped on the outskirts of town and called from a convenience store. My father's wife Clementine answered. I told her who I was and asked if I could come by and see him. There were muffled voices on the other end of the line, then she came back on and said that I should stay put and she'd send someone out to lead me to the house.

A few minutes later, a couple of young men in a beat-up blue car came by and motioned at me. I followed them down the main street and over railroad tracks to a run-down neighborhood of narrow houses and potholed roads without sidewalks.

We got out of the car and went into a tiny, shuttered house whose living room was illumined only by a small television set. I introduced myself to Clementine and we talked about my father for a minute or two. She emphasized that the man I was about to meet was very old, quite ill, and easily confused.

When she led me into the bedroom, I saw him, sunk down in the mattress, a bag of bones. His hands and feet were gnarled and knobby with arthritis, but in his face I saw my own reflection.

I bent over and touched his arm: "How are you feeling today?"

He looked up at me uncomprehendingly: "All right."

"You know who I am?"

Seeing that he was lost in his fog, Clementine said, "It's Billy," using my childhood nickname. He looked at her and then at me.

"Oh, Billy," the voice was thin and wavering. "How long you're staying?"

I told him I couldn't stay long.

There was an awkward silence as I waited for him to say something. But he just stared at me. We looked at each other for what seemed like a very long time. Finally, a lifetime's worth of questions came tumbling out.

"Did you ever care how I was doing?" I asked him.

"No," he replied uncertainly.

"Did you ever try and get in touch with me?"

"No," he looked at me blankly.

"Did you ever even care what happened to me?"

"No."

At this point Clementine intervened: "I don't even think he knows what you're asking."

I knew she was right. I stood there a moment, resigning myself to the situation. I would never get an explanation for his absence from my life. Then Joseph, one of the young men who'd guided me to the house and who I now realized was my half brother, beckoned me out of the room. In the hallway, he asked if I'd like to visit some of my other relatives living nearby. I said yes and he took me outside. We walked next door to a small, three-room house. He told me that this was where I had been born, a claim that I later learned was inaccurate. We then crossed the street to another narrow house. When we stepped up on the porch, an elderly woman was waiting for us. Joseph introduced her to me as my Aunt Ethel. She cordially invited us in.

Ethel had married my father's brother and served as the family's unofficial archivist and historian. As we talked, she asked if I knew anything about my father's family. I said no. Ethel showed me some photos. She told me that his mother, born in 1890, was named Fannie Self Conerly, and that they spelled it with one *n* then. She said that Fannie's mother was Sarah Ford Lovely, who had lived in the small town of Amacoco, Louisiana. She died at the age of 98, when I was a boy. This Sarah Lovely, my great grandmother, had been born a slave.

It was eerie. The day before, when I was debating William Gray at Tulane, one of our exchanges was about slavery. Gray said it was still very close to us today, and I had argued that it was actually quite far away. Now, this sudden disclosure of my own relationship with human bondage. Who was right?

After an hour with Aunt Ethel, I walked back to my father's house and sat for a while beside him as he moved fitfully in and out of a nap. After he woke, I stood and said to him, "I came back to say good-bye. I've got to be going. You take care of yourself."

"You too," he said. "You ever coming back this way again, Billy?"

I smiled and waved and left without answering and without asking him the one question that was still on my mind: Did you beat my mother like they say? Did you hasten her death and thus deprive me of both of you?

On the drive back to New Orleans I thought about my discoveries—this sickly old man who was my life's most intimate stranger; the fact that his blood and mine had once been owned by another human being. I felt subtly altered, but still the same. My father's gift to me, if you could call it that, was not some spurious deathbed bond or even the unexpected revelation about my own connection to slavery. It was an even more profound epiphany: it is not the life we're given, but the life we make of the life we're given that counts.

THREE

WE HEAR A LOT TODAY about black people living in dysfunctional families where the instinct for nurturing has been lost in a haze of crack smoke and welfare squalor. But this was not my experience fifty years ago and I think it is actually not the experience of very many blacks today. Like many black families then and now, when someone close to them was broken by life, my people gathered around and picked up the pieces. They did this without making a big deal of it, or strutting their sacrifice. It just came naturally. My father's desertion and my mother's death may have left me feeling as though my heart had been pulled out by the roots, but I never feared for one instant that I would lack for love, or that I wouldn't be taken care of.

My grandmother was my link between a damaged past and an unknown future. In her middle age, Mom was an energetic woman with a bronze complexion and freckled skin. We lived in a "shotgun" house—a long and narrow structure in which it was necessary to pass through the living room to get to the kitchen, and the kitchen to get to the bedroom. My most vivid memory of Leesville is of sitting on the front porch of this house whose thigh bone was connected to its knee bone, and of taking walks with Mom on airless summer afternoons so suffocatingly hot that some invisible hand seemed to be pressing down on us. When a sudden rain arrived it was as if the sky were sweating.

These images of Mom are very different from those presented by Barry Berak, the reporter who located my father in the course of doing the *New York Times* story about me. In his article, he quoted my father's wife Clementine, who claimed that Mom was a racist: "Roy was too black for the Sonieas. They were high-yellow people." Clementine implied that my grandmother was a bigot who had tried to break up Roy's marriage to my mother because of her own dislike of blacks. Berak then got in touch with other distant relatives of mine who opposed my stand against racial preferences and they, too, said that my politics were my inheritance from Mom's bigotry and self loathing.

Their accounts don't square with my own memories of my grandmother, whose house was always filled with dark-skinned black people from her church and other community organizations and who never in her life graded anybody by their melanin content. She was one of those strong women who, then and now, provide the emotional cement that keeps their families together. She was full of life and had a bubbling laugh. But it is also true that she didn't suffer fools lightly, whatever their color.

Mom was constantly teaching—addition and subtraction, elementary reading—to get me ready for school. She was afraid that my father would one day seek custody as capriciously as he had abandoned me, so she took steps to become my legal guardian. I remember little of this process except for the day when two social workers, a white man and a white woman, came to our house to talk to us. When they came through the front door, I ran into the kitchen and hid under the table, and they literally had to get down on their hands and knees and drag me out for an interview.

Even though she got custody, Mom kept worrying that Roy Connerly might try to snatch me. After fretting for several months, she finally called one of her daughters, my Aunt Bert, who was then living in Bremerton, Washington, and told her to come get me.

Aunt Bert came one night on the Greyhound. Then she and I got on the next Greyhound out of Leesville. It was 1944. I assume that we rode in the back of the bus, at least until we finally escaped from the magnetic field of bigotry that held the Deep South together at that time.

— —

Aunt Bert was married to James Louis. They were introduced to each other by a friend of my mother's when James was working as a deckhand on a ship based in New Orleans. But Mom had not allowed them to date until James came to the house and formally presented himself to her. Mom decided that he passed muster, and the courtship was allowed to go forward. After their marriage, they migrated to Bremerton because James had gotten a wartime job in the Puget Sound Naval Shipyard. He always said that the day he left the South was his personal emancipation proclamation, and the minute he got out of Louisiana he knew he was never going back.

At about six feet tall, James was a powerfully built man with a warm smile and a hearty laugh. He was far darker than my Aunt Bert, who was quite fair skinned. He was born in Mississippi and probably had almost as much Indian as African in him. His genealogy didn't really interest him, however. The only thing James wanted was for the world to respect him and regard him as a man, a word he pronounced with his down home accent as *mane*.

James loved to hunt and always kept hounds, even when he lived in the city. Before he moved up North to work, he hunted all through Louisiana. Bear, deer, possum, rabbit, coon—they were all fair game for him and his baying dogs. He loved country and western music, a taste I acquired from him, and he especially loved the blues. The blues tapped into a reservoir of pain and longing—but never self pity—that he kept well hidden from the world.

James never got past the fifth or sixth grade and was sensitive about his lack of education, especially when some of his Soniea in-laws patronized him. I remember my Uncle William once called him with jocular condescension "an ignorant son of a bitch" in the course of some argument. Uncle James immediately jumped up and said, "You ever say that again and I'll kick your ass." William was bigger, but he knew better than to tangle with James Louis.

James would take on anybody who threatened his family, his property, or his sense of his own worth. My Aunt Bert always worried that his pride would get him into trouble. I remember one night after I had just come to live with them in Bremerton, when her worst fears almost came true. She and I always went to pick James up every night after his shift at the shipyards ended. On this particular evening, he was getting into the car when a couple of white guys came by and made a derogatory remark. Worse yet, one of them banged his fist on the hood of the car. Suddenly, Uncle James grabbed a chain that he kept under the front seat and jumped out and started swinging. The next thing I knew the whites were on the ground cowering in terror and pain. James got back in the car with a satisfied look on his face and said, "I'll bet you by God they don't mess with me again."

On the way home, Aunt Bert reproached him: "James, you could have gotten us all killed!"

He shook his head stubbornly, "I'm not going to let that trash mess with me. A *mane* has got to defend himself!"

This was a lesson he taught me too. Once when I dragged myself home from school after getting whipped in a fight, he told me, "You don't defend yourself next time, Wardell, and you're going to get *two* ass-kickings—the one you get at school, and the one you get from me when you come home."

I first understood the power of racism by seeing the way it affected this proud man. In 1954, after we had been living on the West Coast for a few years, James' father died and we drove down to Nachez, Mississippi, for the funeral. By this time, I was a teenager, full of swagger that was linked in some way to my perception of James's manhood. On this trip it disturbed me to see him so nervous. As we went further into the deep South, he became increasingly quiet and agitated. We had to look long and hard to find a place to eat and when we finally located one, Aunt Bert always went to the side door while James and I remained in the car. Without being told, I knew the reason why Bert was the one to go: she was a woman, and more importantly, she was fairer skinned than James. If the restaurant was crowded or if a white diner voiced an objection to the presence of a "nigger," she would be turned away. But if business was slow she would return to the car with a sack of take-out food, which we shared as we drove deeper into what seemed to me, long before I'd heard of Joseph Conrad, a heart of darkness.

Bathrooms were also a problem on this trip. Whenever we found one that was not a segregated sty, James would say to me, "Boy, you better go now whether you got to or not. You never know when or where you'll find the next toilet." More often than not, we would pull off the main highway and relieve ourselves in a secluded field, James and Bert taking turns standing as sentinels beside the car to make sure that no one surprised us.

Whenever we pulled into a gas station to refuel, Aunt Bert counseled me to be quiet and keep my eyes straight ahead. She then turned to my uncle.

"Now James," she'd hiss at him when the attendant approached his window, "you watch your mouth!"

At one stop, a young white man who looked like he had too many recessive genes sauntered over to the driver's window, sneered down at James in a challenging way, and said, "Whatchu want, boy?"

This word "boy" caused James to flinch as if slapped. He paused for a minute and assessed the situation before replying: "Fill her up, please."

As the attendant walked to the pump, James rolled up the window and railed at Bert. "How old do I have to be before a little son of a bitch like that stops calling me a boy?"

"Hush up!" Bert gave him a hard stare. "You'll get us killed!"

As we were driving off, James was so angry he was almost in tears. "That little snot-nosed piece of trash! I'd give all that's in my pocket to get a chance to kick his ass! He called me *boy!* He wouldn't know a *mane* if he bumped right into one!"

I could sense that something had happened to James in that encounter. It was like he had suffered an invisible amputation. We drove on in silence for several hours afterwards as he tried to regain his normal size.

— —

James was the trailblazer in our extended family. Not long after I moved in with him and Aunt Bert in Bremerton, postwar spending cutbacks slowed the shipbuilding business. James heard about opportunities in California, and in 1947 he decided that we should try our luck there. He chose Sacramento because he'd heard that there was work there. After we had been there a year or two, some of my other aunts and uncles followed, settling near us in the working-class area of Del Paso Heights. My Aunt Cleo and Uncle Frank, for instance, rented a place four doors down from ours. After they were established, Mom left Louisana to join them. All together, we created a Leesville-in-the-North.

We had dinner together every Sunday afternoon. We were neighbors as well as family. Our petty quarrels and reconciliations were the equivalent of town news and gossip. Mom was the central figure and matriarch. She always made it clear to me that she was not only my grandmother but my legal guardian as well, and that I was living temporarily with James and Bert only on her sufferance. I saw her every day. She had a flock of chickens and I delivered the eggs she sold throughout the neighborhood. Members of her church, who called her "Sister Mary," were her best customers. They bought the eggs because they were fresh and reasonably priced and also because they wanted to support her industriousness.

One afternoon Mom came to our house with a look of jubilation on her face and told me that she had qualified for a home loan of $3,500 at Dolan's Lumber Company. "We're going to have our own house, baby."

I told her that I was happy where I was.

"This house will be ours," she cajoled. "We'll *own* it. You'll have your own room."

I shrugged sullenly. I couldn't tell her that I couldn't bear the thought of not living with my Uncle James. I felt safe with him. I felt protected by his strength and courage but also bolstered by his quiet dignity and the sense he conveyed of knowing right from wrong.

In the years I'd lived with him, James had tried to pass on his moral code to me in indirect ways. For instance, he got me a dog not only because he loved animals but also because he thought they taught their owners something. "If you don't feed old Shep," James would say, "that poor dog is going to die. You're all he's got." He based my allowance and the degree of personal freedom I got on how well I took care of Shep and did my other chores. Like other uneducated people, he was convinced that achievement in school was the key that unlocked one's future. "You go on and get yourself an education," he'd say when I complained about homework. "They can't take an education away from you." I didn't know who "they" were or why they would consider coming to take a little learning away from me, but I never questioned him.

In many respects, James Louis was the best man I ever knew. He was certainly the hardest working. As soon as we moved to Sacramento, he got a job working at the sawmill in a little company-owned town called Oregon House. It was just outside Grass Valley, in the Gold Country, about fifty miles north of Sacramento. I tagged along with him in the summer, after school was out. We would leave Sunday afternoon, just the two of us, in his old Model A. During the two hour drive, we listened to country music and James presented me with a philosophy of life. I can still hear him holding forth on the importance of pride, hard work, and personal responsibility. This last item was of particular concern to James. He always said that you could tell a responsible person by whether he shined his shoes, took care of his car, mowed his lawn, and looked after his dog. James's shoes were always gleaming; his car, however old it might have been, was always spotless; and his dogs loved him unconditionally.

I can still see James standing on top of these ten-foot lumber piles up at Oregon House. He is dressed in overalls, in the middle of summer, to keep from getting splinters from the green lumber. The sweat is pouring off him. He has a big grin on his face as he drags a red bandanna out of his back pocket to mop his forehead. He is a figure of power and confidence, and he embodies what the great novelist Ralph Ellison once called "heroic optimism," the belief that a combination of work, endurance, and the ultimate goodness of this country would bring him—and all of us—through.

They worked in twos at the sawmill and by the time the sun was at its zenith, his partner would beg him, "Come on, James. Let's stop and rest."

"Naw," James would say as he looked down at me with a wink, "I gotta get that boy there some shoes."

Finally, after his coworker had badgered him for an hour or so, he'd pause for a minute and dig into his pocket. He'd toss me down a dime and get the other black workers on the crew to do the same thing. I'd gather up the money and go to the store to get them all Nehi sodas. James Louis would chug-a-lug his without taking the bottle away from his lips so he could quickly get back to work. When the workers threw down the empty bottles I gathered them up and took them back to the store. The penny deposit on each of them was mine to keep.

I helped Uncle James cook our meals after work. After eating, we'd sit outside enjoying the stillness of the night and the country and western music twanging softly on the radio. Some of the other workers would come by and I'd listen in as James talked with them. The cadences were as important as the words themselves. It was the easy, satisfied talk of men who'd put in a good day's work and felt, however intangibly, that by doing this they'd put a thumbprint on their world.

I have often thought of these men in the years since, when I have heard honest wages being degraded as "chump change" and honest work devalued as "slavin' for the man." James would not have put up with such talk. For him, work meant empowerment and independence, not subservience; he regarded it as an exercise of his freedom.

After the sawmills went out of business, James stayed around Sacramento and did construction jobs or dug ditches. There was never a day in his life he didn't work. He never got a job with a title, but he was always the best worker wherever he was, and the white foremen always acknowledged this by padding his paycheck a little bit.

— —

I wanted to be like James and looked for part-time work myself. By this time, Mom had started building her house on the lot she'd bought in Del Paso Heights. The lot was at the corner of Grand Avenue and Branch Street, six blocks from where James and Bert lived. She'd hired a local black carpenter named Herbert Powell who brought me on as his helper at fifty cents an hour.

Mr. Powell was proud of his craftsmanship and disturbed by the fact that he had so much trouble getting work from other black people. "They think that because I'm a black man I'm no good at what I do," he'd grumble through the nails he kept in his mouth while hammering. "Now, ain't that a hell of a thing?"

Every day after school and Saturdays, I worked with Mr. Powell at the building site, hauling materials, straightening bent nails so they could be reused, and doing clean up. I wanted James to be proud of me, and I think he was, although he also was a little concerned that perhaps I was doing too much.

One Saturday after I'd been working part time on the house for weeks without break, I decided to go to a movie with my friends. (Saturday matinees were my passion as a boy. I identified with cowboy heroes like Gene Autry, Roy Rogers, and, especially, the Lone Ranger, even though I knew I looked far more like Tonto.) My Uncle William, who participated in the building effort on weekends, ordered me to stay on the job and help him. I had already resigned myself to another day of drudgery when James came by to check things out.

"I thought you were going to the show today," he said.

"Uncle Bill wants me to stay and help," I answered.

James looked at me for a minute and then got William's attention.

"The boy's going to the show," he said.

William started to argue.

"No, the boy's going to the movies," James repeated. "He's worked all week and he needs to spend some time with his friends. I'm telling him to go, and if you don't like it, then let's you and me settle it."

William heard the edge in his voice and didn't pursue the matter any further. I ran off feeling like I'd made a jail break.

— —

I stayed close to my Uncle James all his life. Many years later, when Proposition 209 was being fought out, he was in his eighties and finally retired in the Sacramento suburb of Rio Linda, where he and Aunt Bert bought a house. James got caught up in the excitement of the campaign and the fact that I was in the middle of it. I'm not sure he understood all the intricate details of 209, but I know he was clear on its core issues because they were also at the core of his life: the importance of earning respect and not taking handouts; of being a *mane* and taking care of yourself and your family; and knowing that your achievements are really yours because you've earned them.

During the campaign, I sometimes drove out to his house during periods when the ugly character of the debate and the accusations coming my way about being a traitor to my race had me feeling down. James would come out of the house the minute he saw me drive up. First he'd inspect my car to see if it was clean and check out my shoes to see if they were shined. Then he'd listen while I told him how things were going.

"You're right on this, Wardell," he'd say after I finished unloading my frustrations. "You stick to your guns. You're right to be doing what you're doing."

James Louis died in the spring of 1996, at the age of eighty-two, a few weeks before Proposition 209 passed in a landslide vote. The doctors said the cause was heart trouble and complications from diabetes, but I think his decline may also have had something to do with his exposure to asbestos in the naval shipyards up in Washington during the war. When I spoke at his funeral, what I said came from deep within me: "I never told you enough how much I loved you. You weren't educated but you made sure that I was. You didn't father me, but you became my father."

— —

In 1951, when I was eleven years old, Aunt Bert and Uncle James finally had a child of their own, my cousin Phyllis. Soon after she was born, Mom came over one day to take me away.

"Our house is done, so you're going to come live with me now."

I started crying and told her that I didn't want to go.

"Your Aunt Bert has a baby of her own now," Mom said firmly. "She doesn't need to take care of you too. Anyway, we have our own place now."

"I belong here," I pleaded. By now, Aunt Bert was crying too.

"No, you belong with me," Mom replied. "I'm your legal guardian, and I've been through a lot for you." I knew from the set look on her face that there was no point arguing. She started packing my things and after she was done, we walked to our new house, which was about six blocks away.

Aunt Bert always said that things would have been different if James had been there the day Mom came. But James was at work, of course. When he got home that evening, Bert later told me, he seemed to sense something was wrong.

"Where's Wardell?" he asked right away.

"Mama came and got him today," Aunt Bert said.

"I'm going to go bring him back," James said, immediately heading for the door. "That's just not right."

Bert said calmly, "No, you don't want to do that."

Something in her voice stopped James. As she told me later on, he stood there at the door for a while shaking his head and saying, "It's just not right." Then he went into the living room and sank down into his chair. In time, he accepted the new situation and, like all the rest of us, lived around it; but I know that the way I was taken always rankled him.

Why did Mom come for me? For one thing, she really did feel that I was her responsibility, which she believed—erroneously, as it turned out—she was finally in a position to accept. Also, she was probably lonely, even though she always had a house full of people and numerous children and grandchildren within a mile radius of her. Perhaps most importantly, I think she had made a pledge to the memory of her dead daughter, my mother, to personally see to my upbringing, and she was now in a position to keep her word.

James had monitored my behavior outside the house closely, knowing that the street was a potentially dangerous place for a boy on the edge of his teenage years. Mom gave me more freedom, but was stricter in other ways. She had three basic rules. I had to do my homework every night and get good grades; I had to go to church; and I had to read scriptures or some other uplifting reading material each day. I could break rules two and three and live to tell about it. But if I broke rule number one, there was hell to pay.

Mom had a regimen that I had to satisfy each day before I could go out and play with my friends. I had to learn to spell a certain number of words, memorize my times tables, and read out loud with clear enunciation. I remember one occasion when I was having particular difficulty spelling a certain word, primarily because my mind was preoccupied with being outside and playing baseball. After I muffed it several times, Mom told me to hold on a minute. She left the scrub board, where she was doing the laundry, went out into the backyard, cut off a small limb from a willow tree, and returned. She told me once again to get the word right. I stubbornly insisted that I couldn't do it. She said, "Oh, yes, you can!" and switched the backs of my legs.

Right after that I spelled the word correctly. She insisted that I spell it over and over until she was convinced that I had it. Then she said, in words used by so many authority figures of that era, "Now, you listen to me, young man. Someday, after I'm gone, you'll thank me for this." And in fact I did thank her, after she was gone, for this and the thousand other little things she did to put me in control of my life.

I know that today the values that were part of the lives of people like Mom and Bert and James—hard work, self-respect, independence—are out of vogue with those in the intellectual elite who claim to speak for the "black community." They prefer to talk instead about victimhood and powerlessness, recrimination and reparation. I know too that these older values will have to be reasserted if black people are to complete the long march to freedom and bring with them the urban underclass, which nobody these days, liberal or conservative, seems to care very much about at all.

— —

Del Paso Heights had once been cropland. It was gray in the winter and broiling in the summer. It was divided neatly into black and white sections with Rio Linda Boulevard as the dividing line. It was custom, not law, that kept people separate, and this made the separation feel like choice instead of compulsion.

James was interested in the Southern civil rights movement and followed its progress by radio, which remained his favorite information medium until the end of his life. (In his old age in Rio Linda, he was an enthusiastic listener of Rush Limbaugh, for instance, having discovered Rush in his early days as a local Sacramento radio personality.) Yet, while he was sympathetic to the struggle, he also had been so deeply scarred by his experiences in the South that he didn't feel the region was worth struggling for. When he heard about Freedom Riders being beaten and demonstrators being set upon by police dogs and fire hoses, he would always shake his head and say, "Why don't those people just get the hell out of there?"

A couple of my aunts were maids in white homes in the William Land Park development. I have to report that they were not secretly surly or resentful about their lowly position. They got on with their employers and were, in fact, thankful for the work. They felt that having come to California they were halfway to what Dr. King had called "the Promised Land" and that if they worked hard their children would complete the journey. As James used to say to me sometimes, "I'll shovel shit all my life if it means that you won't have to shovel any shit at all." He and my other aunts and uncles were glad to have stepped out of segregation and to have positioned the family for a future whose promise they believed in without reservation. In this respect, they were like other immigrants who sacrifice themselves so that their children can have a better life.

Racial animosity so rarely broke through the surface of our lives in Del Paso Heights that when it did we were all taken aback. I remember walking to school one morning after a windstorm had littered the lawn of a beautiful house I passed every day with walnuts from a large tree. Some of them had fallen on the sidewalk outside the picket fence that enclosed the lawn, and I bent over to fill my lunchpail. Suddenly an elderly white man came storming out of his house calling me a "little nigger" and accusing me of "stealing" his walnuts.

I stood there as if hit by a stun gun; I couldn't move. But then a little girl I'd never seen before suddenly appeared and pertly informed the old man that her father had told her that anything on a sidewalk was public property. Then, she grabbed my arm and said, "Come on, let's go to school."

From that day, Mildred Tittle and I were friends. She was sparky, with pigtails and freckles. We walked to school together, sat near each other in class, and walked home together. Sometimes, the white boys would taunt her as a "nigger lover," and she would grasp my arm more tightly and say, "Just don't pay any attention to them, Wardell." But the racial animosity cut both ways. I remember one afternoon when we left school, a group of older black girls followed us. As we neared Mildred's house, one of them, a very large and intimidating girl, grabbed both of Mildred's pigtails and yanked them hard in milking motions. Mildred started to cry. I shoved her tormentor down on the sidewalk.

Later that evening, the father of the large girl paid my grandmother a visit. He was angry and complained bitterly that I had "stood up for the white girl" and hurt his daughter.

Hurting a girl was forbidden, and when I saw the look on Mom's face I knew I was in a world of trouble. After the father left, I desperately began to explain that this girl actually outweighed me by twenty pounds and had a few inches on me too. Then I explained who Mildred was and what had really happened. Mom listened like a judge considering a closing argument. I knew there was a good chance that her verdict would be to send me to the back yard for a session with a willow tree switch. But instead, she reached into her purse and pulled out a dollar bill, which was like a brick of gold bullion in those days, and handed it to me.

"You did the right thing," she said. "You should stand up for what's right, and what's right isn't a matter of color."

— —

Moving in with Mom turned out to be a step downward socially. James's household was middle class by the standards of the day in the black community. He and Bert were by no means spendthrifts, but there was always a sense of adequacy around the house. Living with Mom, on the other hand, was less certain. She was too old to look for a new career and too young to qualify for Social Security, so there were times when the cupboard was bare. I recall many delicious dinners of homemade rolls, roasts, mashed potatoes, and pies. But I also recall days, sometimes several of them in a row, when I went to school without much breakfast and with very little in my lunchpail, and when dinner was a slice of sweet potato, a glass of milk, and, if it was summer time, some collard greens picked out of the garden in our back yard. My Uncle Bill, Mom's eldest son, worked nights in the kitchen of the El Rancho Hotel after getting off his day job at the McClellan Air Force Base. The head chef at the El Rancho befriended him and sometimes gave him the meats that had been cooked but not eaten by the end of a shift. Uncle Bill would stop by our house on the way home and we would have a feast.

Mom could not afford a car, so we walked everywhere we had to go. I didn't mind the exercise, but it became a problem when my shoes wore out and Mom couldn't afford new ones. I lined the soles of my old shoes with cardboard to keep from walking on pavement.

The only time we didn't walk was when a relative gave us a ride or on Sunday. Then the Macedonia Baptist Church bus driven by "Brother Dumas" or "Brother Luster" would arrive at our doorstep and take us to the service. I can still remember stepping inside the church. It was like going from black and white to technicolor. There were shouts and whispers, a great communal hallelujah. The sliding chords of the piano would draw the babbling worshippers to their feet and make them move through the aisles, snapping their heads like chickens. Midway through the service, the first fainter would look up at the ceiling, her eyes would flip white, and she would go down. A team of men would quickly assemble to handle her, and all the fainters who followed, with precision—one cradling the head, another smoothing the dress to keep the undergarments from showing, a third batting at the face with the fan bearing the logo of the Morgan Jones Mortuary, and others working like pall bearers to lift up the stiff body and carry it outside to fresh air.

Mom had been operating for years on the money she'd gotten from the sale of her property in Louisiana, supplemented by money from her egg-selling business. But building the house had eaten up her meager savings. One day, when I came home from school, she told me we had to have a talk. I sat down and she admitted to me that her back was against the wall. She still owed on the house, and she had borrowed from the church's "Poor Folks Fund" and was in no position to repay it. She said that the only solution for us was to go on "public assistance." She had been resisting this option for months, but now there was no alternative.

I could tell from the way it came up that this was a grave subject. Then Mom delivered the punch line. She herself was not eligible for welfare. But, as a minor child just over thirteen, I did qualify, and so it was I who would have to sign up for help.

I was embarrassed and humiliated at having to take a step that was against everything I had learned not only from Uncle James but from Mom herself. I tried to argue her out of it, but it was like arguing against inevitability. I vividly remember the day Mom and I trooped down to the Sacramento County office to make our formal application. As we rode downtown on the bus, I kept my head averted from the people getting off and on the bus, fearful that they would be able to take one look at me and see my new dependency written all over my face.

For the next year and a half, we got a monthly check of $60, which took care of the $35 house payment, with just enough left over for food. With this check also came a monthly visit from our case worker who interviewed us and evaluated the way we were using the money. I think welfare was probably a better program when it came with "strings" like these and was seen as "assistance" rather than a "right." But these interviews were degrading torture for me. They made me feel impotent and infantile. I couldn't imagine my Uncle James ever putting up with the probing questions, much less ever accepting a handout from a stranger. You just didn't act that way, not if you considered yourself a *mane*.

During one visit, as we sat with our social worker discussing our budget and what we planned to spend our small surplus on this month, something in me snapped. As I listened to the bureaucratic drone and saw the submissive look on Mom's face, I suddenly stood up and announced that I would not accept another check. The case worker looked at me incredulously and Mom tried to hush me. But I couldn't be stopped. My fifteenth birthday was just around the corner. I was sick and tired of living this way.

"I'm not going to take another one of these checks," I told the social worker. "Just don't you even bother sending them because I don't want them." Then I stormed out through the front door.

I ran directly to see Mr. Lester Brown, the father of one of my friends, who had considerable stature in the neighborhood. At that point, there was a collaborative arrangement in the Sacramento area between Jews who owned a substantial number of the retail outlets in the downtown area and blacks who worked for them doing shipping, delivery, and other functions. Mr. Brown was something of a talent scout in our neighborhood for prospective employees for these Jewish businessmen. Fortunately, he happened to be home on the day I stormed out of Mom's house.

"I've got to have a job," I told him.

Mr. Brown gave me a once-over but didn't ask any questions about my personal situation. He told me he'd look around and let me know.

That same day, I later discovered, he called one of his contacts, a man who owned Kaufman's IXL Men's Store, and asked if he knew of anyone who might need a hard working teenager. The reply was that Manny Schwartz over at the Fabric Center needed a kid to do cleanup, but that Schwartz was sometimes difficult to please.

The next day Mr. Brown came to my house after he got off work and gave me Schwartz's name and address. I caught the bus after school the following day and went downtown for an interview. Manny Schwartz hired me on the spot, and I went to work as a stock boy at sixty-five cents an hour. I made about $80 a month. This was $20 more than we'd gotten from welfare, but it felt like thousands. From this time onward I was the provider in our family, and Mom and I never took another handout.

Manny Schwartz was a no-nonsense kind of guy who rarely smiled or said anything more than "good morning." (And there were days when you didn't even get that out of him.) His son, Joe, was different. He was garrulous and good natured, and often asked me about how I was doing in school and whether I planned to go to college. I realized later that the store could have used a full-time clerk to make deliveries and do other small jobs, but that the

Schwartzes arranged their needs to fit with my part-time availability because they wanted to help me. This is not to say that they pampered me—after three years I was making seventy-five cents an hour—but they gave me work, a set of human relationships, and a view of the wider world.

I met many good people at the Fabric Center. Some of them took an interest in me—like the clerk whose name, I'm sad to say, I've forgotten. I have not forgotten her kindness, however. She felt I was underpaid and clocked me in a few minutes before my actual arrival and out a few minutes later than my actual departure so that I could earn an extra two or three dollars a month.

The schedule I agreed on with Joe and Manny was designed to give me as many hours of work as possible without losing any school time. Classes were out at 2:30 and I had to catch the 2:40 bus to be downtown by three o'clock. But I had to go home first to pick up my dinner, and it took ten minutes, running full speed, to get there. Mom designed a protocol. I'd take off running from school the moment class was over. She'd be waiting on the lawn with my dinner in a paper sack. I'd take it from her like a Pony Express rider grabbing the mailbag and keep going, just barely making it to the bus stop before the bus pulled away.

The bus driver was a white man. After a week of seeing me climb into the bus sweating and out of breath, he struck up a conversation with me. I thought he was just making small talk and told him about how, if I didn't make the 2:40, I couldn't get to my job on time. He didn't say much in return. But I soon noticed that he began arriving at the bus stop about five minutes late. Soon, I came to count on the extra minutes and took time to dash inside our house and use the bathroom and, perhaps, change my shirt before running to the bus stop. After I boarded, the driver would speed through the rest of his stops to get back on schedule. It finally dawned on me that he had been purposely slowing down on my part of the route.

This experience occurred in the early 1950s when the relationship between blacks and whites was distant, to say the least. But what I learned from it reinforced what I'd already begun to understand: simple human decency doesn't have a color.

— —

Recently, I drove out to Del Paso Heights one Saturday morning to see the old neighborhood. There were many changes of the sort that remind you that at a certain point in your life you acquire a past comprised of used-to-be's, parts of a former self that you then carry with you the rest of your days.

The municipal bus I used to ride is now regional, but it maintains essentially the same route as it did forty-five years ago. The driver I saw was a white female instead of a white male, but ironically, the vehicle was parked at the same turn-around point that it used during the days when Mom would anxiously track its pace as I came running home from school.

The place where Uncle James used to get his tax returns prepared by a white accountant is now owned by a Hmong woman whose salon installs false fingernails. The white-owned ice cream parlor where we would go as kids to get milk shakes is now the St. Stephens AME church. Its windows are barred.

As I drove down Grand Avenue, one of the major thoroughfares in the Heights, I saw the old house of Dr. Clarence Wigfall, the only black doctor in our old neighborhood. It was one of the few two-story structures in the area, and most of us regarded it as if it were Tara in *Gone with the Wind.* Now the house seems to have shrunken and doesn't look like a mansion at all.

I went by North Avenue Elementary School and Grant High School, past Aunt Cleo's house on the corner of Clay and Grand where she and Mom lived when they first came to town, and down the street to 3729 Clay, where I once lived with James and Aunt Bert. The house Mom built at 3744 Branch Street was still standing, but beginning to show its age. Still, the garden was freshly plowed, and its soil was still ready to produce tomatoes, green peppers, and collard greens, just as it did for us.

The block where Mildred Tittle used to live is now integrated. But it's not just blacks and whites who live there together; there are a variety of other ethnicities. And the old Taylor Street school Mildred and I attended before North Avenue Elementary was built is still there. The slides where we played are still in use, but the merry-go-round where I would spin her until she became dizzy is gone.

The vacant field Mom and I crossed when we walked to the grocery store, and which provided me a shortcut that day I went to see if Mr. Brown could help me find a job, has been developed with public and private housing. The railroad tracks that separated most of the black section of the neighborhood from the white section are now a bike trail. In fact, all the old lines between black and white, which were never that pronounced in Del Paso Heights to begin with, are now gone. I noticed, for example, that middle-class blacks own some of the better homes, while lower-income whites now rent some of the most run-down dwellings, with non-functioning cars jacked up on blocks in their front yards.

The neighborhood is now not only black and white, but also Russian, Hmong, Filipino, Latino, and, yes, mixed race. Because of my involvement in the national argument about preferences, I paused in my drive through the Heights to wonder which of the people I saw there would be regarded as most deserving of the benefits of affirmative action. The low-income whites whose children were running barefooted down the sidewalks? The middle-class blacks? The Latinos working on their well-kept houses? The industrious Hmong?

Not long before the passage of Proposition 209, the California state legislature tried to define the "socially and economically disadvantaged persons" eligible for preferences and came up with the following Orwellian formulation: "Women, Black Americans, Hispanic Americans, Native Americans (including American Indians, Eskimos, Aleuts, and native Hawaiians), Asian-Pacific Americans (including persons whose origins are from Japan, China, the Philippines, Vietnam, Korea, Samoa, Guam, the United States Trust Territories of the Pacific, Northern Marianas, Laos, Cambodia, and Taiwan)." Under this definition, the son of an upper-income Hmong family living in Del Paso Heights would receive a preference, while the daughter of a low-income Russian would not, even if both arrived in the United States at the same time.

Is that fair? Are some racial and ethnic groups to be put on a list and treated like endangered species? Is this what America has become?

As I drove out of my old neighborhood, an elderly black man waved at me, and a black teenager spit in the direction of my car. I wasn't sure what to make of any of this.

FOUR

WHEN I WENT THERE, Grant Union High School had the best athletes in Sacramento and a rowdy school spirit that calls to mind the face-painted fanaticism of the rooting sections at today's college basketball playoffs. I also remember Grant as a casbah of teenage melodrama. Kids would enter steady relationships that mimicked adult marriages and undergo "divorces" that traumatized the whole school; strive desperately for popularity, the adolescent equivalent of wealth; and wrestle over whether or not to break The Rules which, back in the mid-fifties, still had the power to break them in return. Many of my classmates believed that they were enjoying the best years of their lives and that they would never again have experiences as intense as those they had in high school. I always had a feeling that I was passing through, and that the best was yet to come.

One teacher at Grant High School who strongly influenced me was a tall, energetic man named Clark Dominquez. Mr. Dominquez taught math and practiced tough love before the concept was discovered. He was a hard taskmaster and made us stand and deliver the way Jaime Escalante did for his advanced math students in the *barrio* of East Los Angeles. The compliments he handed out for hard work felt like battle ribbons; the more potential he saw in a student, the more demanding he was. Mr. Dominquez pushed me remorselessly to get to the next level—making it a challenge, a demand, and a dare the way all good teachers do. I ran into him recently, and the first thing he said, after all these years, was, "I read about you in the newspapers. God, I'm glad to see that someone made it out of the Heights!"

There was another teacher at Grant—the only one, as a matter of fact—whom I strongly disliked. His name was Sherman Chavoor and he taught P.E. I was never one to be on the lookout for evidence of racism; in fact, I probably missed expressions of it that were obvious to others. But I always thought that Chavoor didn't like the black students at Grant. A grim-featured man with a buzz haircut, he considered Grant the ghetto and eventually left it to found the exclusive Arden Hills Swimming and Tennis Club, where he achieved fame by training Mark Spitz, Donna deVarona, and other Olympic champions.

Mr. Chavoor made no secret of his prejudices, one of them being his belief that blacks were incapable of being good swimmers. He once told me when I said I wanted to be a swimmer that I'd better not because I would "sink like a rock." When I asked him why, he replied, "Because Negroes are built for running, not swimming." He put this theory into practice not only by trying to keep us out of the water, but also by forcing us to do quarter-mile laps around the football field whenever he thought we were inattentive in P.E. I remember running endless laps as Chavoor stood on the infield glowering at us and mumbling under his breath as we passed, "Run, you damned clowns!"

Ideas—even stupid ones—have consequences. Thanks to Sherman Chavoor, it wasn't until I was twenty-five years old that I finally went to the YMCA to force myself to learn to swim in case my young child fell into the pool of the apartment complex where we were then living. When I entered the water I felt terrified: it was not my medium and I would sink to the bottom of the pool like a rock. I always tell young black students this story when I hear them say that achievement tests are for white people, and blacks will drown in their complexity.

By some miracle, I was befriended at Grant by Charlie "Choo-Choo" Johnson, one of the greatest running backs ever to play for the Grant High Pacers. Blessed with great speed and built like an oak, Choo-Choo got his name because he ran over opposing players like a locomotive. He certainly would have been a star in college and perhaps even in the pros, but he was a poor student with such a volatile temper that even the teachers were afraid of him. Yet he was one of those archetypal fifties characters—the bad boy who longs to be good. And though feeling doomed himself, he respected someone like me who, as he saw it, had the potential to escape the neighborhood. In one of those crystal-clear teenage memories, I can still see myself on that day when I was about to have to fight a mean black kid named Raymond. He had been tormenting me for weeks, and I was ready to get it over with, although my prospects weren't very good. But just as we were about to have our showdown, Choo-Choo came up to Raymond and said, "You hurt him and I'm going to kick your ass." And that was that. I was saved as if by divine intervention.

I lost track of Charlie after high school, but then, many years later, when I was collecting rents on some properties I owned in an area named Strawberry Manor, I knocked on the door of one apartment and Choo-Choo answered. He had fallen far from the old days when he was the most admired—and feared—boy at Grant. That rock-hard body was bloated and soft, and the look in his eyes told me how down on his luck he was. When he said he didn't have the money to pay me, I told him to forget it. It was a rare opportunity to pay an old debt.

As my life filled up, Mom became increasingly active in church to keep herself occupied. By 1955 she was getting Social Security, and this, along with what I earned, made us feel comparatively well off. Having once been the beneficiary of the church's Poor Folks Fund, she was now running it and dispensing money to others living on the edge. As my graduation neared, she kept after me about college. I told her I was going, I just didn't know where.

If some counselor had come to Grant and said that I needed certain classes to be eligible for a University of California campus, or had helped me apply for a scholarship for needy students—in other words, if there had simply been some kind of outreach—I might have wound up at Berkeley or UCLA, schools my grades and test scores qualified me to attend. But there weren't any advisors or scholarships. (In many inner city black schools there still aren't. And of course the strident defenders of affirmative action certainly never show up there to offer poor students person-to-person help.) So the school I wound up attending was determined by a trivial issue—transportation. There were three other Grant seniors from my neighborhood who planned to go to American River Junior College, because they didn't have the grades to go anywhere else. Not having a car of my own, I went where their carpool took me.

I started out at American River with a strong sense that I—one of the first in my family to graduate from high school and the first to attend college—was entering an unmapped life. But while I knew I had a future, I didn't yet know what it was. For the first couple of semesters at ARJC, I was like someone walking in a fog: it was clear right around me, but hazy up ahead. Possibly because of all the time I had spent doing sums with Mom as a kid, or perhaps because of the math problems I'd solved with Mr. Dominquez, I got it in my head that I ought to be an accountant. My first semester in junior college I took double-entry accounting, business law, and other courses. Then I fell under the influence of an English teacher named Edith Freleigh.

She was in her late thirties, tall and somewhat schoolmarmish, but attractive. For some reason she decided to make a project out of me. She saw that I was reticent about participating in class discussions and took pains to draw me out. She gave me books to read in addition to the usual assignments and encouraged me to try my hand at creative writing. One afternoon after class she asked me about my ambitions. When I told her I was headed toward accounting, she got a sour look on her face. I still remember what she said: "That is a nondescript, empty suit of a profession."

Miss Freleigh had a favorite Chinese proverb she got me to memorize:

> He who knows not and knows not that he knows not is a fool - shun him.
> He who knows not and knows that he knows not is willing - teach him.
> He who knows and knows not that he knows is asleep - waken him.
> He who knows and knows that he knows is wise - follow him.

Back then, at American River Junior College in 1958, these words seemed like a summary of human wisdom. Even today, forty years later, they still seem to be a useful approach to the good life.

Edith Freleigh was one of those people you bump into in life whose influence is so subtle as to be almost imperceptible—a person who changes who you are and what you become without either one of you knowing that this is happening. And although this white woman certainly didn't "look like me," as they say about the need for color-coded role models in higher education these days, she gave me something to shoot for. Because of her I understood that education was an end, not a means, and I gained enough confidence in myself and my ideas that I wound up giving one of the commencement speeches at the American River graduation ceremonies in 1959.

— —

When I transferred to Sacramento State College that fall, I had saved enough money from my job at the Fabric Center and from other odd jobs—cleaning the restrooms at the neighborhood service station and mowing lawns among them—to buy a 1950 Chevy. In a literal as well as a figurative sense, I now felt I could go anywhere I wanted.

During my first week on campus, I got caught up in Pledge Week. I had never even remotely considered joining a fraternity; there were none at American River Junior College, and "Greek life" was not something we learned much about in Del Paso Heights. But the idea of a group of organizations competing to have me as a member was appealing. I wound up joining Delta Phi Omega, which subsequently went national and affiliated with Sigma Phi Epsilon.

DPO had never had a black member before. I didn't know this until after I'd made my commitment and my sponsor casually mentioned one day that we were going to break a racial barrier. That was the first and only time during the nearly three years I lived in the DPO house that my color was ever mentioned.

I must admit, however, that I was sweating bullets during the initiation ceremony. There was none of the violent hazing or near-homicidal alcohol abuse one hears about today, but it was scary for me. The musty basement where the initiation took place was pitch black. I walked down a long aisle after my name was called, going to the front of the room, as ordered, past all the assembled members. Then the president of the fraternity asked, "Is there anyone who will sponsor this man?" No reply. A little louder he asked, "Is there anyone who will sponsor this man?" Still no reply. I began to worry. "I ask, again, is there anyone who will sponsor this man?"

As the third repetition of the question hung there in the silence, the thought went through my mind that I had been brought there only to be blackballed. But then, after a long silence, a voice behind me said, "I will sponsor this man" and I felt a firm hand on my right shoulder. From that moment forward, I felt that I belonged.

The members of Delta Phi Omega ate and studied together, lived in the same house, and were constant companions at social events. Yet we were all very different and had become "brothers" by choice, not some accident of color. I believe that there was far more real "diversity" in that fraternity house than in the voluntarily segregated living arrangements that one finds on many college campuses today.

The day I moved out of Mom's house for good, I was helped by two of my fraternity brothers. Mom cooked us a huge dinner. I could tell that she liked my friends. She didn't say much when we drove off in a couple of cars filled with clothes and boxes of possessions, but it was an emotional moment for us both; a moment beyond words. She knew I was on my way now and that in some sense I would have to leave her behind. It was that tragic perception felt by anyone who has had children: you know how well you've succeeded by how well the family you built falls apart.

In my first semester at Sac State I was lucky enough to take Dr. Robert Thompson's course, Elements of Western Political Theory. Dr. Thompson was tall and gangly, with a craggy, bearded face and a laconic manner. The term Lincolnesque fit him perfectly. He was one of those natural-born teachers who instruct indirectly—not so much by what they say as by who they are. Dr. Thompson had a way of questioning—tilting his head forward and staring down over half-glasses—that made you look inside. He taught in partnership with Dr. John Livingston, a more ironic individual and politically more of a liberal. It was Dr. Livingston who got me to join the ACLU and the NAACP during my time at Sac State.

The year after I took his course, Dr. Thompson hired me as his reader to help grade undergraduate papers. We spent a lot of time talking about the problems and promise inherent in the American Dream, a popular subject in the late fifties. Sitting in his cramped office one day after a lecture, I challenged the premise that I had been created equal to some other students who were born with silver spoons in their mouths. During summer vacations, after all, I worked from eight at night until three in the morning on the assembly line at Continental Can Company and then went back to the fraternity house and caught a few hours sleep before working a half day as recreation supervisor at a local children's home. Most of the other students didn't have to work at all; they had nice cars and ample allowances, and had entered life well ahead of me.

"Mr. Connerly," Dr. Thompson replied—in all the years I knew him he never called me by my first name—"life is imperfect, and the ideal of all men being created equal is as important as the reality. What we want is for our government to *believe* you and I are equal and treat us accordingly in its transactions. Then in the most basic sense we are, indeed, created equal."

Dr. Thompson was a realist. He pointed out—and this was in the flush optimism of the early civil rights movement—that equal opportunity, when it finally came, wouldn't necessarily lead to equal outcomes, and that this was sure to cause problems. But he was also an idealist and believed that the egalitarian spirit in America would prevent the formation of rigid economic classes and ultimately allow people, all people, to move upward in the social and economic order based on their individual talents and efforts. I'm sorry that his perspective is so out of fashion in the academy today.

The only time I recall Dr. Thompson mentioning my race was at dinner at his house one evening in the fall of 1959. We had been talking about the revolution Martin Luther King was beginning to create in the South and Dr. Thompson said if it succeeded in its aims, it would redeem America. Then he looked at me over his glasses and said, "Mr. Connerly, when the day comes that I can call you a son of a bitch without you thinking that I am a racist, or thinking about my color in relation to yours, that will be the day when true equality will have been achieved."

It was largely because of Dr. Thompson's influence that I became involved in school politics. At the end of my first year at Sac State, I was elected vice president of the student body. I also joined the Cosmopolitan Club, which was primarily comprised of students from other countries. One of the members of the club—I don't remember his name—was a middle-aged student majoring in engineering from the Far East who had a wife and five or six children back home and planned to return to them at the end of the school year. One morning, this student was killed when he was hit by a truck while riding his motorbike to the campus.

For most people, this was an unfortunate accident. For those of us in the Cosmopolitan Club, it was a social tragedy. We knew that our friend had tried to rent an apartment in River Park, a neighborhood within walking distance of the campus, but had been turned down because he was a "dark-skinned foreigner." He was forced to take a place several miles away and had to make a long trip on his motorbike every morning in dangerous traffic.

We were outraged by this death and thought that the school should do something. We went to the student council, which voted to create a Student Committee Against Discrimination in Housing and appointed me as the chair. Our first action was to define the extent of the problem. We sent "testers"—minority and white students—to apartment complexes and houses in River Park where vacancies had been advertised. We verified beyond any doubt that units available to whites were suddenly no longer vacant thirty minutes later, when someone with dark skin showed up.

As our committee was preparing its final report, I was contacted by the office of Jesse Unruh, at that time the "Big Daddy" of Democratic party politics in California and the Speaker of the Assembly, and asked to testify before the legislature. I said I would like to appear. Shortly afterward, as if by coincidence, I got a call from the office of Dr. Guy West, President of Sacramento State, inviting me to dinner.

It was the first time I'd ever been to the presidential residence, an elegant house whose backyard sloped down to the shores of the American River. Mrs. West was pleasant and nondescript. President West was a balding man who looked a little like President Eisenhower. He was a legendary figure at Sac State, having been the individual most responsible for getting the campus established a few years earlier.

I went to the dinner without any suspicion that I was walking into a hidden agenda. The evening began pleasantly enough. We discussed my coursework and similar topics. But then, when coffee was being served, President West abruptly changed the subject.

"You know, Wardell," he said smoothly, "we're not Berkeley here. We have an excellent relationship with the surrounding community. We don't like our students to be involved in off-campus issues."

He didn't say anything more specific than that. He returned to the social superficialities of our previous conversation, obviously thinking that giving me a glimpse of the iron fist under the velvet glove would be sufficient.

The next day I went to Dr. Thompson and told him what had happened.

"What should I do?" I asked after finishing the story.

"You've got to consult your 'knower,'" Thompson smiled.

"What's that?"

"Your heart, your conscience, your gut, your *knower*," he shrugged. "What does your knower tell you to do?"

"It tells me that I don't like the implication of what President West was saying."

"Well, he can certainly make life miserable for you," Dr. Thompson said.

"I don't want to back down," I replied.

"Well," he chuckled, "listen to your knower."

My knower told me to testify before the legislature, which I did. Afterwards, our Committee Against Discrimination released its report. It caused considerable comment and helped give a push to the passage of the Rumford Fair Housing Act, which ultimately outlawed the kind of housing discrimination we had documented in Sacramento.

Instead of causing the ostracism President West had subtly threatened me with, these events actually increased my standing with other students, and at the end of my junior year I was elected student body president of Sac State. As the first black to hold this position, I was sometimes referred to as a "trailblazer." I didn't think of myself in these terms. (To be honest, one of the reasons I wanted to be president was that the job paid $35 a month.) I didn't see my own color; if others did, that was their problem.

But Dr. West was right in one regard. Sac State was not Berkeley, which even in those pre-Free Speech Movement days was a mecca for student activism. As a student government officer, I didn't have many big issues to deal with. In fact, the burning question during my term in office had nothing to do with war and peace or discrimination. It was whether Sac State would eliminate boxing as an intercollegiate sport.

This issue was dramatized by the presence on campus of Terry Smith, a nationally ranked white middleweight who'd come to Sac State from England to train under legendary boxing coach Hank Elespree. Hank had made our program one of the best in the country, but the belief that boxing was inhumane and must be banned was prevalent among liberals on campus. The leader of this movement was a student councilman named Phil Isenberg, who later went on to a successful career in the Democratic leadership of the state assembly. Most of the student body—me included—agreed with Terry Smith that boxing should continue and that Sac State should contend for the national championship. But Phil, showing the talents that would eventually make him a valued lieutenant in the liberal "machine" soon to be built by Congressman Philip Burton, engaged in a series of parliamentary maneuvers that kept the student body from voting. The student council, where he was in control, passed the ban.

I have run into Phil Isenberg now and again over the years, almost always looking at him from the other side of the political fence. We clashed politely, but seriously, in 1995 when I testified in hearings he held before his Assembly Judiciary Committee on a bill that would have outlawed racial preferences in California. Phil took pride in being able to bottle up this bill and keep it from getting to the floor of the legislature for an up or down vote, just as he had kept the students at Sac State from voting on boxing. This time, however, Phil's vote-quashing maneuvers amounted to little more than a Pyrrhic victory, since they forced those of us who opposed racial preferences to take the issue out of the legislature's smokeless rooms to the people of California in a statewide initiative. I've always wondered if Phil is aware of the irony: by killing the preferences bill, he helped Proposition 209 get started.

— —

At the end of my senior year in 1962, Dr. Thompson, acting on his own, got me an application for graduate school at Syracuse University, his alma mater, and even went so far as to set me up for a doctoral scholarship there. I kept making excuses to him for not applying, usually having to do with being awash in debt. This was true enough, but the real reason I didn't want to go to Syracuse was that I was in love.

I met Ilene when I gave the welcoming speech at the Freshman Orientation ceremonies in the fall of 1961. When I finished talking, I wandered through the crowd meeting the new students. At one point, I ran into this pretty blond woman with a smile that lit up her whole face. She blushed when I introduced myself. I made a mental note of the fact that she was living on campus in the women's dormitory.

Later that week, I was driving from my office in the Student Center back to the fraternity house. As I edged into the crosswalk, lost in thought, I almost ran into her. She shot me a look of puzzlement as I drove by.

A few days later, I created a pretext for going to the women's dorm. From the lobby, I rang Ilene's room and she came down, playfully accusing me of trying to run over her. As we sat talking in the living area, the chemistry between us immediately started to work. She was open and innocent—not naïve, but ready to believe the best about people. She had grown up in a solid working-class family in a small rural northern California town and had chosen Sacramento State because it was only a few hours from home.

Unlike some other students who regarded college as a place to "find themselves," Ilene was serious about having an education and a career.

I kidded her about being from the sticks. But as we talked I understood that in many ways she was far more experienced than I, having traveled widely on vacations with her family, while the only time I'd been out of Sacramento was when I went to Mississippi with Uncle James and Aunt Bert. We were both aware that there was social distance between us, but we knew that it had less to do with race than with background and life experiences. At the end of that first conversation, I had a feeling that we were going to narrow this distance considerably.

The first couple of times I saw Ilene, I pretended that my only interest was in making her feel welcome on campus. It soon became clear that if this was the case, she was the only freshman female that I wanted to feel at home at Sac State. I finally asked for a formal date—to a party at the fraternity house. She accepted. Within a few weeks, we were spending most of our time with each other.

Up to that point, I had dated white, black, and Latino women. But I had never gone out with someone like Ilene. She was attractive enough to make me feel puffed up to be seen with her. But from the moment we met, I was also aware of how solid a person she was—bright, a voracious reader, the sort of individual who works through an issue meticulously and then commits herself unflinchingly to the results of her inquiry.

I saw also that she was moral to the core, a quality that has always made her my compass. Not long after we were married in 1962, for instance, we drove to Los Angeles for a weekend. We were waiting at a stop sign on Sunset Boulevard when a Cadillac convertible with the top down pulled up next to us. I looked over and there was rock and roll singer Little Richard, cuddling in the arms of a white male driver. I made some crude comment about homosexuals. Ilene looked at me and asked: "Why would you say a thing like that?" I blustered out some answer meant to keep my male pride intact, but I felt small and petty.

As I think of it, there is probably a straight line—although at times an invisible one—from that experience to my decision over thirty-five years later, in the fall of 1997, to support "domestic partner" benefits for employees at the University of California. This had been a sleeping issue all during my term as a UC regent. The faculty had voted for these benefits, and staff studies had shown that they would not be that expensive. But the new president of UC, Richard Atkinson, didn't want to risk the political flare-up he thought a vote would cause. I saw domestic partner benefits simply as an issue of fairness and decided to force his hand; he couldn't very well keep it under wraps any longer if someone like me—a "reactionary" in the eyes of the liberal press because of Proposition 209—was for it. So I arranged for Duncan Mellickemp, the faculty representative on the board, to press for a discussion of the issue before his term expired and promised to give him my strong support.

The vote on domestic partner benefits took place in one of the most dramatic meetings I've ever attended during my time on the UC Board of Regents. The measure won by one vote after an impassioned and intelligent debate. I was portrayed in the press as being the "swing vote" for the measure, although the same might have been said of anyone who voted yes. The fact is that the issue probably would not have surfaced in the first place had I not worked with Duncan to get it on the agenda and had he not had the courage to pursue my recommendation.

My friend Pete Wilson, who was on the opposite side of the

issue, knew of my role in getting this proposal approved. I was having a chat with him several days later and he said, "I thought you'd just cast your vote and let it go at that. I didn't realize you were going to argue publicly against me."

"I felt it was the right thing to do," I told him. "And because it seemed right to me I didn't think I should stay in the background."

My friendship with Pete withstood this test and is still going strong. It is a testament to this friendship, in fact, that the governor, with whom I agree about most things, never asked me why my position on this issue was so different from his. If he had asked, however, I would have told him about that day in southern California when Little Richard pulled up beside me on the Sunset Strip, and I got a lesson in humanity from my wife and friend Ilene.

— —

Our marriage has been a good one, but I won't pretend that there weren't some rocky moments at the beginning. Even then, however, the problem was not between us, but between us and other people.

A few weeks after we met, when it was already clear to both of us that we had embarked upon something serious, Ilene's parents drove down to Sacramento one Saturday afternoon to check out the campus and the dorm. Ilene had told them about me and said she wanted us all to meet. Because of the emotions we had already begun to kindle in each other, I was a little wary. But as it turned out, all four of us made an unspoken tactical decision about how to comport ourselves during our little get-together: keep it light and dignified; don't ask too many questions; and act as if I were just another college friend of Ilene's. It worked. The day was a success.

Ilene's mother was quite outgoing and friendly. Her father was more reserved, much like Ilene herself. I wasn't sure how he had reacted to me. But Ilene reassured me afterward that things had gone well, and I allowed myself to believe her.

A few weeks later, the two of us used the excuse of attending a local rodeo to return the visit. At this point, the idea that we were "just friends" was wearing a little thin. We both knew that the relationship was more than that and felt guilty at the deception. It made being with her parents difficult.

Not long after this trip, Ilene's sister Charlene, who knew the truth about our relationship, told them that we were serious about each other. They reacted with shock and dismay and spent long hours on the phone with Ilene trying to keep the relationship from developing further. Hoping for support from my own relatives, I went home one weekend and told Mom about Ilene. She never seemed to notice when I had dated white girls in the past. But now, seeing how serious I was, she was cold and negative. "Why can't you find yourself a nice colored girl?" she blurted out. This comment stunned me so much that I walked out of the house and didn't contact her for a long time afterward.

Ilene and I now felt secretive and embattled. The fact that our relationship was "forbidden" gave it added drama, but the isolation was disturbing. In addition, the end of the school year was approaching, which put me at a crossroads. I could go on to graduate school at Syracuse, but this would mean leaving Ilene behind. I knew I was more interested in her than in preparing for a university teaching career, so I popped the question.

Marrying "outside your race" was no easy decision in 1962. In fact, many states still had laws against interracial marriages at that time. (It was not until 1967 that the Supreme Court ruled such statutes unconstitutional.) And those states took this position with the full support of some churches, which backed such bans on the grounds that mixing of the races was contrary to the will of God, eroded family values, and weakened civilization—arguments remarkably similar to those applied to same-sex relationships today.

It was decidedly more difficult for a white woman in these inter-marriages than for a black man. The stereotyped assumptions about why a white woman would seek such a union were vile but widely accepted. By entering wedlock with a black man, a white woman stepped over a line that was decisive for many Americans, a line that separated respectability from degeneracy.

I knew that Ilene had no qualms about challenging social norms. But I was less sure that she could deal with exclusion by her family, which seemed to me a real possibility. Nonetheless, she said yes to my proposal and we were married on August 17, 1962. The wedding was performed in the living room of Reverend C.M. Cummings, pastor of the Macedonia Baptist Church. No family members were there.

I called Mom the day after the wedding and told her we had married. She apologized for what she'd said earlier.

"It wasn't Ilene," she said. "I just didn't want you getting married at all. I felt you were too young and a wife was going to slow you down just when you're getting started. If you'd come around with a fiancèe who was black, I probably would have said, Why can't you find a nice white girl?"

Ilene's parents were not so quick to alter their position. For months, the lines of communication were down between their house and ours in Sacramento. Our only contact was through Ilene's sister Charlene. She told us that they missed Ilene, but, in essence, that they did not want her to come home for a visit as my wife.

Ilene got along well with Uncle James and Aunt Bert. But I could tell that it hurt her to be estranged from her own family. Sometimes I came home from work at the end of the day and found her sitting on the couch crying.

Finally her parents agreed to see her, but not me. I drove her up to their house and waited in the car while she went in. As the hours passed, I seethed. At one point I started the engine and took off, but I didn't know the city and so, after circling the block, I came back to where I'd been and parked again. When Ilene finally came out of the house, I tried to find out what had been said during her visit. She said very little about it, but I got an idea of what had gone on when she cried for nearly the entire return trip to Sacramento.

Today, people would rush to hold Ilene's parents guilty of racism. But even when I was smoldering with resentment, I knew it wasn't that simple. These were good people—hard working, serious, upstanding. They were people, moreover, who had produced my wife, a person without a racist bone in her body. In a sense, I could sympathize with my new in-laws: there were no blacks in their daily life, and they lived in a small town of coffee shops, bowling alleys, and cloying gossip, where everyone knew everything about everyone else. Our marriage was a leap nothing in her parents' lives had prepared them to take. But their reaction to me still rankled. After having to wait in the car that afternoon I vowed never to go near their house again.

For a long time we didn't see Ilene's parents. But we did see her Aunt Markeeta and Uncle Glen. They were wonderful people. Glen, dead now, was a salt-of-the-earth type who worked in a sawmill, and Markeeta had a personality as piquant as her name. They integrated us into their circle of friends, who became our friends too. One of these friends was Tony Miller, who many years later ran for secretary of state in California as a gay Democrat. Remembering those healing days when we all functioned as an extended family, I unhesitatingly supported him in his bid.

If I had to pick the moment when our family problems began to resolve themselves it would be the day our son Marc was born. It was not long after this that we were asked to come for a visit. This time I was included in the invitation. I remember sitting stiffly through the event, which had the tone of the recently released film, *Guess Who's Coming to Dinner?* I was supremely uncomfortable, but I also sensed that the fever had broken. And indeed, after Marc was born, a peace process was put in place. The visits become more frequent. The frigid tolerance gradually thawed into welcome.

There was no single dramatic moment that completed the reconciliation, no cathartic conversation in which we all explored our guilt and misconceptions. Instead, we just got on with our lives, nurturing the relationship that had been born along with my son. It grew faster than he did. Within a year we were on our way to becoming what we are now—a close-knit, supportive family. Today, my relationship with my in-laws could not be better. I love them very much, and I know that the feeling is mutual. As I write these words, I see on my desk a foldout birthday card I received from them a few years ago. It is about as close as we have ever come to an examination of our situation. The cover says, "Son-in-law, we sure didn't make a mistake letting you in the family..." Inside, there are dozens of goofy looking people—some cross-eyed, some with plants on their heads, some in bizarre postures. The message across the centerfold reads, "Nope, you have no one to blame but yourself!" The card is signed, "Love to you. Mom and Dad."

The moral of my relationship with my in-laws is clear. Distance exaggerates difference and breeds mistrust; closeness breaks down suspicion and produces connection. My life so far tells me that our future as a nation is with connection.

Ilene and I rarely talk about those early days together any more. Nor do we spend much time analyzing our relationship or its social meaning. We just love each other. But I think we both know that a successful interracial marriage is by its nature an exercise in color blindness. You see that other person you wake up next to every morning not as a representative of a race, but just as a person with high and low moments. You stop thinking: this is a white woman. You begin thinking: this is my wife. Then the kids come along. You don't think: that child is part black and part white. You think: we made that; it is some of her and some of me—the best part of us both.

This is not to say that Ilene and I haven't had to cope with *the look* when we've been out together. We have. Sometimes we still do. At times it has been filled with contempt. As often, I think, it is filled with curiosity. It used to be that I got the look primarily from whites, but in the last few years, as I have become identified with the struggle against racial preferences, it is mostly blacks, and particularly black females, who stare daggers at us.

For some, the marriage is living proof of my race treason. In one attack against me, a black San Diego City Councilman, George Stevens, commented pointedly in open session that Clarence Thomas, former Reagan administration official Clarence Pendleton, and I had all married white women. (He might also have included conservative intellectuals Shelby Steele and Thomas Sowell on his enemies list.) Stevens went on to imply, in a bizarre twist on "Mandingo" thinking, that our wives had somehow worked their white magic to influence our thinking on subjects such as affirmative action.

But Stevens was subtle in comparison to California State Senator Dianne Watson. Because she was a leader of the anti-209 fight, we often opposed each other in print and television debates. At a climactic point in the campaign, Watson told Amy Wallace of the *Los Angeles Times*, "Connerly wants to be white. He doesn't like being black. That's why he married a white woman."

Soon after this interview, Wallace came up to me at a Republican convention in Burlingame, California. "You're not going to believe what's going to be in my story," she said. Then she repeated Watson's comment, adding, "I'm not asking you for a quote, at least not yet, but I thought it was an outrageous thing for her to say and that you ought to know about it."

A few days after this, I attended a joint meeting of the state senate and UC regents on the subject of affirmative action called by Senator Tom Hayden, head of the state senate subcommittee on higher education.

"What's *he* doing at a senate meeting?" Watson, demanded, looking over at me as she entered the hearing room in a huff.

"He's a regent, I invited him," Hayden replied.

Then Watson gave me the evil eye: "You wouldn't be where you are if not for affirmative action. You're turning your back on your kind. Yes, *your kind*, Mr. Connerly!"

"You're a bigot, Senator Watson," I shot back. "Moreover, you're a lightweight."

After the meeting ended and we were all standing in the hallway outside the senate meeting room, reporters buzzed around me asking why I'd called Watson a bigot. I explained that it was because of the comment about my wife, which Amy Wallace, who was there too, confirmed Watson had made. At this, the journalists left me and rushed over to Watson, who was standing a few feet away, and began questioning her. Because a reporter for the *Los Angeles Times* verified that she had made the comment, Watson could not very well deny it and stood there sputtering as she tried to explain herself.

As I walked out of the state capitol building that afternoon, I felt that I had just been part of a closet drama that spoke volumes about race in America.

FIVE

I'D HEARD ABOUT PETE WILSON long before he telephoned me one morning in the fall of 1968. Since being elected to the state assembly from southern California a few years earlier, Pete had acquired a reputation as a young man in a hurry. His aggressiveness didn't sit particularly well with the mossbacks in the legislature who expected junior members to wait their turn and yield the right of way. Democrats regarded Pete as a "comer" and plotted ways to stage a crib death for his career. Even Republicans used words like "brash" and "cocky" to describe him.

He had just been made chairman of the assembly's newly created Housing and Urban Affairs Committee, and he was calling because he wanted me to come to work for him as chief consultant. I was tempted. I was not quite thirty years old, and this was a job that marked the person who held it as a player in California's housing arena. But I was aware that the Republicans held a precarious 40–39 majority and could easily return to their accustomed role as the minority party in the assembly after the next election. In that case, Wilson would be out of the chairmanship, and I would be out of a job. After talking it over with Ilene, I called him back and declined his offer.

I was probably too cautious. But for the past few years, I'd been working on something that was starting to look like a career, and, already a conservative by nature if not yet by politics, I feared making that one careless decision that could derail my forward motion.

I had begun with the Redevelopment Agency of the City and County of Sacramento, where I started to work on a Monday morning in June, 1962, after graduating the previous Friday afternoon from Sacramento State College. I took this job in part because of the money—$440 a month, which seemed like a king's ransom at the time—but also because I thought that the work, first as a trainee and then as assistant to the director, would allow me a front row seat at the reconfiguration of downtown Sacramento then taking place. My involvement with the campaign against housing discrimination at Sac State had made me aware of the almost invisible way government policy affects residential patterns, which, in turn, have the potential for reinforcing a variety of inequalities. As a result, I had come to see Sacramento not just as my home base, but as a civic organism that was acted on in ways that would make it grow or atrophy, develop or decay, enfranchise all its residents or keep them walled off from each other. Working at the Redevelopment Agency would allow me to see these changes and perhaps even have an influence over them.

It was clearly a moment of transition. California was coming of age, and it required a capital city worthy of the state. So Sacramento was trying to shed its sleepy, cow-town identity and the inferiority complex it had developed after so many years of being referred to as the hick cousin of San Francisco. A decision had been made by the city fathers to redevelop a large part of the downtown area bounded by the riverfront and the rail yards which was "blighted"—to use a word then in vogue—by boarded up buildings and flop houses.

One of my jobs at the agency was to interview those to be dis-possessed. They were typically referred to as "winos," but each of them had a story filled with tragedy, alienation, self-pity and, some-times, humor as well. The human interest in these stories made a deep impression on me, particularly because Ilene and I had a new apartment and were starting to breathe the air of the lower-middle class. I won't claim that I flagellated myself by thinking when I saw these down-and-outers, "There but for the grace of God!" But they did give me a deepened awareness of the fact that being alive is to roll the dice.

I went into the agency's office early and stayed late. I worked hard to master the mechanics of urban renewal and carefully watched the negotiation process between the city and corporations like Macy's, which planned to put a huge department store into the redeveloped downtown area. The decision makers I dealt with were mainly white males whose power clung to them like a strong cologne. I expected them to be sharkish bottom-liners. As I worked with them, I saw some of that, but there was creativity and vision too, qualities the popular culture of the day did not associate with businessmen. Either because of brashness or naiveté, I didn't see the world in which they moved as being *their* world. I saw it as potentially my world too, and, even if it wasn't exactly my oyster, I felt certain that I could pry up the edge of the shell and make space for myself inside.

Money was important to me. Part of me was still—and I suppose always will be—the poor kid living with his grandmother and with memories of an empty lunch pail and cardboard soles in his shoes. (This background probably also made me hesitant, when I became a University of California regent, to vote for salary raises for UC administrators and fee increases for UC students.) Yet, while I wanted to make money, I wasn't interested so much in becoming "rich" as in putting a thumbprint on my social world. At this point in my life, I hadn't heard the quip attributed to Joseph P. Kennedy: "Life is a game, and money is the way you keep score." But I already knew I wanted to hit a home run.

So did a friend I made at the Redevelopment Agency, Ken Williams. In my first few years there, Ken and I spent a lot of time analyzing the success of the big developers in Sacramento and talking about how we could make it too if we only had capital. (I remember one of the other employees gesturing dismissively at us as we sat talking intensely in the lunchroom one afternoon, "Wardell and Ken: always scheming to become zillionaires.") To make it clear to ourselves and everyone else that we really meant business, we finally designed a plan to make a zillion *without* capital.

We saw that the federal government was beginning to acknowledge that the expansion of public housing in the postwar era was a disastrous experiment. It had given rise to inhuman structures which were little more than dense breeding grounds for crime and social dislocation. In the mid-sixties, Washington policy makers came up with the innovative plan of using vouchers to get people out of these grim warrens—"dispersing the poverty inventory" in bureaucratese—and into single-family dwellings.

Ken and I saw these changes in process. We also knew from our work at the Agency that some of the tracts that had sprung up in the Sacramento area like toadstools during the boom of the fifties were now standing vacant. Presumably, these tracts had been built with upwardly mobile minorities in mind as the ideal clientele. Many of them bore fantasy names like "Strawberry Manor," which were cruelly ironic given the fact that the developers had never planted yards or trees. The construction was so shoddy that residents lived in them a few years and then just walked away from their minimal investment, leaving behind wasted dreams, and, for the savings and loans associations that had held the mortgages, worthless paper.

Ken and I got a commitment from the Housing Authority to lease these tract homes to the poor people it was trying to remove from public housing projects. Then we called the S&Ls and convinced them to make us 110 percent loans (the extra 10 percent was for rehabilitating the structures) on about sixty units that we bought for nothing down. Soon, all the buildings were occupied, and we were the owners of a large number of houses worth less than the mortgages.

Now I knew why Mom had been so happy when we built our place in Del Paso Heights. Ilene and I still lived in an apartment with our new son Marc, but we "had property." I looked to buy other derelict houses on my own. I remember taking my lunch hour one day to look at one property in Rio Linda, one of the nicer—and whiter—suburbs of Sacramento. It was a relatively spacious suburban home and I explored it carefully, ignoring some of the neighbors who were standing across the street with their arms crossed, glaring at me. When I came back the next day, a message had been scrawled in paint on the stucco No Niggers Wanted— and someone had poured concrete into the toilets. I bought the house anyhow and immediately leased it out to tenants from the Housing Authority.

In 1968, Ken Williams moved to another part of California, and Ilene and I became the sole owners of these properties. Over the years, they became a burden for me, however, taking me away from the family at all hours to deal with leaking plumbing and other tenant complaints. We finally sold them at a small profit to an investor from the Bay Area, one of those guys who'd made a lot of money by staging seminars on how to parlay investments in real estate into millions. Shortly after he bought them from us I heard he went to jail for tax evasion, a cautionary tale for a would-be zillionaire.

— —

The sixties were a strange time for me, as, I guess, they were for many people. It was a time of possibility and also of wasted potential; the best of times and the worst of times. I was excited by the success of the civil rights movement in the early part of the decade. The dialogue about equality and brotherhood, and the national drama of opening opportunities and increasing personal freedom were themes being played out in microcosm in my own life. I believed that I was living day by day inside Martin Luther King's dream. I saw this country as basically generous and enriching. I considered myself more an American than ever before, and a proud American to boot.

It disturbed me that such emotions should be considered naïve or even "collaborationist" by the radical blacks—some of them really only radically chic—who had increasingly begun to call the social tune during the sixties. I was profoundly alienated by the increasingly militant behavior and "heavy" rhetoric that seemed to call all of the accomplishments of the civil rights movement into question. I couldn't understand the insults black radicals directed at King, and I was appalled when these same people used King's murder as an excuse to go on a violent rampage in cities across the country. It seemed that just as black people were finally about to reach the Promised Land, the seductive voices of nihilism were telling them that the last steps of the journey weren't worth the effort.

In 1967, when Huey Newton brought his Black Panthers to demonstrate in Sacramento, all of them armed and sporting uniforms of black leather jackets and berets that made them look like a ragged honor guard for some Third World dictator, the imagery was as foreign to me as Huey's homemade Maoism. I didn't consider myself politically sophisticated at this point in my life, but I knew in my gut that this hatred of America was not the prize I'd been keeping my eyes on. I did not see anything of myself or my aspirations in the gun-toting theatrics of the Panthers or in the separatist rant of Stokeley Carmichael's black nationalists. The historical moment felt bizarre, almost hallucinatory: black people were being asked to agree that America was a "concentration camp" just at the moment that they were completing their great stride toward freedom.

I realized later on that the 60s juxtaposed in particularly stark terms the radically opposed visions of America that have been present in black culture over the past century. One side was represented by Booker T. Washington, who preached a gospel of black enterprise and believed that black people would win a seat at the American table by sheer doggedness and hard work. Washington didn't underestimate the virulence of white racism, but he believed, perhaps somewhat naïvely, that whites would ultimately be forced "to respect a Negro who owns a two-story brick house." As he said in his famous 1895 Atlanta Exposition speech, rhetoric ought to take a back seat to "progressive, constructive action."

The other side was symbolized by W.E.B. DuBois, who regarded Booker T. Washington as an Uncle Tom. DuBois believed that blacks would be saved by their "exceptional men," people like himself who were intellectuals and activists, at home in the world of ideas. He scorned Washington's reliance on black investment—financial and emotional—in America, embodied in the famous plea to the black common man to "cast down your bucket where you are." DuBois proposed instead that a "talented tenth" of the black population would direct a political struggle through elite institutions such as the NAACP, which he helped found.

Washington stood for black capitalism and black economic power; DuBois stood for black rights and black political power. Washington urged blacks to look inward and live lives of personal responsibility; DuBois urged them to focus their efforts on changing the system, which he held liable for all their ills. Both men were right, and for decades, black progress rested on a balance between these two competing visions. (The civil rights movement talked DuBois's language, but it grew out of and was partly financed by an increasingly prosperous black middle class in the "Bookerite" tradition.) But in the sixties, Washington and others who followed him in working within the system were subjected to withering contempt, stigmatized as "sellouts" for having tried to give black people the tools of survival that would help them go the distance on the road to freedom. DuBois became the radicals' patron saint, although less for having helped inspire the modern civil rights movement than for the symbolism of his later life, when he turned his back on this movement as a Marxist, a member of the Communist party, and an obsessive anti-American who died in an exile of pan-Africanism in Ghana.

All these issues, and the disorienting effect the sixties had on blacks' perceptions of their place in America, were brought home again to me recently. I had just finished a speech at Harvard (where DuBois became the first black to win a PhD). I received the mixed reception I have come to expect from audiences with large numbers of black people. But afterward, a young man came up to shake my hand and surprised me by introducing himself as the great-grandson of Booker T. Washington. He told me that he believed his ancestor had been "smeared" by black radicalism and would ultimately not only be rehabilitated but vindicated by black progress and integration into American life. Then he told me, "Your message is basically the same as his. Stand on your own two feet, rely on yourself, and stop blaming the world for your problems. I believe that you'll be vindicated too."

I had never thought of it that way. But I came away from this brief encounter feeling that I was glad that I had cast down my bucket here in this great country, which, for all its flaws, has given black people far more freedom and opportunity than they ever could have found in any African homeland, real or imagined.

— —

In 1966, I left the Redevelopment Agency to take a job as a Community Development Coordinator with the newly created California Department of Housing and Community Development. My job was to visit local communities and help them deal with urban decay, redevelopment, growth management, and other problems. Over the next couple of years I traveled to cities all over California, getting to know the state from the inside out. I also became the Department's liaison with the state legislature, explaining our programs, testifying on legislation, and getting to know the political players in the state's building industry.

It was an interesting moment in California history. Because of countercultural maneuvers in San Francisco's Haight-Ashbury neighborhood and elsewhere, California was increasingly regarded as a "state of mind" by the rest of the country, a fantasy place where a Hollywood actor governed a political Disneyland. Yet something more profound was happening in California than experiments in hedonism and hallucinogens, the radical alienation growing out of the antiwar movement, and the beginnings of what would become the human potential movement. A seismic shift in population, the rapidly growing aerospace industry, and explosive economic growth were among the factors making California a place where the future was being born and where the present carried new political power and influence.

This was the state of things when Pete Wilson made his first call asking me to join his Housing and Urban Affairs Committee. As I've already said, I initially declined the offer primarily because of status anxieties. Still, I was disturbed by the factionalism inside the Committee, where Pete was opposed by another young assemblyman, Willie Brown, who would be his political antagonist and rival for years to come. By the mid-sixties, Willie had become an important cog in the liberal machine assembled by Congressman Philip Burton, his brother John, and lieutenants such as George Moscone, the future mayor of San Francisco. On a social level, however, Willie's role was somewhat similar to the one Sammy Davis, Jr. played in Frank Sinatra's Rat Pack.

Pete and Willie seemed to move in parallel universes. They were two of the most promising figures in the assembly and were both looking for ways to become their party's leader in the next generation. But from my perspective, while Pete was a young man on the move, Willie was a young man on the make. When Pete was named chairman of the Housing Committee, Willie pitched a fit and made it known that he believed he had a "right" to the position because housing, after all, was primarily a "black folks" issue.

A few days after I initially declined Pete's offer, he called again and asked me to come to his office for a face-to-face meeting. When I got there, he greeted me with a strong handshake and bustling energy. I'd heard he was an ex-Marine, and I could sense his resiliency and toughness. But there was also something boyish in his hesitant way of speaking and his lopsided smile. As we gave each other the once over, I noted that he was about my age. I worked hard not to fall under his spell as he urged me to reconsider his offer of a job.

"If you're chief consultant to the committee, you'll have an opportunity to make an impact on state housing policy," he said. "Maybe you can do something big."

This opportunity to do "something big" obviously clinched the deal as far as he was concerned, and he sat behind his desk waiting expectantly for me to capitulate. When I mentioned my worries about job security—Ilene was expecting our second child and we had just begun to build a house after living in a succession of apartments—he shot me a look implying that he pitied me for my faintheartedness. I left our meeting promising to reconsider his offer.

The decision was not as easy as he seemed to think it was. If I remained where I was in the Department of Housing, I'd have the security of a state civil service job. After fifteen or twenty years, I might be making as much as $50,000 or $60,000 a year, assuming cost-of-living increases. If I went with Wilson, it might turn out that I had given up this security in return for very little. Committee consultants serve at the pleasure of the chairman, and it was widely believed that the Democrats would regain control of the assembly in the next election in 1970—meaning that Willie Brown would replace Wilson, and I'd be out on the street. I was tempted to call Pete back and ask him what kind of big influence I could have on state housing policy as the head of a homeless family. Instead, for reasons that were difficult to explain at the time, even to myself, I decided to take a chance and went to work for the committee on the first business day of 1969.

The week I started, Pete and I traveled together to a housing conference in Seattle. He went to learn more about housing—he was a quick study and was able to expand his knowledge of this area considerably in the course of the meeting—and I went to learn more about him.

I immediately saw Pete's virtues as a person—among them an

aversion to showy gestures and self dramatization—although it was not yet clear how much of a hindrance their absence would be for a politician in an era increasingly defined by sound bites and imagery. Pete's keen political instincts and pragmatic cast of mind would also hurt him in the future by making the positions he developed issue by issue sometimes appear opportunistic. Yet, in fact, his beliefs were fiercely held. It was clear from the way he reacted to the housing issues we discussed that he believed deeply in the free market and in competition—believed in them viscerally, not just as part of some imagined Republican Party loyalty oath.

In the course of our trip, Pete told me about having worked as an advance man for Richard Nixon, whom he admired for his political canniness. (Later, Nixon came to regard Pete as something of a protégé and frequently counseled him about proper career moves.) One night over dinner, he told me about what he hoped to achieve in public life and then asked me about my political philosophy. I told him I had been in the ACLU, NAACP, and other liberal organizations while in college, but that watching the cynical operations of Democrats in the state legislature had made me change my voter registration to independent.

"What about your long-range plans?" he asked.

"I'll probably wind up going back to the Department of Housing after my assignment with the committee is over."

"Jeez, why would you want to do that?" he said in the flat, raspy voice that would become familiar to a generation of Californians. "That seems like a very limited view of your future. Have you ever considered going to work in the private sector or going into business for yourself?"

I admitted that I hadn't.

"Why do black people so often gravitate to government jobs anyway?" he continued to probe.

"Government is a safe haven," I told him. "Civil service is the one place where there's stability and blacks don't feel that they can be fired on the whim of some bigot."

"Yeah, I can see how they'd think that," Pete reflected. "But it seems to me that you're selling yourself short. You're underestimating your ability. You ought to consider getting out there on your own some day."

This conversation was probably not particularly memorable for Pete. But it continued to echo faintly in my mind over the next few years. It caused me to question my fears and to think about the possibility of life outside the vocational box into which I'd placed myself. It took me a while to act on it, but when I did it was because of a process Pete Wilson had helped set in motion.

Over the next year or so, Pete and I became friends as well as colleagues. After a hard week, we often got our families together on weekends for dinner and movies. Sometimes Ilene and I went over to the house he rented a couple of blocks away from where Ronald Reagan lived. Sometimes, he and his wife Betty (whom he later divorced) came to the place we had built near Sacramento State College. The four-way chemistry between us worked very well. Ilene and I both liked Betty a good deal. She was an attractive blonde with a smoky voice and a sneaky sense of humor. She was a few years older than Pete and had a witty, teasing manner that kept his ego in check. She was always kidding him, for instance, about his fears that he was too bland. On one occasion, he decided to grow a mustache to look more interesting, but the hair was too sparse to make an impact on his upper lip. Every morning, Betty would come close and make a show of inspecting his upper lip. She would always tell him that nothing had happened overnight, and Pete would then run off anxiously to find a mirror.

Betty had children by a previous marriage. (Many years later, in the middle of the war over Proposition 209, she called and asked if I would allow her grandson, a writer for the UC Berkeley student newspaper, to interview me. I did and the *Daily Californian*, in a gesture of truly gritty journalistic independence, wrote an editorial against racial preferences.) She and Pete had no kids of their own. Pete hadn't made room in his life for such a commitment, but I could see in the way he enjoyed playing ball with my son, Marc, in our backyard and in the way he admired our new baby daughter, Tracy, that he would have made a good father.

What I liked about Pete then, and still do, was that he had strong opinions but was secure enough to be able to change his mind if events proved him wrong. When he first got to Sacramento, for instance, he had voted against the Rumford Fair Housing Act, not because he was for segregated housing but because he believed, along with Barry Goldwater and other core conservatives, that the federal or state government should not try to dictate outcomes in areas involving freedom of association. But by 1969 his legislative experience with housing issues had convinced him that a different approach was required. He got me to draft legislation that would give tenants of public housing the opportunity to become homeowners—a unique and creative idea back then—and to have a greater voice in the governance of their public housing complexes. But the transition from public dependence to private ownership he envisioned would require government involvement, which put us on a collision course with Republican party orthodoxy and, more specifically, with Governor Reagan himself.

We drafted what we thought was a good bill, which called for the creation of a secondary mortgage market, backed by government bonds, for private institutions interested in making housing loans in "red lined" neighborhoods. But we heard rumblings that

Reagan would probably veto the legislation even if it managed to get to his desk. Pete came into my office one day and said, "We need to straighten this out. Let's go see the governor."

As we entered Reagan's private office, I was struck by one thing. The surface of his large executive desk was absolutely clear. It was huge and shiny as a mirror. There wasn't a piece of paper or a file or a folder on it, just a pen and pencil set and a jar of jelly beans reflecting on a large expanse of polished wood. The governor immediately passed the jelly beans around as if offering hors d'oeuvres. Then he told a couple of stories whose exact subject matter escapes me, although I remember that famous Reagan charm floating through the room like laughing gas. But the governor was in a businesslike mood that day. Pete sensed that we had a limited window of opportunity once the initial pleasantries were over and quickly asked me to explain our bill.

Reagan sat expressionless behind his desk during my presentation, giving me no inkling of whether I had been persuasive. After I finished, Pete said, "Governor, it is important for the Republican party to be a leader in solving the housing problems of our state. My bill represents a responsible role for government in the secondary housing market. It allows our party to be *for* something involving low-income people."

As Pete sat back with a hopeful look, Reagan tilted his head to the side, gave the familiar agreeable half-smile, offered us some more jelly beans, and then said with surprising directness, "Well, that's not my view of the proper role of government." As a stricken look came over Pete's face, Reagan went on to talk about how he didn't like the state competing with private markets and soon digressed into a story about how, in the aftermath of the great San Francisco earthquake, people had quickly gotten together and rebuilt the city without government help or handouts.

Pete protested gently that there was a big difference between 1906 and 1969, but Reagan had spoken. Without losing his affability, he gave Pete a look that showed he meant what he'd said.

"You're out of step on this issue, Pete," he said firmly. "Private industry will solve this problem, not government." Then he added, "You're listening to the wrong people," and shot a significant look in my direction, as if I was one of them.

At this point, a Reagan aide who'd been sitting anonymously in the background during the discussion stood up and spoke briskly, "Well, it looks like the Boss has spoken." This was our cue to exit. As we stood to leave, the governor gave us a genial handshake and a no-hard-feelings smile.

Walking out of the executive office, Pete and I looked at each other with wonderment. We knew we had been routed, but neither of us felt that we'd been smacked down. On the contrary, in the meeting Reagan had conveyed power, principle and also basic good nature, all at the same time. It was like encountering a force of nature. As we talked on the way back to our office, we agreed that this was a man who knew exactly what he believed in, even if he sometimes expressed it in hokey parables, and would always act on his beliefs.

I couldn't help contrast Reagan with Willie Brown, whom I now saw in action almost every day in assembly hearings. As a member of Pete's committee, Brown did everything he could to prevent bills from being reported out, even if it meant helping to kill a piece of legislation that would benefit the poor. Brown just didn't want Pete to get any political credit. And he made it clear that he considered me a sell-out for working for the committee—a preview of the "house nigger" attacks that he and others would subject me to years later during the struggle over Proposition 209. Willie wanted Pete to fail, and he made it clear to me that in his opinion, it was a racial betrayal for me to be working to help Pete succeed, even if the ideas we were putting forth were socially beneficial.

Willie and I never had a major confrontation. We were polite to each other, but suspicious, like a couple of dogs with ruffs standing up on their necks. I knew he presumed that the two of us should share a viewpoint because we shared dark pigmentation. But Willie's way of operating was foreign to me, and I had no sympathy for his ideas. Because he was generally so successful with blacks, his inability to sway me bothered him. Whenever we were together, I could tell he was trying to decipher my code. It amused Pete that I got under Willie's skin. "He race-baits the rest of us," he once told me, "but he seems threatened by you."

Willie Brown was presumed to be my friend because we'd both come into this world with "colored" on our birth certificates, but I liked Pete Wilson far better as a person. Willie and I were presumed to share ideas because we shared skin color, but for me Ronald Reagan's forthrightness and his belief in individual initiative were far preferable to Brown's deck of race cards.

Thinking about Pete, Willie and Reagan as the seventies began, I realized that I had to make a decision about my political life. I stopped thinking the unthinkable and did the undoable by becoming a member of the Republican Party.

$\sim$ $\sim$

At the time, signing up with the Republicans seemed a little like buying a stock just as the bottom was dropping out of it. Not long after our meeting with Reagan, the Democrats did indeed recapture control of the legislature. Shortly before that, Pete told me he'd had it with the legislature and was moving back to San Diego to run for mayor. As he explained it, the decision made sense. San Diego was growing rapidly and was well-positioned to be a major player in California's economy. Moreover, there was a good possibility that the next national Republican convention might be held there, spotlighting the city and its mayor. Pete also said that he had no desire to be in the minority of a Democrat-controlled Legislature, particularly one in which Willie Brown was likely to become a member of the leadership.

None of this surprised me. But I couldn't help feeling that I'd been cut loose. Because we'd gotten so close, I assumed Pete and Bob White, his administrative assistant, and I were a team. But here he was letting me know something I should have seen by myself: that a public person's first concern is his own future. As part of our discussion about his next career move, Pete said that of course after he was elected he'd bring me to San Diego. But Ilene and I had a new baby and a new house, and we didn't want to leave what had become comfortable territory for an interracial couple. Moreover, I knew that if I accepted Pete's offer to relocate, I would become the tail on his kite. There was a large semantic territory between the words "friend" and "aide." When I told him I wouldn't be going to San Diego with him, he didn't insist. In fact, I think he was glad to see me assert my independence.

One of my options was to stay in the legislature and work for the assembly's Office of Research. Such an assignment would have probably resulted in a salary reduction; it definitely would have defined me as a political "hanger-on" subject to Willie Brown's whims. For this reason, if no other, I would rather have flipped hamburgers for a living.

Instead, I decided to return to the Department of Housing and Community Development, this time as chief deputy director. The Department was now headed by a man named Don Pinkerton. Don and I established a good relationship based on a joint commitment to using government to promote home ownership among the poor. But our philosophy was somewhat to the left of the administration's. In fact, Reagan's aides made it clear that they viewed our department as a pork barrel created by the Democrats and wanted to see it dismantled. The problem, however, was that they wanted to avoid the fallout by having Don and me perform a mercy killing from within. Eliminate positions, downsize the budget, ignore existing responsibilities, and propose statutes to do away with important functions: this was the mandate they gave us. And don't let staff members know that it is the administration doing these things, because if they found out they would whine to their Democrat friends in the legislature, who would, in turn, leak it to their friends in the press and there'd be hell to pay.

Neither of us had the stomach for this kind of deceit and after nearly two years of nerve-wracking tension between us and the governor's office, Don came into my office one day late in January 1973 and said that he'd had enough. I immediately said, "Me too." We both resigned on the spot. I knew I'd just worked my last day as a civil servant.

— —

The idea of starting my own business had been planted during that conversation with Pete Wilson a few years earlier in Seattle. And so when Ilene and I began Connerly & Associates on February 1, 1973, we felt, in the words of the hippie saying of the era, that it was the first day of the rest of our lives.

Our office—about a hundred square feet in a building with several other offices and a shared receptionist—wasn't big enough for two people, so Ilene did the books and other work at home. In starting the business, I was gambling that after ten years of work in the field, I knew about as much as anyone about the field of housing. The niche I saw for Connerly & Associates was in providing expertise to businesses and communities forced to work their way through the increasingly complex maze of government policies.

My first—and for a long time my only—client was the California Builders Council (now the California Building Industry Association), the building industry's statewide representative. I analyzed legislation for them, went to hearings, and, along with Paul McCarron, the organization's executive vice president, generally functioned as their eyes and ears in the capital. Working on an hourly basis we made about $1500 a month. It was less than my salary as a state employee, but from my very first bite of private enterprise, I loved the taste.

After about six months we got another client, California Building Officials, for whom we provided staff services as well as policy analysis. When this contract was signed, Ilene and I breathed a joint sigh of relief: for the first time in months we were sure we'd be able to pay the mortgage and feed the kids.

After scraping along for a year or so, our big break came in 1974. The growing environmental movement had made protection of California's coastline a major political issue. When the state legislature failed to enact protective laws, a statewide initiative was passed creating a commission whose mandate was to design and adopt a comprehensive coastal zone plan. The kinds of regulations that would be implemented were a matter of grave concern to numerous segments of California's economy. And so, to maximize their impact on the policies about to be born, a number of industry associations—homebuilders, realtors, cattlemen, farmers, landowners, and others—decided to form a coalition and hire a consultant to assess the ways in which these regulations would affect each of them.

Connerly & Associates got the contract. It was for $250,000, many more zeroes than I'd expected to see behind a set of numbers this early in our business. Ilene and I hired her sister, Charlene, as our first full-time employee, and sub-contracted with environmental planners, biologists, attorneys, and several other consultants and still came away with enough profit to open a bigger office and begin marketing our business in earnest.

Through all this, I continued to watch Pete out of the corner of my eye. Getting elected mayor of San Diego had become the good career move he thought it would be. In the early seventies, people around the state were starting to pay attention to him and getting accustomed to the notion that he'd be running for higher office. I supported Pete throughout his ascension through California politics—not as an "aide," but as a friend. Like most politicians, Pete appreciates loyalty, but unlike most politicians he also hates yes-people. The relationship we developed had enough give and take to accommodate disagreement. When he was mayor, for instance, Pete designed a controlled growth plan for San Diego as a way of establishing his credentials in the area of environmental protection. But, he needed to address growing criticism from land developers and contracted with Connerly & Associates to do a study on the impacts of the plan. Unfortunately, our report concluded that the plan would cost jobs. This was not the conclusion Pete had in mind and he let me know it, whereupon I reminded him of our conversation in Seattle when he had urged me to be my own man. At this, Pete gave a wry smile.

One of the reasons our relationship has remained strong is this smile and the down-to-earth sense of humor that goes along with it, which I've seen a lot of over the years. By now I've watched a lot of politicians in action, white and black, and Pete Wilson is one of the few who have managed to be in the profession for the long haul and yet remain emotionally whole.

I supported him when he ran for the U.S. Senate. As he took up residence inside the beltway, I was becoming more deeply embedded in California than ever. We didn't see each other that much, but there was still a sense of connection that survived the distance. I passed political tidbits on to his chief of staff, Bob White, who had been with Pete since he first came to the legislature. Pete would occasionally call with something for me. In 1975, for instance, he called one day to tell me about a new bill—a community development block grant program that would send money back to the states as part of Nixon's "New Federalism." Pete said, "I wanted to give you a heads-up on this. You probably ought to take an interest." I immediately made contacts with cities and counties all over the state telling them about the bill and how they could control their own lower-income housing activities. Connerly & Associates established many relationships then that continue today.

Over the next few years, Connerly & Associates became well established, employing fifteen or so people full time along with dozens of outside contractors. I won't deny that I relish the financial independence this business has given me. But it has always been less the money than the act of entrepreneurship itself that has given me satisfaction: the act of making something and seeing it grow, that sense of accomplishment the poet Gerard Manley Hopkins calls "the *achieve-of* of a thing."

I regret that Mom didn't live to see the full success of Connerly & Associates. I think she would have seen it as a vindication of the sacrifices she had made in raising me, although we never really talked about such things. Mom was not one to live vicariously through others, even her own children. As she often said, "The Lord has given us all our own work to do."

Mom's work involved her family and her church, and she was always a lightning rod for both. She had read certain passages of scripture so often that she had them virtually memorized; she had a quote from the Bible ready for every occasion. As she grew older, those qualities always present in her character—seriousness, conviction, irony—grew more pronounced, as did her Indian looks. In the early seventies, she suffered a stroke and afterwards suffered friends and neighbors and family members to take care of her.

I stopped by frequently to see her at our old house on Branch Street, which over the years had taken on more and more the look of a museum of my past. Mom always sat me down and queried me, as she had when I was a teenager—still teaching, still searching for evidence of sound judgment in me, still worried about my moral well-being.

"Are you going to church?" she would ask every time I visited.

"Not really, Mom," I'd stammer. "I've been pretty busy."

Then she'd get that stern look on her face I remembered so well.

"Are you telling me, young man, that you are too busy for the Lord? Nobody's *that* busy!"

Mom died in the spring of 1977 at the age of eighty-five. Her voice lives on in the back of my mind, becoming especially loud when I give in to self-pity or weakness. I wish that what it says could be heard by all young black people: "You stop your complaining, hear? Get to work! Take charge of your life right now, young man!"

In 1990, Pete came home to run for governor against Dianne Feinstein. The California Republican Party united behind him and he won, even though, as usual, he began as an underdog. Ilene and I were among his major donors and we helped him raise money for the race. There was talk among reporters that I would become part of the Wilson "kitchen cabinet" if he were elected. The term made me smile. Ronald Reagan might have relied on such a group when he was governor, but if Pete had ever formed one it would have had very few meetings. He wasn't one for extensive consultation or governing by committee.

The day after the election, I got a call from Bob White, still Pete's right-hand man. After preliminary chitchat, Bob indicated that Pete wanted to see me. When I showed up at the transition office the next day, Pete and I danced the minuet familiar to potential appointees.

"Business good?" he asked.

"Very good," I replied.

"Happy with what you're doing?"

"Very happy."

"Want to go back into public service?"

"I can't afford to leave my business."

The role Pete had in mind for me was Secretary of Business, Transportation and Housing. If I had been backing him simply in hopes of a political payoff, as some later suggested, I would have jumped at this high-profile job. But Connerly & Associates needed me and I let Pete know I couldn't take a full-time position.

"You'll do volunteer stuff?" he asked.

"Of course," I replied.

A couple of days after this conversation, Bob White asked for a meeting.

"We want you to be our go-to guy," he told me.

I asked what that meant.

"You will be our guy outside the administration to serve as a liaison with the private sector," White said. "You want to do it?"

"I guess," I answered.

At this time, California was still mired in a serious recession. Businesses were leaving by the dozens and people were leaving with them. The problem was so serious that a common joke around Sacramento was that the only growing industry in the state was the moving industry. Pete felt something had to be done to turn things around. He established the Council on California Competitiveness and appointed Peter Uberroth as chair and made me a member.

After meeting for several months, the council released a report in 1992 with several important recommendations, among them a call for a reform of workers' compensation insurance premiums, which were driving businesses crazy—and driving them also to relocate in Montana and Colorado. But much of the impact of the report was blunted by the competition that had sprung up between Pete and Uberroth, who was still something of a star as a result of his role in the 1984 Olympics and seen by some Republicans as a possible future rival to Pete. Uberroth did small irritating things that further strained the relationship. For example, he tried to have the press conference unveiling the report in Los Angeles rather than Sacramento; he tried to present the report to the governor and the legislature, rather than just the governor; and he had his aides, instead of the governor's, plan the publicity. And then, when the report was finally released and all the members of the Council were supposed to go around the state marketing its conclusions as a way of stopping the "job-killing machine"—as our report put it— that state government had become, Uberroth suddenly quit to become chairman of another committee, Rebuild Los Angeles, established in the wake of the Rodney King riots.

Not long after the Council on California Competitiveness had completed its work, I was at a hotel across the street from the state capitol building attending a fund-raiser for a shrewd local politico and genuine character named B.T. Collins. B.T. was a Vietnam veteran who'd emerged from the war with a prosthetic arm and leg but with his big heart and a raucous, profane sense of humor fully intact. He had gone into state politics years earlier as Jerry Brown's chief of staff and become one of the most quotable sources during the cosmic weirdness of Brown's "Governor Moonbeam" phase. Perhaps the most outspoken advocate of veterans in California, Collins had also become increasingly conservative over the years. When Pete was elected, B.T. wanted to join the new administration. (Knowing that I was the "go-to guy," B.T. called me out of the blue one night and made his wishes known in his own inimitable way: "I wouldn't mind helping Wilson out, but if that little son of a bitch thinks I'm going to kiss his ass to get a job he's crazy.")

I told Pete and Bob White about the content of the conversation (without quoting B.T. directly). To his credit, Pete was willing to ignore the fact that B.T. could be something of a loose cannon in order to profit from his creativity and experience. Knowing of Collins' sympathy for troubled kids, Pete named him to head the California Youth Authority.

Pete can seem a little stiff in public, but in private he has a wicked sense of humor, and he came to love B.T.'s larger-than-life persona, his crusty, unorthodox style, and especially his way of sticking it to the liberals. When a crucial seat in the state assembly became vacant in 1992, Pete convinced Collins to run for it. The race was an expensive and particularly vicious one. B.T. barely won and the effort may, in fact, have hastened the heart attack that killed him a year or so later.

The fund-raiser for B.T. took place in 1993, and its purpose was to help retire B.T.'s campaign debt. The guest of honor was Rush Limbaugh. ("Connerly, you bastard," B.T. had growled into the phone when he invited me to attend, "you'd better get the hell over here. I've got a real star this time. It's Limbaugh, not a phony, candy ass like the rest of you sons of bitches.") I had just begun to talk with Rush, in fact, when Tom Hayes, one of Pete's aides, came up to me and whispered, "The governor would like to see you."

I walked to Pete's office. Following a brief discussion about some innocuous redevelopment bill, Pete leaned forward in that earnest way of his and said he wanted to appoint me to the University of California Board of Regents.

"How much time would it take?" I asked.

"No big deal," Pete shrugged. "Maybe a couple days a month."

I told him I'd think about it.

I was still mulling over Pete's offer a few days later, when I received a call from Julie Justus, the governor's appointments secretary. Julie read me a press release announcing my appointment. I chuckled that I still hadn't made up my mind.

"But the Governor really wants you to take this appointment," she said. "There are a lot of problems on the board that need solving."

I missed the warning implicit in this last sentence and told her to go ahead and send out the press release.

— —

I assumed that I was being tapped for the same reason that most regents are selected—not so much for any expertise in issues of higher education but because they are major donors, or have close or long-standing ties to the governor. I qualified on both counts. But several days after the appointment was announced, I received a bundle of reading materials intended to help me prepare for a hearing scheduled before the legislative advisory panel that reviews and comments on the qualifications of prospective regents. Included in the package of materials were transcripts of the state senate confirmation hearings of the regent who had been appointed just before me, John Davies, Pete's roommate in law school and his personal attorney.

As I read through this material, I discovered for the first time that when John, who is white, was appointed, an understanding had been reached between the governor and the senate, which has the power of confirmation, that future appointments would reflect greater "diversity."

None of this had been mentioned in discussions about my appointment. I'm sure that Pete was aware that if it had been mentioned I would have walked. Although I knew that he wouldn't have chosen me for a high-profile position unless he had absolute confidence in my ability, it nonetheless bothered me that race was a part of the mix. A white appointee would be presumed to have gotten the job because of who he was. Would I be seen as the "black" regent?

Ironically, in the days following the press release, as the nature of my complicated relationship with Pete was scrutinized by the press, the issue of race took a backseat to the issue of "cronyism." I was actually relieved to be seen as just another political appointee being given the nod because of longtime personal and financial support for the governor.

Why feel less stigmatized by cronyism than "diversity"? Well, consider the example of Vernon Jordan and Bill Clinton, a relationship that preceded Monica Lewinsky and will presumably continue long after she has become an agate type footnote in the history of the presidency. The Jordan-Clinton relationship is not based on Jordan's color or his standing in the "black community." It is based on his independent power and the traction he has achieved in the wider world, and it shows that black people can become political insiders with access to decision makers similar to that of other corporate and business leaders and irrespective of race. Cronyism is at least based on one's individual qualities; diversity is based on factors that render individuality irrelevant.

Once I had sorted out these problems, I came to the Board of Regents with a sense of possibility and optimism. It was supposed to be one of those honorific jobs that gives heft to a career, and it was in this spirit that I took it. Pete may have had an idea that there were a few "problems" on the board, but neither he nor I had any idea that he had put me in a place that would soon become the cockpit of California's racial politics.

SIX

THE MEMBERS OF THE UNIVERSITY of California's Board of Regents may not be household names, but they are all heavyweights nonetheless, politically savvy and aware of what it takes to operate successfully behind the scenes. The board is not exactly a center of intrigue, but it is a center of power, and, as such, it promotes a subtle jockeying for position among its membership. By the time I was sworn in, I knew that some members were more equal than others, and that these "players" gave the board its distinctive personality.

Howard Leach, for instance, was a wealthy entrepreneur from the Bay Area who had been appointed by former Governor George Deukemejian. Sharp and thoughtful, Howard is a tanned, silver-haired, aristocratic-looking man who has worked in the upper echelons of the national Republican Party, including a stint as finance chairman of the Republican National Committee during the Dole-Kemp campaign.

Dean Watkins, who has since left the board, was appointed by Ronald Reagan. He too is wealthy, reserved, and very conservative. A strong supporter of the UC administration, he felt that the most significant thing the regents did was select the president of the university. Dean had a simple philosophy: the board should let the president do his work without meddling, and if this approach didn't sit well with the board, it should fire him and get someone else.

Frank Clark was the last of Jerry Brown's appointees. He was in his late seventies when I came to the board, and was stern and serious. A powerful corporate attorney for major companies, Frank was the ultimate fiduciary who read every financial report word for word. He had been more influential on the board in the past, but retained power by the knowledge he acquired in his dogged pursuit of facts and figures.

Meredith Khachigian was usually identified as the wife of Ken Khachigian, one of California's leading political strategists and a chief aide to George Deukemejian, who had appointed her. But people who saw Meredith simply as Ken's appendage drastically underestimated her. She had been deeply involved in alumni affairs and other aspects of the university for years and carried considerable weight on the board.

Roy Brophy, a big, flush-faced man with white hair and a blustery manner, had made his money as a home builder and had also been appointed to the board during the Deukemejian administration. Roy bragged that he was the only person ever to have served on all three governing boards of higher education in California: community colleges, state universities, and the University of California. I saw immediately that he was quite influential with the other regents and accustomed to getting his way.

And there was, of course, the UC President, Jack Peltason. In his late sixties when he was hired for the job, Jack was a one-time political science professor who had risen to the chancellorship of UC Irvine. He was seen as something of a transitional figure, someone who would keep the seat warm for a successor who would presumably have longer tenure. I came onto the board thinking that most college administrators were a bad combination of Neville Chamberlain and Saul Alinsky. But Jack proved me wrong. While he was adept at riding the political and ideological updrafts of higher education, at bottom he was a man of calm conviction who, even if his office sometimes made him evade the hard questions, was still never one for easy answers either.

I felt that becoming a member of this board was like being called up to the big leagues of public service. A University of California regent's term is twelve years, but it feels like a lifetime sinecure. There is no salary, but the perks are world-class. From the outset you are made to feel like minor royalty, cosseted by university administrators who look after you in the ritualized way of workers tending a queen bee. The board is steeped in tradition, and your colleagues initiate you into a ceremonial world that seems almost like a secret society. It is the plush world of power, second among such nonelected bodies in California only to the state supreme court. Yet signals are clearly given from the moment you're sworn in that this power is contingent on being a team player. You *will* suppress potentially embarrassing questions; you *will* regard the smooth functioning of the university as the highest good; you *will* avoid comments or controversies that open the board to the prying eye of the media. The table you sit at may be oval, but it is top heavy with senior regents at one end. It is one of those bodies in which you're supposed to spend a season or two being seen and not heard. At least, this was the structure that existed upon my arrival.

I saw all this clearly on the day of my very first meeting. It was at UCLA in the spring of 1993. I arrived late because of delays at the Sacramento airport. When I walked in, all of the other regents were already conducting business. I was introduced as a new member of the board and politely applauded. I sat down and tried to keep an intelligent and alert look on my face. Because one of the agenda items was a possible increase in student fees, there were a large number of students in the audience, and the atmosphere was tense. During a discussion of this issue, a couple of hecklers shouted out remarks and Roy Brophy, who was chairing the meeting, suddenly stood and ordered us to adjourn. "Okay, we're leaving now."

As everyone else withdrew, the student regent, a young man named Alex Wong, and I hung back to talk to the angry students. After chatting with them for a while about fee increases and other issues, I walked back to the lounge where the others had gathered. When I got there, Brophy was waiting with a choleric look on his face.

"When I say we're leaving the room," he said to me, "we leave the room! We all act together!"

"Look, you don't tell me what to do," I interrupted him, "and you don't tell me who to talk to."

The other regents who were nearby watched us with looks of shocked disbelief. As Brophy stood there glaring at me, I realized that this was someone who wouldn't forget this confrontation.

If the context had been more civil, I would have explained to him that while I hadn't become a regent to cause controversy, I didn't intend to meekly follow orders. I didn't want to break ranks with the rest of the board, but I wasn't going to be a rubber stamp either. And, during my first few months as a regent, when the contentious issue of raising student fees finally came to a vote, I stood against it—with the student regent, I was the only one on the board who did—because it seemed to me that the university administration was not serious about cutting costs and wanted students' families to subsidize the self-indulgent status quo. I didn't mind being in the minority on this or any other vote, but the pressure to achieve consensus on every issue disturbed me. I wrote a letter to my colleagues in which I questioned the deferential atmosphere.

Despite this static—or perhaps because some of the other regents actually agreed with some of the issues I raised—I was elected head of the Finance Committee. Ironically, given what was to come, I had first been asked to serve on the Affirmative Action Committee, but said no, not because I had a strong position on the issue—I didn't yet—but because I didn't want to be seen as the "black" regent who was automatically given the "black" portfolio.

Finance is considered the board's most important committee, the central nervous system for the whole operation. It oversees a budget large enough to operate a small country. The financial decisions it makes determine the university's future. But in addition to riding herd on the numbers, I found that the Finance Committee also spent an inordinate amount of time settling lawsuits. Some of the issues had large social implications. The medical school at UC Irvine, for instance, had stepped into a potential hornet's nest when it was revealed that some of the professors and researchers in the fertility clinic there were secretly extracting healthy women's eggs and then later dispensing them to the infertile on what amounted to a eugenics black market. The idea of some young person showing up twenty years after the fact with an attorney and saying "I was that egg and my life has been screwed up because of what you did" gave university lawyers bad dreams. In my first few years on the Finance Committee, we settled several lawsuits stemming from this practice.

But most of the legal matters we dealt with were much less weighty. The University of California's reputation as an institution that doesn't want to go to court, combined with its deep pockets, makes it an inviting target, and it seemed to me that it didn't take much of a complaint to get a sizable settlement in this era of political correctness and inflamed gender relations. In one case, for instance, a supervisor in one of our maintenance departments left a female co-worker he had been living with to take up with another woman whom he supervised. The first woman claimed that he was now discriminating against her in terms of job assignments, and the university settled with her for a substantial figure. Later on, the supervisor left the second woman, who also sued and settled. And then, when the administration finally told the guy to get it together, *he* threatened to sue UC for invasion of privacy!

It is not only the responsibility for protecting the university's reputation that keeps a new regent anxious. The legislature's peculiar delayed confirmation process also contributes to one's unease. The state senate has a year to confirm or reject a new appointee. If the senate doesn't act, it is the equivalent of a pocket veto and you're out. The legislators usually take several months to decide, which gives a new regent time to acquire a record. This record, along with the appointee's background and qualifications, is scrutinized when the final decision is made.

Some regents warned me that being outspoken during my probationary period might threaten my confirmation, but I think it actually helped me. Lester Lee, a regent Pete Wilson appointed the same day he appointed me, said very little during his first year, and yet he was rejected for confirmation because he was presumed to be a tool of the governor.

As part of the confirmation ritual, I went to see Tom Hayden, chairman of the state senate's Committee on Higher Education. Oddly enough, I'd met Tom when he ran for the U.S. Senate in the late seventies. At that time, even though his candidacy had seemed marginal, I'd invited him to give his views on housing issues to a state builders' group represented by Connerly & Associates, and he had reciprocated by inviting me to attend a fund-raising cruise on the American River with his then-wife Jane Fonda. These had been casual contacts, but we both remembered them.

When I appeared at his office, Tom and I chatted for a moment about these events from several years earlier. Then, he got down to business.

"I've got two reservations about you," he said. "One, you're too close to Wilson. And two, the Nexus search my staff did shows that you've made some comments critical of affirmative action."

I knew exactly what he was referring to. In 1991, a law had been passed requiring contractors doing business with state government to subcontract out 15 percent of the total contract to minority-owned businesses and 5 percent to women-owned businesses. At the time, I didn't pay much attention to it, dismissing it as just another vaguely distasteful government regulation. But then I got a call one morning from a white contractor who wanted to form a joint venture with Connerly & Associates. We would be the minority consultant on the project, for purposes of satisfying the minority requirement, and he would allow us to choose what 15 percent of the work we wanted.

I felt like telling this man that he could go and have carnal knowledge of himself. The notion of being another firm's fig leaf betrayed every commitment I'd made in building a business that had succeeded by doing better work at a lower price. It was also not a very good business proposition. If I could buy off all of my major competition by giving them 15 percent of the business, I would truly be rolling in financial clover.

A similar experience occurred later that same year, when a member of my staff received a call from a San Francisco contractor who was bidding on a toxic waste clean-up project in that city. The contractor, who was white, wanted to set up a joint venture with us to make his bid more competitive. The fact that Connerly &

Associates specialized in housing issues and had no particular expertise in toxic waste management did not seem to be terribly significant to him. All that mattered was that I was a "minority" and thereby met the most important threshold requirement for the bid. I told one of my aides to call this contractor back and inform him that our firm did not respond to bid requests for which we were not qualified and did not participate in minority business programs.

I was annoyed enough by these experiences to sound off in a 1991 profile done by the *Sacramento Bee*, which was the item Hayden's Nexus search turned up. "I'm opposed to it," I'd said there of affirmative action. "For me, it's the ultimate insult. I don't need any brownie points from anybody. I don't want any from anybody. And to my knowledge we have never taken advantage of it."

When Hayden read my quotes and asked me about them, I told him I hadn't changed my mind since making these statements.

"Well, I disagree with you," he shook his head dubiously after thinking about it for a moment, "but I'm going to support you anyhow."

I was confirmed by the state senate without a dissenting vote. The *San Francisco Chronicle*, which later labeled me a tool of the governor during the campaign to eliminate race-based admissions, called me "a breath of fresh air."

Hayden was probably right to think that I would be okay on this issue. At this point, affirmative action was a social policy I generally disagreed with, an annoying intrusion of racial bean counting into the business world. In my limited experience, it seemed to me a philosophy that corrupted both the white businesses that called in minority firms to help get contracts and the minority firms that participated in the farce. But, to the degree that I thought about it, at this point I regarded affirmative action as a bureaucratic rather than a moral problem, and it concerned me only when it was in my face. Without knowing much about it, I accepted affirmative action as a part of the world in which I lived; a more or less invisible and certainly unchallengeable policy with a life of its own; the white noise of our everyday social transactions.

I regarded the idea of "diversity" in the same way. It was one of those concepts that sounded so good, a notion that called up images of different people standing joyously on a mountaintop singing "We Are the World." How could you oppose it? Of course, later on I understood that the people who use this word define it in a very narrow way. For them, diversity means people who have dark skin or wear a pants suit and unquestioningly support their "progressive" political line. "Diversity" (this is one of those contentious words it is impossible to use without quotes) is really about forming group caucuses and has nothing to do with the individual's heart and soul, which is where true diversity exists. Once on the board, it wasn't long before I was responding to bureaucrats who told me that we needed an even more diverse faculty at UC. I told them that I'd acknowledge the importance of this concept when I heard that they wanted to hire an evangelical Christian, say, or a woman who is pro-life, or, for that matter, a Republican.

I know exactly when my attitude toward confronting affirmative action began to change. It was one morning after I'd been on the board for a little over a year when I received a call from fellow regent Clair Burgener. A former member of Congress, Clair was well respected by the board, a consensus-builder there as he had been in the House of Representatives. In his late seventies, Burgener was a good-looking, witty man who prided himself on his ability to defuse volatile situations, and I liked him from the moment we met. In this call, he was asking for a favor. He had just met with a couple of his "constituents," Ellen and Jerry Cook from La Jolla, who had assembled a "report" on how the university was discriminating against Asian and white applicants in our medical schools. Because he feared that they might try to sue us, Clair asked me, as chair of the Finance Committee, to meet with the Cooks and try to understand what had gotten them so worked up.

At this point in time, the question of who got into UC—or, more to the point, who did not—was causing a good deal of discussion (grumbling would actually be a better word) around the state, with Asian Americans in particular beginning to claim that the admissions game was rigged against them. Yet at this juncture, the same university administrators who would later defend preference policies as vitally necessary to build a just society were not even willing to acknowledge the existence of such practices. I believed them when they said that race played a fairly insignificant role in the admissions process and saw myself as the good soldier whose duty was to defend the institution. I agreed, therefore, to have a reassuring talk with the Cooks. I expected to give them a sympathetic hearing and then send them on their way.

They flew to Sacramento and met me in my office in late August, 1994. It was one of those airless, sweltering days that paralyzes the Central Valley in mid-summer. After sitting down, they remained motionless for a moment, allowing the air-conditioning to revive them. When we began to talk, I saw that Ellen, who teaches accounting at the University of San Diego, a Catholic liberal arts college, was reserved and professorial, while Jerry, who trained as a physicist, works in private industry and has taught in the UC system as a form of community service, was just the opposite: voluble and kinetic, and giving off so much energy that electricity seemed to crackle at his fingertips.

Later on, Jerry told me that he had first begun to wonder about affirmative action when he was asked to teach a course in quantitative methods at UC San Diego in the late eighties. The course was designed for graduate students studying international relations, so he wasn't expecting much mathematics expertise. But neither was he prepared for what he did find. It turned out that the class was virtually bisected by ability, with about half performing well and the others unable to do even elementary algebra. In the lower group there were a disproportionate number of black students. Jerry reports mentioning this to the Dean, who said to him, "Oh, those are my a.a.'s." Jerry asked him what he meant by "a.a.'s." The Dean said, "My affirmative actions," and then gave Jerry a small stipend to buy remedial materials for the low-achieving members of his class.

Jerry didn't mention this experience in our first meeting. The story he and Ellen focused on was far more personal, revolving around the experience of their son James. I knew from my own experience that parents tend to exaggerate their children's accomplishments. But if even half of what Jerry and Ellen told me was true, James Cook was an exceptional student and person. While still in high school he completed 16 university courses at UCSD, was on the National Science Olympiad Team, and was a National Merit Scholar. He graduated from high school at sixteen with nothing lower than an A on his transcript. He then enrolled at UC San Diego, where he graduated in 1992, having earned Phi Beta Kappa as a computer science major. He co-authored three published articles in medical journals, and volunteered on medical relief missions to Mexico. James wanted to be a doctor and had outstanding scores on his Medical College Admissions Test.

James's elderly grandparents lived in San Diego and he had originally hoped to attend medical school at the University of California campus there because it was close to home—just down the street, in fact. He applied to all five UC medical schools and also to the Harvard Medical School/MIT Joint Program in health sciences and technology, and to graduate school at Cal Tech in Computer Science. Harvard/MIT admitted James and offered him a fellowship for medical school within five days of interviewing him. Cal Tech admitted him to its PhD program, along with a $29,000 fellowship, within hours of his interview. But all of the UC medical schools rejected him.

Although he was disappointed, James attributed his rejection to the luck of the draw. As his father told me, "He just shrugged and said, 'The people that got in must just be better than me.'" He decided to attend Cal Tech for a year and consider his options for realizing his dream of a medical education.

While doing his first graduate year at Cal Tech, James reapplied to the five UC medical schools and to several out-of-state schools as well. He was immediately admitted to the prestigious Johns Hopkins Medical School—one of only two California residents offered admission that year. By June 1993, however, when James was completing his Masters thesis at Cal Tech—the first student in the department ever to get a graduate degree in one year—he was once again getting rejection slips from the UC system. But with one exception: this year UC Davis, alone among the five medical schools, offered him admission. Preferring to be a brief airplane ride away from his family rather than on the other side of the country (and because Johns Hopkins would have cost about $150,000), James decided to attend the campus whose rejection of Alan Bakke fifteen years earlier had led to the growth of an affirmative action establishment in the U.S.

Later on, I came to see that the Cooks' story was typical in many ways, not the least of which was their initial reluctance to pursue what they had unearthed because they didn't want to be seen as selfish parents trying to seize an advantage for their kid.

Incredulous at the idea that there would be systematic bias against whites and Asians, the Cooks, in fact, had initially made excuses for the UC system. But once James was admitted to Johns Hopkins, perhaps the best medical school in the country, they began to smell a rat and decided to investigate more closely.

Jerry went to the UC San Diego campus and got copies of the records of all the UCSD students over a several-year period who had applied to medical school. There were no names, but there were racial data, test scores, grades, and information about where the students had applied and where they had been accepted. Jerry brought the materials home, sorted out the UCSD grads who had been accepted to UCSD Medical School (to reduce the variables and get an "apple-to-apple" comparison) and then entered the numbers into a computer. He put the results into a scatterplot—a square field with high grades on the right side and low grades on the left, and high test scores on the top and low ones on the bottom. The students, represented according to race by black (for blacks and Hispanics) and white circles (for Asians and whites), were placed in the field according to their marks.

When he handed me the scatterplot, the results needed little interpretation. There were a few black circles in the upper-right part of the square, but most were white. The circles in the lower-left part were almost all black. I asked Jerry what he thought the figures meant and he gave me a statistician's response: "If you look at grades in required premed courses and at the scores in the Medical College Admissions Test, the average affirmative action admit ranked in the lowest one percent relative to the Asians and whites admitted."

"Put it in practical terms," I said.

"Say you're six feet tall," Jerry replied. "Fairly tall for the general population, but if you played in a college basketball division of one hundred players, you might be in the lowest one percent with respect to height."

Then Jerry asked, "Do you play poker?"

I nodded.

"Well, put it another way then. Even if you ignored all consideration of grades and test scores and simply drew names out of a hat, given that there are only 13 percent of the applicants classified as 'under-represented,' you are 180 times more likely to have four aces and a king than you are to have this many under-represented applicants picked. It's a stacked deck in a crooked game."

As I studied the scatterplot, Jerry told me that the preponderance of black circles in the lower-left part of the figure bothered him far more than white ones clustered in the upper-right corner. He explained that his father had been a sharecropper in Missouri, while Ellen's father was a laborer in Kentucky before he went into the army during World War II. The fact that there were no white circles in the lower-left part of the square meant that "their people," poor whites who needed a boost too, were never given a break under affirmative action.

After analyzing the UC San Diego data, Jerry Cook visited the medical schools at UCLA and UC Irvine, obtaining and analyzing similar placement statistics. The results were the same, indicating a rigged system. Rigged in more ways than one, in fact. Jerry's outrage increased when he discovered that the kids of the heads of the outreach program and one of the residential colleges at UC San Diego, both white, had gotten into medical school. What's more, the son of a high-ranking black administrator in the UC system, with a salary of $219,000 and additional outside consulting income of nearly that much, had been brought into the undergraduate "Bridge" program, where underprivileged students get free housing, food and books.

As Ellen told me, "James was fortunate to finally get admitted to UC Davis, but it's clear that many, many young people like him are having their chances in life radically diminished because they're of the wrong race. In one year's worth of UC San Diego medical school applicants, we found fifty applicants who were better qualified academically than the *best* affirmative action applicant admitted to UC San Diego Medical School. Yet, *none* of these applicants was admitted to *any* medical school in the entire United States."

Armed with their facts and figures, the Cooks approached UC administrators, believing that they would correct this injustice once it was made clear to them. But when they presented their case, they were not only told that the bias they had discovered was a mirage, but they suffered petty harassment as well. When they asked for more data, for instance, they were presented with hundreds of photocopied pages rather than the disks they had previously received. This was clearly intended to make computer analysis more difficult for them. In addition, Jerry told me, a UC Davis campus policeman once accused him of having hacked his way into the university computer system and warned him that this was potentially a prosecutable offense.

Increasingly doubtful that anything would be done, but wanting at least to expose what was taking place, Jerry sent copies of his detailed analysis—it would become known as "The Cook Report"—to the attention of the UC president's office late in 1993. After months had dragged by without a reply, he finally told his story to my colleague Clair Burgener. Clair made a call and shortly afterward, the Cooks received a letter from a staff attorney of the UC General Counsel's office. It stated, "Our conclusion is that the procedures and criteria at each school should pass legal muster under the *Bakke* case. Our review *found nothing clearly unlawful.*" This last phrase, which I have italicized, has always struck me as similar to the sentence Al Gore blurted out—"There is no controlling legal authority"—when he got caught with his hands in a different sort of cookie jar.

Jerry Cook told me later that his heart fell when he walked into my office the first time. He didn't know I was black, and when he saw me he thought that Burgener had sent him to me as part of a skin game. As for me, I was dumbfounded by the end of our meeting—unable to believe that something like this had happened to someone like James Cook and that it had been so hushed up.

The last thing I wanted was to become embroiled in racial politics on the Board of Regents. But once I heard the Cooks' story and read the material they gave me, I said to them what I couldn't deny in my heart: "This is wrong." I told them I would pursue the matter, and this simple decision changed my life.

The first thing I did was call Clair Burgener. "We need to put the question of the role played by race in the admissions process on the agenda," I told him, "or at least get some kind of real response to the Cooks' report."

Clair agreed. We decided that each of us would send a copy of the Cooks' material to the UC president and then call him so that there would be no question later on that it had been received. When I spoke to Peltason he agreed to issue a series of reports devoted to the subject of admissions and to address what the Cooks had to say in our November board meeting.

But when this meeting took place, I sensed a certain cockiness on the part of the administration—almost as if this matter was a nuisance it was annoyed to have to deal with. After a brief summary of medical school admission policies, President Peltason noted that over the past twenty-five years all of his predecessors had committed themselves to the idea of diversity and that the regents had also backed this goal. As he spoke, a kind of surrealism crept into his words, as if he were speaking in allegories. He kept referring, for instance, to the administration's efforts to "affirmatively seek qualified minority students."

Peltason was followed by Cornelius Hopper, one of his vice presidents. A self-confident black man, Hopper proceeded to give us a little lecture on the benefits of minority enrollment in medical schools—making doctors for underserved communities—and on the social implications of the *Bakke* decision, with some snide allusions to Alan Bakke himself.

(I remembered Hopper's comments a couple of years later when the case of Patrick Chavis burst into the news. A black medical student admitted to UC Davis med school about the same time that Alan Bakke was being turned down, Chavis eventually became a poster boy for affirmative action and for the sort of community service Hopper had discussed. Working as a doctor in a poor, black section of Los Angeles, Chavis appeared on the cover of the *New York Times Magazine* (which praised him for being the antithesis of Bakke) and was pictured as a hero by Sen. Edward Kennedy in an extravagant speech on the Senate floor. But then, in 1998, news reports revealed that Chavis's "service" consisted of performing liposuction operations—after taking a four-day preparation course—at such high risk and with so little competence that some of his patients died or suffered crippling injuries. When California authorities finally stripped Chavis of his medical license, Alan Bakke was continuing to serve unobtrusively in a hospital in Minneapolis with a multiracial working class clientele. As all this became public knowledge, I felt like calling Hopper to ask him what he thought the moral of the story was.)

After Hopper finished speaking, a pair of administrators from the UC Irvine and UC San Francisco medical schools ended the administration's presentation by talking soothingly about how race was "only one of many factors" (a "bump" was the term they used) in the admissions process. As soon as they finished, all the staff people sat back with smug looks on their faces that suggested they were confident that they'd put out the Cooks' little brush fire.

But I was agitated by what I'd heard. During the presentation, I'd felt my "knower" kick in. For all the talk about "building diversity," what had been described, as far as I was concerned, was the scaffolding of injustice. When the board chairman asked if there were any questions, my colleagues glanced at each other with noncommittal looks on their faces, ready to declare themselves ready to move on. It was a crucial moment: a time when the issue of preferences at the university might well have gone away before it even became an issue. I wanted to say something, but wasn't sure that my reaction was right. I told myself that this might be a time to go along to get along. In fact, I made almost a physical effort to prevent my lips from moving. But I couldn't do it.

"What we've just heard," I finally said, "doesn't sound right and doesn't sound fair. You're rationalizing what you're doing, but you're not telling us why you're doing it. You didn't address the questions raised by the Cook Report."

I will never forget the pall that fell over the room after I finished talking. I had heard a good deal about "political correctness" and, like many people, considered it something of an exaggeration. But now I saw what a powerful sanction on behavior it could be. Judging from the pained reaction to my comments, one would have thought that a skunk had just entered the picnic area.

After an uncomfortable silence, Dean Watkins spoke up. "I'm not sure about this 'educational diversity' business either," he said. "It sounds like you're saying that our students can't learn without a certain number of minorities present."

"Learning is a much richer experience if they are present," Hopper answered smoothly.

Watkins shrugged and said, "Hmm," in a way that made it clear he was not convinced.

Then, another regent, Leo Koligian, a prominent lawyer from the Fresno area and my good friend and ally on the board, said, "I agree with Ward. I think we're practicing quotas here."

The administrators present looked at him as if he were a little tetched.

No one else said anything and the meeting ended with the status quo apparently intact. But we had all crossed a Rubicon even if we didn't know it at the time. This November 1994 meeting of the regents had let the genie of race preferences out of the bottle previously kept hidden away in the UC chamber of horrors.

— —

A few days after this meeting, on Thanksgiving Day, I got a call at home from Pete Wilson. He was still basking in the afterglow of his recent come-from-behind victory over Kathleen Brown in the 1994 governor's race and told me he was giving thanks once more to people like Ilene and me who had helped him

"So, things okay on the Board?" he asked as that part of the conversation began to wind down.

"They're shining us on, Pete," I said, still frustrated by the rhetorical shell and pea game of the last meeting.

"They who?"

"They, the university administration."

"Shining you on how?"

"This whole admissions issue," I said. "When we raised the issue of discrimination against whites and Asians, they really didn't deny their conduct; they just tried to make it disappear. Worse, they acted as if we were being disloyal and disruptive for even trying to figure out what they were up to."

Ironically, given the fact that he would later be accused of micromanaging the Board of Regents to produce a wedge issue, Pete at this point had not really followed the issue of preferences very closely.

"Shouldn't we be addressing the problems of all needy students," he finally asked, "and not letting some in because of their color and ethnic background? What about blacks and Hispanics from wealthy families?"*

"Right now I'm more bothered by the fact that we're not getting good information," I told him. "It feels like a cover-up to me."

"So, what are you going to do?"

"I'm not sure. I might pursue it."

"Well, if you want to, I'll be with you," he said. "It's your call."

I did more soul-searching from the time of this conversation until the end of 1994 than I can ever remember having done before in my life. All of my fragmentary and inchoate thoughts about race and history in the U.S. and my own "race" and history, in particular, rose to the surface of my mind. I had always been on my own, making my own way. Yet, I knew that the good things that had happened for me couldn't have happened without the civil rights movement. I felt incredible pride at what had been accomplished

---

* I didn't really pick up on it at the time, but Pete was onto something. Three years later, in 1998, in the furor following the scrapping of affirmative action, there was talk of reviving the policy, this time using sociological rather than racial factors. Advocates of this position assumed that such a policy would achieve the same ends—admission of more blacks—since most black applicants presumably came from disadvantaged social backgrounds. But Herma Hill Kay, dean of the UC Boalt Hall Law School and a leading defender of preferences, was forced to acknowledge that the premise was faulty when the subject came up: "Generally, African Americans who apply to our law school are not disadvantaged. Their mothers and fathers are professionals with good family incomes."

by this movement, yet bothered by the fact that it had now been commandeered by people pushing ideas like affirmative action that were hostile to its entire spirit. I felt that whatever I did in this situation would be seen as wrong and that my color, which I had always tried to make a secondary matter in my life, would soon become primary if I made the wrong decision.

I knew the smart thing to do would be to stand aside. The University of California is a large institution with significant power to mobilize against those it sees as posing a threat to its operations. But, I also knew that if I remained silent I would become in some basic moral sense an invisible man, like the character who skulks through Ralph Ellison's great novel. After a couple of weeks of reflection, I decided that I was responsible only to one constituency, and it wasn't the civil rights professionals or the UC administration: it was the students and students-to-be at the University of California and their parents. My compass throughout my weeks of thought was set by the example of my Uncle James and by the simple worldview of that gray-haired old woman, my grandmother, who reminded me all through my childhood that I should "never judge a book by its cover."

On the first business day of 1995, I called Leigh Trivette, secretary of the regents, and requested that she put affirmative action on the agenda of our January meeting.

— —

A few minutes after I made this request, I got a call from Jack Peltason.

"What do you have in mind in making this request?" he asked.

"To be honest with you, I'm still pretty pissed about the snow job we got at the November meeting," I said. "You guys didn't respond to the issues raised by the Cook Report. I'm not just concerned about medical schools now, but about the whole process of admissions, university-wide."

"Our staff didn't understand what information you wanted," Pelatson tried to soothe me. "Give us a chance to study these questions more intensively for a few months before you make any motions."

Peltason suggested a six-month review of the admissions process, and I agreed to wait before making it an agenda item.

At the January 19, 1995, regents' meeting, I merely noted that I had been disappointed by the quality of information offered in November and pointed out that what we had heard then did not seem compatible with the statement printed on the bottom of all the university's official documents: that we did not discriminate in terms of race, color, or background. I said that I agreed with Peltason's proposal for a six-month review, but that during this time I planned to conduct my own inquiry.

This seemed like a fairly moderate statement to me. Yet, when I finished speaking, the mood in the room was sufficiently tense that Clair Burgener admonished everyone to "keep cool." But a couple of people ignored this plea and broke the board's first commandment: thou shalt not speak ill of a colleague in public. Roy Brophy, still seething over our contretemps months earlier at UCLA, made a disparaging comment. Then Alice Gonzalez, a Brophy ally, accused me of using the affirmative action issue to build a future political career. She said that I was an "ambitious young man," which I guess was at least half a compliment.

From this moment onward, the minuet of decorum that had always governed the regents' deliberations was gone. In its place was what would sometimes become the rhetorical equivalent of slam dancing.

After the meeting, I was swarmed by the press. What was a black man doing raising questions about policies that helped black students? Why had I made this quixotic gesture of questioning something as deeply embedded in the university's philosophy and governance as affirmative action? What did I expect to accomplish by my divisive comments?

On the way back to my office, I felt as though I'd made a tremendous blunder. I feared that few would support my position and that I had exposed myself to ridicule for no real gain. But, when I got to my desk, I found more than fifty telephone messages waiting for me. They were from people who had heard the news—students, faculty, and members of the general public—and were thrilled that someone had finally raised the taboo subject.

The next several months were the regents' equivalent of the Phony War. The administration issued a series of papers—on admissions practices, employment, and contracting—at our March, April, and May meetings. They were somewhat impenetrable, filled with bureaucratese and endless statistical tables. But they all repeated the familiar refrain: in all these areas, race is only one of many factors. The subtext was clear: we shelter quite comfortably under the penumbra of the *Bakke* decision.

But these reports were so lacking in candor and objectivity that other regents' skepticism increased. First, it was Dean Watkins and Leo Kolligian. Then came Steve Nakashima, a Japanese-American regent from San Jose who was concerned not only about race preferences at UC but also at San Francisco's elite Lowell High School, where high-performing Asian students were being turned away in droves in the interest of "diversity." Nakashima was joined by Glenn Campbell, a former head of the Hoover Institution, who, though politically conservative, had previously been a strong supporter of the administration's admissions policies. Eventually, he became one of my closest friends on the board.

As the administration was deluging the regents with paper, I decided to conduct my own investigation. Throughout that spring I had visited nearly all of the university's campuses. In each case, I had the chancellor advertise my presence and invite students and faculty members to come and discuss the issue of fairness in admissions. Those who showed up were primarily blacks and Latinos, along with faculty members from the ethnic studies departments. Their message was uniform: we are living in a multicultural society; we must celebrate diversity; and our campus must, as Bill Clinton had said of his cabinet, look like America.

If, rather than merely listening, I questioned the need for preferences, these conversations often became confrontational. I found myself changing as a person. I became more hardened to criticism, to be sure, but I also became more critical too—especially toward those blacks who clearly wanted preferences not because of fairness but because of power. It seemed to me, among other things, that they were affecting the way the rest of society—even other "people of color"—perceived black people. They were saddling all of us with baggage it would take generations to shed.

My campus sessions became abrasive enough that I was eventually assigned security guards. But while it was sometimes uncomfortable for me, I learned what arguments were being made on behalf of affirmative action. I also got valuable insights from those students who came to these meetings and usually said very little until afterward when they took me aside and told me what I began to think of as "horror stories" about how the preference regime worked on their campuses.

At the same time that I was making these visits, I was also receiving dozens of calls a week from people who'd suffered from preferences, and every day my mail contained letters with tips and even official documents, often sent anonymously out of fear of reprisal. For instance, in March, I was sent a flyer advertising an administrative position that concluded with the sentence, "The affirmative action goal for this position is an African American male." When staff members from the president's office released their statistics about university employment in the regents' April meeting and repeated the mantra about race being one of many factors, I handed Peltason a copy of this document. As he read it with a stricken look on his face, I realized that even he had no idea of how deeply engrained preferences were in the university's daily routine.

In April, I had a conversation with Pete Wilson, who was becoming more and more interested in the issue. I told him one of the conclusions I had reached was that "affirmative action"—an attempt to reach out to qualified students and help them gain admission to the university—was not what was going on at UC. Rather, we had created a system of "preferences"—a commitment to put a certain number of black and ethnic students into the university, even if their admission meant discriminating against those who were better qualified.

"So affirmative action *is* race preference?" Pete asked.

"That's the way it seems to me," I replied. "But most people hear 'affirmative action' and they think in terms of 'equality of opportunity.' The term has been out there so long, been used in so many ways, that it has ceased to mean anything. We've got to begin to call this discrimination for what it is."

Pete agreed with me, and from this point on we made a point of using the word "preferences" when talking about this issue. It wasn't just an arguing point and a way of redefining the nature of the debate. It was the truth.

The crucial document that came to me that spring—also arriving anonymously—was something called the Karabel Matrix. This was a guide for admissions put together a few years earlier by a team of faculty and administrators headed by a sociologist on the Berkeley campus named Jerome Karabel. Its existence and contents had never been made public, and as I read it, I realized why. The Matrix proposed a sliding scale for assigning points for admissions. There were 8,000 points possible. Whites and Asians had to have over 7,100 to be admitted. "People of color" could be below 6,000 and still get admitted. This was one of the smoking guns that showed race was not one among many factors, but *the* factor. After reading it, I decided that I would introduce a motion calling for the UC system to end all race preferences.

In May, as I was beginning to build support for my position, the president's office suddenly issued a press release in which it admitted that the Davis, Irvine, and San Diego campuses had been automatically admitting all "underrepresented minority" students who applied.

When I read the story, my jaw dropped. Here the university was confirming everything it had been so vehemently denying a few months earlier. I suspected that it was a calculated release meant to get some of the bad news out and preempt any information I might reveal at the next meeting. But I knew it would make critics only wonder what else was happening that they weren't being told about. I could imagine the reaction of some of my colleagues on the board, many of whom had started to become more vocal about race preferences during the spring: Why weren't we informed about this until now?

By this time, the UC administration knew there was going to be a showdown and that it would probably take place at our June meeting. In late May, Peltason called and asked if we could put off the issue until July. His reason was that the legislature was still dealing with the university's budget, and if there was some alteration in affirmative action policies, the Democrats might retaliate by making funding cuts.

I agreed to reschedule the discussion and was about to hang up, but I could tell that Peltason had something else on his mind.

"Something else you want to talk about?" I asked.

"Yes, there is."

"What?"

"Maybe we could phase this thing out over time," he finally said.

"You're talking about phasing out preferences?"

"That's right."

For the first time I had a sense that perhaps I was dealing with a paper tiger.

"Jack, why didn't you bring this up back in January when I first wanted to have an honest debate about affirmative action?" I asked.

He paused for a moment and then said, "Because back in January we didn't think you might win."

SEVEN

I CELEBRATED JULY 4 1995 with a heightened awareness of
the personal freedom at the core of our nationhood. When the
Founding Fathers said that we were all created equal, they were
proposing an audacious theory that ultimately inflamed the rest of
the world. By fits and starts, Americans had tried to make that theory into a reality, with abolitionism, the Emancipation Proclamation, and, of course, the civil rights movement, which instituted
sweeping revisions of the law that have brought us ever closer to
the fulfillment of the promise of our national life. I felt in my heart
that race preferences—by whatever name—were not a continuation of that progress, but an obstacle in the road to freedom and
equality. At best a diversion, and at worst a giant step backward,
affirmative action preferences caused us to lose sight of the task we
inherited from the Founders—creating *equal* as the only category
that counts in America.

The next morning I released my proposals to reform the race-
based polices of the University of California. It was two weeks until
the next regents' meeting, ample time for my colleagues to review
the four pages of text that were being called resolutions SP-1

(admissions) and SP-2 (employment and contracting). Jack Peltason was still trying to find a compromise. To some degree, he was reacting to pressure from activist students and faculty to "save the system," but in fairness to Jack, I think he also wanted to save the Board of Regents from being thrust once again into the public eye. The last time this had happened was almost exactly thirty years earlier, during the Free Speech Movement of 1964. In that jarring experience, student demonstrators invaded and disrupted the regents' meetings and published Marxist diagrams attacking individual board members as being compromised and corrupted by personal holdings that were "interlocked" with the major economic interests of the "power structure." It was an experience that put this sedate body, which has always liked to pursue its deliberations invisibly and liked to think of its individual members as anonymous benefactors of the commonweal, squarely in the public eye and on trial. Although it was rarely mentioned, I understood that what had happened during the FSM lingered in the organization's institutional memory as a warning and a curse, a sort of academic *Kristallnacht* never again to be repeated.

Hoping to avoid a similar crisis, Peltason faxed me a confidential memorandum that contained several provisions he felt would give me most of what I was seeking. Among his most important concessions was an agreement that all applicants for undergraduate admission to Berkeley and UCLA, the elite campuses of the UC system, would go through the same review process that would not give significantly greater advantages to designated minorities. He also agreed that UC Davis and UC Irvine would discontinue the practice of automatically admitting all eligible "underrepresented" minorities. In addition, all UC campuses would discontinue the practice of reserving certain faculty positions solely for minorities and women, and the University administration would create a task force of business leaders and others to develop a significantly enhanced program of academic outreach.

I was elated. Reading between the lines of this document, it was impossible to miss the admission that our campuses had been using racial preferences in a big way. For the past six months, I had been vilified for suggesting that this might be the case. On *This Week with David Brinkley*, for instance, Elizabeth Toledo of the National Organization for Women had essentially called me a liar when I said that race was a dominant factor in UC's admission process. The "facts" she used in her attack against me had come from University administrators. The brick wall I had been banging my head into had seemed so solid in its denials that race was more than a slight "bump" that I'd sometimes wondered if I was misinterpreting the situation entirely. Now there were no more doubts.

From Peltason's point of view, his deal was worth making because it would avoid an up-or-down vote on affirmative action and preserve the administration's illusion of control over its own house. And, in truth, it would have given me much of what I was seeking. But one thing it wouldn't give was certainty. Could those who had essentially created the present system be trusted to drastically alter it? I didn't think so. Nor would this compromise change the culture of the university, which is what I was (and am still) seeking as much as anything else. There would have been no public exploration of the evils of racially biased admissions, no full disclosure of the way in which the invisible system of preferences worked. And most important, making such an agreement behind closed doors would have done nothing about the dismal eligibility rate and poor academic competitiveness of black kids —a problem I hoped would be dramatized and corrected by passage of SP-1 and SP-2.

For these reasons, I rejected Peltason's settlement and released the text of my resolutions to the regents along with a letter that explained our negotiation and my reasons for deciding to proceed: "I have no doubt that President Peltason is operating in good faith; however, I have grave doubts about the wisdom of leaving this in the hands of the campuses, considering their failure to be forthcoming about their practices until now, and their absolute insistence on trying to preserve the status quo by whatever means possible…. The University of California has no statutory obligation, federal mandate, consent decree, or executive order which compels us to give racial preferences in employment, contracting or admissions. We are doing so on our own initiative. We are out-of-step with the views and policies of the people of our state…. It seems to me that the leadership which we must show is to get the University moving in a new direction… which makes it clear that race-based decision-making should no longer occur."

Once news about SP-1 and SP-2 hit, my office became a virtual studio for television networks, news reporters, and talk show hosts. From July 5 until July 19, the day before the regents showdown, I spent an average of eight hours each day just responding to the media. Some journalists saw it as a David and Goliath story in which one person was fighting an institution backed by an array of well-paid administrators and faculty, allies in the legislature, and a band of aggressive and highly motivated students for whom protection of the status quo was a holy cause. But most reporters, following the leftish ideological commitments of the media, saw me as a freak of nature—the black man who didn't "think black."

For some of those I thought of as allies, the juggernaut forming to protect the status quo caused a failure of nerve. Not long before the climactic meeting, for instance, I talked to Clair Burgener, board chairman, about how he thought things were shaping up.

After we talked about board politics for a moment, there was an uncomfortable pause. Then Clair said, "You probably shouldn't count on my support."

I felt like I'd been hit in the stomach. I wanted to say: "Dammit, you got me into this thing in the first place because you knew what we were doing was wrong, and now you leave me twisting in the wind!" Instead, I simply told him I was sorry that he had made this decision and ended the conversation.

As it became clear that the resolutions had a good chance of passing, the proponents of affirmative action made this into an apocalyptic battle between good (them) and evil (me). In June, the Office of the President had lobbed a grenade into the debate in the form of a report that concluded that the elimination of race as a consideration in the admissions process would drastically reduce by as much as 50 percent the number of African Americans enrolled at UC, and the number of Hispanics by as much as 15 percent. I tried to make the point that whatever the exact numbers, we were talking about tokenism as well as unfairness.* But the media seemed to be working in collaboration with the UC administrators in forecasting the higher educational equivalent of a racial and ethnic cleansing if preferences were abolished.

Meanwhile, Jesse Jackson seemed to have virtually taken up residence in California. All during the spring, he had shown up on university campuses throughout California urging students to prepare for this "mother of all fights" to save affirmative action. He had made it into a personal contest between the two of us. During an appearance at UCLA, his rhetoric turned rancid, as he called me, among other things, "strange fruit." It was hard for me to understand why Jesse used this term, once applied to the pendant

---

* In 1978, the year after *Bakke*, blacks composed 3.9 percent of the university's admissions. In 1996, after nearly twenty years of social engineering and hundreds of millions of dollars, the rate was 5.1 percent.

bodies of black people who had been lynched, and the title of a famously bitter Billie Holiday song. Was it a joke or a threat?

One morning a few days before the regents' meeting, I received a call from Reverend Amos Brown, a San Francisco preacher and West Coast representative of Jackson's Rainbow Coalition. Brown said that we needed to get to know each other and have a talk, man-to-man. I agreed to meet, but the conversation didn't get off to a very good start. Brown began by apologizing for having character-ized me in one of his sermons as an "Uncle Tom," but he said that the apology was directed to Tom, a slave in *Uncle Tom's Cabin*, not me, because Tom had at least come to the defense of his people against their slave masters, while I was selling them out.

"So you don't actually deserve to be accorded the title of 'Uncle Tom,'" Brown said pleasantly.

Despite his stupid and insulting tone, Brown portrayed himself as a "peacemaker" and earnestly invited me to attend a private meeting on July 19 at his church. He said the attendance would be limited to him and a few other ministers. I told him that I'd share my views with his group, but wasn't interested in walking into an ambush.

"You are coming to my house," he said in a wounded tone. "I don't insult my guests at my house, and I don't let anyone else insult them either." He expressed indignation that such a thought would even enter my mind.

Later in the day, when I told Roger Shelton, a young man who worked in my office and had been helping me get ready for the Regents' meeting, about this episode, he warned me that I was being set up. I thought he might be overreacting until the morning of July 18, when I received a call from a *Sacramento Bee* reporter who asked what I expected to accomplish at my meeting the next day with Jesse Jackson. I said that I had no meeting planned with

Jackson. The reporter then told me that he'd just seen a press release from the Rainbow Coalition announcing that I would be attending a meeting at the church of Reverend Amos Brown in San Francisco on July 19. Also in attendance would be "Brother Jesse" and several hundred others.

I immediately called Brown's office to inform him that I would not be attending the meeting. As one of my employees at Connerly & Associates quipped, Br'er Rabbit had eluded Br'er Fox once again.

— —

When I arrived at my office on the morning of July 19, I was greeted by a dozen or so protestors carrying signs that, among other things, described me as an "angry Oreo."

Throughout the day, I received calls from media representatives from all over the world wanting to know how the next day's vote would go. I told them I thought that about fifteen regents would vote for my resolution relating to admissions and sixteen would support the companion measure on hiring and contracting. This estimate was based on the expected attendance of Doris Allen, Speaker of the California State Assembly, who had committed herself to voting for SP-1 and SP-2.

That night in San Francisco I had dinner with several students who had berated me earlier in the day at a student forum. At one point in the event the student regent, Ed Gomez, asked if I would assist him in putting his resolution on the floor to reaffirm existing affirmative action policies. Gomez's resolution was diametrically opposed to mine, but I agreed to assist him nonetheless. It gave the opposition one more shot at defeating us, but I believed that the students at least deserved to have their resolution formally considered.

Later, when I returned to the hotel, there was a call from my friend and fellow regent, Tirso del Junco. The operator said it was "urgent." When I reached him, Tirso informed me that Roy Brophy had announced that he would be voting against my resolutions and offering an alternative plan. Before I could digest this information, I received a call from one of Speaker Doris Allen's aides saying that she would not be attending the meeting because she had flown to Colorado to be with her mother, who had suffered a stroke.

I climbed into bed around midnight, even though I knew I probably wouldn't sleep very much. I was thinking about my appearance on *Good Morning America* scheduled for dawn and also what I would say at the regents meeting when I introduced my resolutions. As I closed my eyes, the butterflies were moving around in the pit of my stomach the way they had when I was a kid waiting for the big game to get started.

When my wake-up call came at 3:05 a.m. on July 20, my eyes were already open. I dressed and went downstairs where *Good Morning America* had a temporary set. Opposite me on the show was Congresswoman Maxine Waters (Democrat from Los Angeles), one of the shrillest advocates of race preferences and personally one of the most obnoxious politicians in the country. When host Charlie Gibson asked her to what extent the university used race in admissions, Waters ignored him. She held up a piece of paper she claimed represented evidence that my company had benefited from affirmative action, after which she shrilly attacked me as a hypocrite.

It was a lie, of course, just as it had been a lie when Joe McCarthy waved a piece of paper he said contained the names of communists in the government. As I listened to this woman who had eaten from the public trough all her life, from her early days on welfare until now as a member of Congress, I began to realize that Waters and others like her had too much invested in maintaining a system of racial preferences to ever let go of that system without a fight to the finish. I knew from listening to her what was ahead for me the rest of the day and perhaps for the rest of my life.

After our television segment was over, I returned to the hotel room and tried to draft something I could read when I introduced SP-1 and SP-2. I knew that my fellow regents and everyone else would be waiting for me to answer one question: Why are you doing this? The answer was evolving. When I had first begun to review UC's policies and practices, I concluded that they were unfair to Asians and whites, who were victims of a system of race preferences that may have been created innocuously enough years earlier, but over time had taken on a grotesque life of their own. As I began to dig deeper into UC's affirmative action practices, however, I saw an additional and unexpected group of victims—the members of "underrepresented" groups who worked hard and gained entry to UC on their own merits and then saw their accomplishments degraded by policies implying that all minority students get where they do only because of preferential treatment. Finally, I had also become aware of the plight of all those young blacks and Hispanics who are not competitive with their Asian and white counterparts because of the mediocrity of the primary and secondary school education they receive. (In 1994, slightly more than 500 black high school graduates in California out of 18,000 had an academic record that qualified them to attend UC.) Affirmative action was, at best, a microscopic Band-Aid on this cancer of underachievement, and the disgrace of giving these young people a third-rate education was compounded by telling them that their problems came from being victimized by white racism and that they therefore deserved preferences.

I finished the fifth or sixth draft of my statement about an hour before the bus arrived to take us to the meeting at UC San Francisco, site of one of the system's excellent medical schools. I still had enough time to spend a few minutes looking over the line-up of regents to make sure that I knew where we stood. As I went over the list, I was still worried about Meredith Khachigian. Although I thought we could win without her vote, I wanted her with us for a variety of reasons. First, I knew that she would be heavily lobbied by Brophy. Second, she is a very level-headed and conscientious regent whose commitment to change would be critical in the aftermath of the vote. Finally, I knew Meredith was very close to Jack Peltason, and if she could withstand his influence, I knew that our side was in good shape.

Because of my uncertainty about Meredith's vote, I tried to think tactically. As author of the two resolutions, I had the right to present them in any order I wanted. I knew that the opposition would be concentrating its firepower on admissions, so I decided to introduce SP-2 (employment and contracting) first. SP-2 would certainly pass. By putting it first, I would start out with a certain victory and, more importantly, I would find out about Meredith. If she voted "aye," I felt confident that she would support SP-1 too. If she voted "nay," I would still have time to adopt some of the amendments I knew a few regents were itching to introduce as a way of watering down the resolution about admissions.

Having gotten my thoughts in order, I headed downstairs with Ilene and Roger, both of whom had driven down from Sacramento that morning, for the bus taking us to the meeting. It was the first regents' meeting Ilene had ever attended, and I could tell that she was almost as apprehensive about how events would unfold as I was. I was surprised to receive handshakes from several members of the hotel staff and a wish of good luck from my driver.

At the UCSF campus there were dozens of police milling about. It occurred to me that there wouldn't be this level of security unless someone was concerned about something going wrong. As Ilene and I got out of the bus it was clear that we were being more heavily guarded even than the governor, who arrived at about the same time I did. This made my skin prickle.

Inside, Ilene took a seat a few rows from the front of the room, behind a group that turned out to be Jesse Jackson supporters. Pete and I both visited casually with other regents while we waited for the meeting to begin. Tirso del Junco came over to tell us that Roy Brophy had Meredith in a corner and was lobbying her hard to oppose my resolutions. I watched the two of them. Brophy's rigid body language suggested that he was striking out, but on the other hand, I noticed that Meredith was wiping away the tears from her eyes.

As we assembled in the meeting room, the air was electric with anticipation. Many members of the California State Legislature were present, along with other political figures. Every seat was taken and an overflow room was crammed full as well, and the halls outside were crowded with students. Cameras were clicking and rolling, with their lights casting sudden zones of heat throughout the area. I later learned that several camera crews had been instructed to monitor me, the governor, and Jesse Jackson for reaction shots during the debate.

Just before the meeting began, I noticed that Willie Brown, now San Francisco mayor, was seated on a ledge at the perimeter of the room. Although we had been on the opposite side of many issues, perhaps most pointedly on affirmative action, I felt he deserved a better seat so I beckoned for him to come forward and take the seat that had been reserved for the absent Doris Allen.

As president of the regents, the governor was given the opportunity to speak first. Some smiled at the raspy sound of Pete's voice—he was just recovering from a throat operation—but I knew the discomfort he was experiencing and was proud of his characteristically gritty performance. Pete pointed out that the UC application form states that the university does not discriminate on the basis of race, which he said is "a fundamental American principle that must be not only the policy but also the practice of the institution." He went on to add, "It has become clear, despite official claims to the contrary, that this is not the policy nor the practice. As President Peltason acknowledged recently, race has played a central role in the admissions practices at many UC campuses." Pete observed that it takes the state taxes of three working Californians to provide the subsidy to educate a single UC undergraduate. He suggested that these hard-working taxpayers deserved a guarantee that their own children would get an equal opportunity to compete for admission, regardless of their race or gender.

The personal testimony came next. As Johnnie Cochran demonstrated so well in the O.J. Simpson trial, we live in an era when people make their legal and political points less by reasoned analysis than by "story telling." Not surprisingly, therefore, most of the women and minorities who spoke in favor of the status quo called on their personal experiences. In these occasionally maudlin discussions of their preference heritage, they invariably made comments like, "I wouldn't be here if it weren't for affirmative action," or "I'm proud to be an affirmative action baby." The subtext was clear: "I am a success story. By giving me a preference, look how society has benefited."

Some of these personal diatribes were specious. In his talk, for instance, Willie Brown took note of his experiences as a black man growing up under segregation and cited the ways in which affirmative action had contributed to his development. There was one problem: when Brown came to California from Texas and got admitted to San Francisco State College in the 1950s, there weren't any preferences. When he started his law practice representing a clientele filled, by his own admission, with pimps and prostitutes in San Francisco, the term "affirmative action" had not yet been coined. When he was elected to the California legislature in the mid-1960s, the voters in Brown's district may have been influenced by his liberal politics, but not by some requirement to elect a certain number of blacks. When Brown's colleagues in the legislature made him their speaker for fifteen years, they were not filling a quota for blacks. Indeed, his story had a moral quite the opposite from the one he tried to draw. Willie Brown had risen because of his individual talent and drive, not because of a handout, and as I listened to him give affirmative action credit for his rise I had to work hard to keep a straight face.

There were also emotional presentations by other black and Chicano opponents of my resolutions. But the passion wasn't one-sided. When his time came to speak, Steve Nakashima, a regent of Japanese descent, said pointedly, "You people don't have a monopoly on discrimination." He then went on to talk about the internment camps his relatives had endured. Assemblyman Charles Poochigian, another supporter of my motions, told of how his Armenian forbearers had suffered genocide in Europe and discrimination in the Central Valley of California but had never sought a preference.

But the person everyone was waiting to hear was Jesse Jackson. Because of Jackson's prominence, Clair Burgener, in his capacity as chairman of the board, had publicly stated his intention to give him all the time he wanted. Most of us thought this was a mistake, not only because it gave Jackson a license to engage in one of his brain-dwarfing filibusters, but because flattering his egotism would deny others—even others on the pro-preference side—the opportunity to speak. I considered making a formal objection to the chairman's decision, but in the end decided to keep my eyes on the prize.

Like the accomplished showman he is (and man of the cloth when the situation calls for it), Jackson began by asking everyone to stand and join hands in prayer. Then he showed how much more comfortable he is rendering unto Caesar by launching into a diatribe against my resolutions. Jackson jabbed at the governor for his "divisive" politics, and then at me and Regent Howard Leach because of our contributions to Pete's recent reelection campaign. Demanding that "academic freedom not be polluted by political agendas," he said that it had been a "tortuous road since the Civil War" as the nation marched toward "freedom and equality for enslaved and dispossessed African Americans." Apparently missing the irony, he noted that this journey had "taught the nation that it is wrong to suppress people on the basis of their race and ethnicity." Then, in a comment that encapsulated the clash of values underlying the affirmative action debate and also the decline of principle in the civil rights community, Jackson stated that instead of being color-blind, America should be "color-caring."

Jackson's puns and doggerel always yield something memorable, and the phrase of this day that stuck in my mind was, "To ignore race and sex is racist and sexist." The statement caused many in the press gallery to raise their eyebrows, and, indeed, it was mind-boggling.

Although I'm miles apart from Jesse on the issue of how America should handle racial issues, I couldn't help feeling a certain grudging admiration for him as he did his thing. His alleged charisma doesn't work on me, but it is impossible not to be aware of his gifts. I also saw his pathos—someone who had sacrificed the possibility of being a transformational leader to become a defender of liberalism's racial party line. As I watched Jesse repeat what he had said so often before, it sometimes seemed that he was going through the motions, imprisoned in formulaic phrase-making and political cliches. He was so out of step with recent social policy—welfare reform, tougher law enforcement, decentralization of government, a renewed emphasis on personal responsibility rather than collective guilt—that he sounded like a flat earther.

Watching Jesse work himself into a lather, I was also struck by the preposterousness of someone who is limo'd around the country from one cause to another posturing as a tribune of the underclass. (Comedian Chris Rock once scored a palpable hit in a TV interview when he looked at Jackson and said, "So tell me, Reverend, what is it that you *do* for a living, anyhow?") But it is also true that Jackson has energy and determination, and one quality the public sees less of: an earthy sense of humor. During one of the lulls in the endless series of public comments at the regents' meeting, and before Jackson had made his appearance, I took a nature break. To get to the men's room, I had to pass through a meeting room where Jesse and his supporters were lounging on a table. I stopped and we chatted briefly. Just then the governor walked by, also on his way to the men's room. Jackson said, "Pete, you and I should form a ticket to run for President, and appoint Connerly to be our finance chairman."

I said that I'd accept the appointment only if Pete headed the ticket. Jackson said no, he thought that he should head the ticket in the interest of affirmative action. We all laughed at this and returned to the battle.

— —

The people who argued against SP-1 and SP-2 were for the most part representatives of the organizations—NAACP, Mexican-

American Legal Defense Fund, etc.—that compose the preference lobby. Those who argued for these resolutions tended to do so as individuals.

Assemblyman Bernie Richter received a chorus of boos and a tongue lashing from Jesse Jackson when he talked about the legacy of Dr. King and his dream of a color-blind society. As I watched, it occurred to me that one surefire way to tick off an advocate of preferences during an affirmative action debate is to use King's quote about judging his little children by the content of their character and not the color of their skin. Once when I myself invoked this vision, a heckler screamed at me, "How dare you mention Dr. King!" I answered that I dared because his legacy belongs to us all, not to a chosen few, many of whom reviled King during his lifetime as "Uncle Martin." King is an American hero, not a black hero. That is why we rightly celebrate his birthday as a national holiday.

In her testimony Sally Pipes, president of the Pacific Research Institute, said she supported SP-1 and SP-2 because these measures represented a fair and effective way for UC to bring itself into compliance with the principles upon which the nation was founded. She spoke about how affirmative action policies have the effect of heightening ethnic divisiveness. (I thought this comment was right on the money: there is more talk on college campuses today about blood quantum and ethnic membership than at any time since the Nuremberg Laws.) Pipes said she believed that true diversity would be produced through strong secondary education and civil rights legislation, without mandates or quotas.

One of the most dramatic presentations came from John Ellis, professor of Comparative Literature at the UC Santa Cruz campus. Ellis had been instrumental in creating the first affirmative action program for graduate students at UCSC decades earlier, but said that he now saw that this policy had done "great damage to the academic enterprise of the university by bringing in underqualified students who are then psychologically harmed by their lack of preparation." Putting such unprepared students into the same classroom with others with more developed abilities tends to promote rather than dispel racial stereotypes, Ellis said. As a former UC dean familiar with the internal workings of the university, he warned the board that, above all, it should not rely on the present administration to repair the damage that affirmative action policies had caused.

Just as the time for public input was ending, a campus policeman burst in and yelled, "Everyone clear the room!" I was hustled out of a side entrance with the other regents, and I saw Ilene go out the front door. She later told me that she stood around with other observers outside while the room was searched for bombs and bands of protestors marched in circles and sang civil rights songs. They didn't know who she was, and she didn't tell them.

After nearly an hour, we reassembled and the meeting resumed. The time for public comment having expired, the moment had arrived for me to give my reasons for proposing SP-1 and SP-2. After a few introductory remarks, I got to what I thought was the heart of the matter:

> This has been a long, painful, and lonely journey for me. And, my detractors have often been unkind. I have tried to step into their shoes to understand the basis of their frequent lack of charity in failing to allow me to express my views, which are deeply felt. As I said to the students yesterday, sometimes in the heat of battle not only do we forget who the good guys are and who the bad guys are, we forget why we are fighting. Today, I want to sharpen the focus on the issues that I am asking this Board to resolve by way of the resolutions that I will be offering to you....

I believe unequivocally that the goal of this nation and of this state is to have its government institutions blind to the color of one's skin or the national origin of one's ancestors in the transactions of government.... We have been granting racial preferences to remedy some of the historical unfairness and injustice projected upon and practiced upon many Americans, particularly black Americans. The assumption has been made that these preferences would be temporary. But with each passing day it should be clear to us that our system of preferences is becoming entrenched, as it builds its own constituency to defend and sustain it as a permanent feature of public decision-making. It is equally clear to me, as I suffer the characterizations of "traitor," "sell-out," "Uncle Tom," etc., that we are dividing ourselves in America along racial lines, and that we may already have passed the point where we can regroup and think of ourselves as individuals. I am absolutely convinced that our excessive preoccupation with race contributes to this racial divide. And, nowhere is the art of race consciousness practiced more fervently than on our university campuses.

Then I moved for the adoption of SP-2, which eliminated race preferences in contracting and employment. The motion was seconded by Governor Wilson.

Then came discussion on the part of individual regents. Some of the statements—on both sides of the issue—were persuasive and eloquent. After everyone had his or her say, Dean Watkins called for a vote. The secretary called the roll, and SP-2 passed fifteen to ten.

The easy part of the meeting was now behind us. I immediately moved that SP-1 be adopted. Governor Wilson again seconded my motion. Roy Brophy offered a substitute motion that would have effectively killed my resolution, but he was defeated fourteen to eleven. When I glanced at Brophy, his head was lowered and he had slumped down in his chair. I then turned to look out at the audience, particularly at Jesse Jackson to see what his next move would be. He had publicly stated his willingness to be arrested (he was dressed in a casual jumpsuit, his "jail clothes," as some called them), and I knew that if Jackson was going to make a move, time was running out for him to do so.

Just then, one of the hecklers in the back of the room made a statement which I did not hear. Dean Watkins, arguably the most widely respected member of the board, and until then one of the most silent, responded with asperity, at which point all hell begin to break loose. I then saw Jackson sigh, hesitate for a moment, look from side to side, stand, and fold his arms. This was the signal to his allies to follow suit, which they did. Chaos ensued as preachers and students rushed to the front of the room to link arms with Jackson, while others were elbowing their way out of the room in case there was violence.

Once their arms were linked, Jackson's supporters began to sing "We Shall Overcome." The effect was surreal. Was it possible that these people didn't see any difference between those days thirty years earlier when this great civil rights anthem was sung in the middle of attacks by Bull Connor and his police dogs, and today, when they had spent the morning eating cantaloupe and croissants in the regents' VIP lounge before being given pride of place at this meeting? As I was suppressing a laugh at the sight of Lieutenant Governor Gray Davis trying to lip-synch the words of the song, I saw some of the more militant protestors yell and begin to charge down the aisle toward the regents. The police intercepted them. At this point, the meeting was deemed officially to have been "disrupted" and the chairman called for a recess. I gestured at Ilene to come forward and held her hand as the police escorted us to a separate room that had been set aside in anticipation of this disruption.

Jackson and a few of his people were allowed to follow us to our new site. He made an appeal to the regents not to take the action that was now imminent—approval of SP-1. When he caught my eye, he beckoned to me. I left my seat at the table and went to where he was sitting. He hissed, "Connerly, don't do this to *your* people." I told him that what he called affirmative action was part of the problem faced by *our* people, not part of the solution. Then he said, "Connerly, you are throwing rocks on the grave of Dr. King." At this point, I realized that civil and rational discourse was hopeless; I told Jackson that his comment was disgusting and returned to my seat.

Jack Peltason spoke against the motion. As president, he urged the regents to join the chancellors, the provost, the vice presidents, and the university's academic and student leadership in reaffirming UC's thirty-year commitment to the twin goals of diversity and excellence. But he added that whatever the board decided, the administration would carry out its policies. As he spoke, I was struck once again by his grace, humor, and integrity—qualities he had exhibited throughout the several months he and I had been friendly opponents. I felt sad that this controversy marked Jack's final days as president.

UCLA Chancellor Charles Young asked to speak. Senior chancellor in the UC system, in terms of time served, and a man of well-known leftish politics, Young said that he and his colleagues believed that the campuses could properly take race, gender, and ethnicity into account without the use of quotas or set-asides as part of the process. If improper actions have been taken in the name of affirmative action, he said, then these actions should be modified or eliminated. Young urged the regents to allow him and his colleagues to retain the tools that would enable the university to continue along the path to diversity for the good of the institution and the society as a whole.

UC Provost Walter Massey then talked about having been raised as a black man in the rigidly segregated society of pre-1960s Mississippi and attested to his desire for a color-free society. If he believed that race-conscious programs were imperiling or even delaying that goal, he said, then he would be against them. To the contrary, however, he believed that these efforts are an important vehicle in creating a society where race may not matter.

Walter's call for diversity rang a little hollow considering that he would be departing in about six weeks to accept the position of president at Atlanta's Morehouse College, his alma mater. It was all that I could do not to ask Walter to reconcile his premise that quality cannot exist without diversity with the fact that Morehouse is all black and all male. I wondered whether he thought the lack of diversity at Morehouse had in any way disadvantaged its most famous alumnus, Dr. Martin Luther King, Jr.

This long and difficult journey finally came to an end at 8:35 p.m. The vote was called and the resolution to end the consideration of race, sex, color, ethnicity, or national origin as criteria for admission to the university or to any program of study carried by a vote of fourteen to ten. There was no emotional outburst by those of us who had voted in the affirmative, just a feeling of relief. Jesse Jackson might have still been atonally humming "We Shall Overcome," but I wanted to sing that old James Brown song, "I Feel Good."

After the vote, I returned to the hotel room under the protective watch of several San Francisco police officers, one of whom, a black man, shook my hand and said, "Regent Connerly, I want to congratulate you. You did the right thing." I went upstairs and got a snack from room service. Then, I lay in bed surfing the newscasts on the local channels. Almost all of them were covering the regents' meeting and the resulting protests now causing chaos in the streets of San Francisco.

One of the programs led with footage of Jesse Jackson asking the regents to maintain affirmative action because America was racist and blacks could not succeed without it. Then, the picture cut to me at a news conference expressing optimism about America's future and about the ability of black citizens to compete with other Americans. I was proud of the contrast and felt that I had done my part to enhance the image of black Americans as being independent and resourceful, confident in America's ultimate fairness, and capable of finding their own way to success and fulfillment.

EIGHT

AFTER THE REGENTS' VOTE, black *Chicago Tribune* columnist Clarence Page, one of my favorite writers, wrote that I'd gotten my "fifteen minutes of fame" and could now fade back into the obscurity from which I'd come. I suppose that this was supposed to brand me as a freaky flash in the pan, but frankly, given that I'd scarcely seen my family or tended to my business for weeks, obscurity was starting to look pretty good to me. I did have a nagging sense of unfinished business though: I felt that what the regents had done begged some serious questions. For instance, if fairness and equity demanded that preferences be abolished at the University of California, shouldn't they be rooted out of all the other areas of our social and political world as well? But I was in a mood to let others deal with the broader implications of the regents' decision. Indeed, shortly after the vote, when a couple of political newcomers named Glynn Custred and Tom Wood asked me to help them qualify what they were calling the California Civil Rights Initiative for the ballot, I cited Clarence Page's vision of my future and said that I was now in my sixteenth minute of fame. As I recall, I made one of those flippant remarks you later smile ruefully about: "I'm retiring from politics. I want to keep my amateur status."

I first ran into Custred and Wood in 1994, about a year before the regents' vote. State Assemblyman Bernie Richter was introducing a bill to make the state of California color-blind in matters involving contracting, university admissions and hiring, and, knowing that I had become interested in the issue as a result of my talks with Jerry and Ellen Cook, he asked me to make an appearance. The hearings went nowhere, largely because my old classmate from Sacramento State College, Phil Isenberg, was chairman of the Judiciary Committee and had made it a graveyard for measures that didn't pass the liberal litmus test. But Glynn and Tom were present when I gave my brief testimony. They introduced themselves and described the measure they were calling the California Civil Rights Initiative, and we talked for a few minutes before going our separate ways.

Over the next year, Custred, Wood and I moved in parallel intellectual and political universes. As the situation heated up at the Board of Regents, I occasionally got a call or a fax, usually from Wood, offering unsolicited advice and help. The night before the vote, in fact, he called with what he thought was a brilliant idea. He would hire a skywriter the next day—which he believed would be a red-letter day in the history of our "movement"—to promote his initiative. I told Tom that it would do neither of us any good to engage in a dopey PR gimmick at this time. I thought he agreed with me, but when I came out of my hotel room the next morning, I heard the sputter of an airplane engine and looked up and saw a puffy cumulus of letters spelling out "CCRI." This stunt was characteristic of the political amateurism that defined CCRI at the time.

By this time, the press had zeroed in on Custred and Wood, portraying them as the "Angry White Male" personified. This was an unfair and simplistic characterization. A professor at California

State University at Hayward, Glynn became a target for the left as a result of his outspoken criticisms of the forced march toward "diversity." The attacks were sometimes quite fierce. For example, when Willie Brown spoke at the Hayward campus, he urged students who wanted to do something for black people to disrupt Glynn's classroom.

For Tom, the personal was also political. He had never landed a full-time university appointment despite receiving a Ph.D. in Philosophy from UC Berkeley in the mid-seventies. He had become disgusted by the way that diversity capriciously hurt some who were truly qualified—prospective professors as well as prospective students—while giving what amounted to a windfall profit to others simply for having been born into a certain race, gender or ethnic group.

After meeting at a caucus of the conservative National Association of Scholars in the early nineties, Glynn and Tom saw that they had an intersecting agenda and decided that they'd try to make the state of California live up to the letter and spirit of the U.S. Constitution. Seeing themselves as citizen-activists in the spirit of Howard Jarvis and Paul Gann, another tag team that had changed state politics by pushing through Proposition 13 in the mid-seventies, they went to the library, photocopied the 1964 Civil Rights Act, and then began to write an initiative based on its language and philosophy.

The initiative went through many drafts, which they circulated among their academic colleagues, then revised and circulated again. By 1993, Wood and Custred finally settled on the text. It was elegant in its simplicity: "The state shall not discriminate against, or grant preferential treatment to, any individual or group, on the basis of race, sex, color, ethnicity, or national origin in the operation of public employment, public contracting, or public education."

They would be criticized later on by members of the race industry for "stealing" the language of the Civil Rights Act. Their reply was ready made: this great piece of legislation belongs as much to those who honor its sentiments today as to those who claim that their actions led to its passage yesterday. I admired Tom and Glynn's in-your-face gesture in designing a measure that showed the partisans of preferences were guilty of bigotry in their social engineering just as the Mississippi rednecks of the 1950s had been in their violence and intimidation.

During the year that I was putting the preference issue before the regents, Custred and Wood raised seed money to open an office in a Berkeley storefront and hired Arnie Steinberg, a political consultant who had worked in local Southern California races and was looking to expand his reach with a hot statewide measure. Steinberg's early polls showed enormous support for the California Civil Rights Initiative—with over seventy percent of the people supporting its language and spirit.

As CCRI inched onto their radar screen, most Democratic party bigwigs, in the words of state party chairman Bill Press, decided that it was a potential "Armageddon." They were locked into support for the affirmative action status quo because it was the key to maintaining their stranglehold on the black vote. But they had been burned in 1994 by getting on the wrong side of another initiative, Proposition 187, the anti–illegal immigration measure that was widely credited with having sunk Kathleen Brown's gubernatorial challenge to Pete Wilson and elected a Republican legislature for the first time in a decade. They feared that this would be one of those "wedge issues" they couldn't cope with.

The Clintonites were also in a sweat about CCRI. At the end of 1994, after the Republican sweep of Congress and before the president veered to the right, they saw Clinton's 1996 reelection effort as an uphill battle and were nervous about the possibility of having to run against such a measure.

What its opponents didn't know, however, was that at this point in time, CCRI was a paper tiger—enormously popular with the public, but unlikely to get on the ballot. Part of the problem was that Glynn and Tom were, by their own admission, professional intellectuals and political novices. They were far better at formulating ideas than they were in building the networks that would make them succeed in the real world. They simply didn't have the political reach or connections to raise the money required to get CCRI off the ground. Neither did they have the necessary political instincts and organizational skills to oversee a statewide campaign.

Unlike the backers of Proposition 187, who had been able to turn to a long-standing network of organizations to help them qualify their measure for the ballot, there was no existing anti-preference movement to which Custred and Wood could turn. Moreover, they had also run smack into what might be called the "Colin Powell Effect." The retired general, whose possible presidential candidacy hung like a charge of static electricity over American politics during 1994 and 1995, clouded the debate on preferences by seeming to oppose them in his book *My American Journey* and then, as Jesse Jackson and the "brothers" got to him, changing his position to one of aloof support of the status quo. Powell's tremendous popularity and his standing as America's leading black political figure gave his statements, in some quarters, the status of Holy Writ.

As all of these adverse factors came together in the summer of 1995, CCRI became lost in a political Bermuda Triangle. The Republicans didn't quite know how or even whether to get the measure on the ballot; and the Democrats were hoping that it would just go away. Wood and Custred were like a pair of miners who had discovered gold but couldn't find a pick and shovel. Smelling blood, organizations opposing the California Civil Rights Initiative—including the NAACP, the ACLU, and NOW—were emerging from the woodwork in hopes of keeping it from coming to a vote.

— —

I heard that Custred and Wood had gone into a do-or-die mode in September when they officially filed their initiative with the secretary of state's office. Now, the clock was running and they had until the end of February to get one million signatures. By November, the campaign was enveloped in gloom. There were a mere 200,000 signatures, twenty percent of the total needed, and the deadline was only three months away.

Midway through the month, I got a call from Larry Arnn, head of the Claremont Institute, whom Glynn and Tom had appointed statewide chairman of the CCRI campaign. Arnn asked to meet me in Sacramento, and during lunch at a local restaurant called Paragary's, he begged me to take over his role.

"You're already identified with the issue," he said in his soft Texas drawl. "You have fundraising abilities. You're close to the Governor. All these things say you could do it."

"No thanks," I said.

"If you don't get in we're not going to make it, and not making it would be a disaster."

"No thanks," I said again.

"Why not?" Arnn pressed. "You've just gone through a grueling battle on the same issues."

"You just answered your own question," I told him. "It was a grueling battle. As a regent, I had a duty to do something about a situation that was destroying the integrity of the institution I was supposed to be overseeing. But I don't have any duty to get involved in this thing. If I got involved, I'd be out there on my own. Even if it qualified, there'd be a huge national campaign against CCRI. The race industry would use me as a punching bag. My family and my business would suffer. It would be played as some sort of ego move on my part. No way."

Larry tried to keep arguing, but by the end of our conversation, I'd worn him down.

"Well," he said, "I hope you'll at least keep the door a crack open."

I told him I intended to keep the door all the way closed.

I didn't think much more about the matter until the mid-November regents' meeting. But then I picked up a disturbing rumor about my old antagonist on the Board of Regents, Roy Brophy. I knew Roy was still steamed about our decision to end preferences at the university. On the day after the vote, when the regents were finishing their monthly business, he had ostentatiously gone into the audience to speak as a "private citizen" and melodramatically warn us of the dire consequences that would flow from our decision. Along with most of my colleagues, I dismissed this as grandstanding. But now I heard that Brophy was telling some of the other regents that if Custred and Wood failed to qualify their measure, as now seemed likely, it would prove that the regents had been out of line with public sentiment on the issue of preferences. And then, Brophy apparently told people close to him that he planned to introduce a resolution to rescind our vote. I might have dismissed all this as rumor if Brophy hadn't confirmed his intentions in an op-ed piece that appeared in the *Sacramento Bee*.

I could well imagine the board taking his point. If CCRI didn't even have enough support to get on the ballot, it might legitimately be concluded that the people of California had spoken—if only by their silence—on the issue of preferences and, in effect, repudiated what we had done. If they revisited and overturned the vote, the principles we had fought for would be defeated, and the old system of preferences would be reestablished as official university policy, more strongly entrenched than ever.

My Thanksgivings were getting weird. During the previous holiday weekend, in 1994, I was upset because I felt that university administrators had misled me about just how pervasive the preference system was at UC. Thanksgiving 1995 was uncomfortable because I saw that the failure of CCRI to make it onto the ballot could threaten a year's worth of work. I began to reconsider my decision not to get involved.

At one point that holiday weekend, I called Bob White, the governor's chief of staff, to ask what he thought.

"Stay out, Ward," he said. "You know that you're seen as being a Wilson guy. If you were to take it on, it would not be perceived as your thing or a Republican thing, but as a Wilson administration thing. You'd look like a tool. It probably won't make it on the ballot anyhow. It's lose-lose."

Then I called Pete and told him I was thinking of getting involved.

"Did you talk to Bob yet?" he asked.

I told him what White had said.

"Well, Bob has good instincts," Pete replied.

"But if I don't do anything," I told him, "the initiative won't qualify, and then Brophy might try to overturn the regents' resolutions. If he succeeds, then it will be like that whole struggle never even happened."

"You're probably right about that," Pete said after thinking for a moment. "The vote was pretty fragile."

There was a pause. "But anyway," Pete said. "Bob's against you jumping in, and I'm not very keen on it myself."

"I still think I ought to do it," I insisted.

"Well," Pete said wearily, "if you want to do it, I'll be with you. But don't enter this thing lightly. This is going to be the mother of all initiatives. If you do get it on the ballot, you'll get attacked in a way that will make the regents thing seem like kid's stuff. They'll attack me as a racist and you as my black lackey. I guarantee you, it will be shittier than anything you've ever been in."

"I'm still leaning toward doing it," I said.

"God bless," Pete replied.

When I became chairman of the California Civil Rights Initiative, the campaign had less than twenty percent of the one million signatures it needed. While Joe Gelman and the people working in the headquarters Custred and Wood had opened in Los Angeles were committed to the issues, they were politically inexperienced and involved in a hand-to-mouth operation. Debts had piled up, payrolls were barely met, and there was no money left over for political action.

Glynn and Tom had originally envisioned a righteous army of citizen volunteers angered by the injustice of race preferences fanning out across the state to gather hundreds of thousands of signatures. But this hadn't happened. If CCRI was going to meet the fast-approaching deadline, it would have to be a streamlined political effort relying on professional signature gatherers.

I spent all of December raising money. Some of the people I contacted didn't need much convincing. Howard Ahmanson, a southern California philanthropist identified primarily with Christian charities, gave right away. Others were a little more difficult. Ron Unz, for example, who would later design a successful anti-bilingual measure for California, seemed interested in giving support, but only if he became a vice-chair and designated spokesman for CCRI. I told him that I didn't want leadership positions being handed out on a quid pro quo basis, and we agreed to become ships passing in the night.

By the end of the month, I had collected $500,000, and Pete had raised another $100,000. Of this amount, much went to erase past debts the Wood and Custred operation had acquired, and the rest just barely got a signature-gathering firm back in the field.

Throughout January, I was on the radio talking about the initiative, often several times a day. It was not a hard sell. Whenever I was on the air, the phones in the CCRI office lit up, and people committed themselves to sending money and getting petitions signed. But as late as early February, I still wasn't sure we'd make it. Although we technically had to get only 700,000 valid signatures, I felt that we should get over one million to protect against sabotage. (I had been warned to expect an organized campaign by the opposition to blitz our signature-gatherers with false names.) To be on the safe side, we kept working until February 20, the day before the deadline.

On February 21, I went to the secretary of state's office with all our bundled petitions. Along with the governor, Assemblyman Richter, and Quentin Kopp, the respected state senator from San Francisco who had courageously supported CCRI, I turned them over to the clerks.

As it worked out, we submitted 1.2 million names. A few days later the secretary of state's office did a random sample of the signatures for authenticity and said that we'd qualified. The California Civil Rights Initiative now had official standing as Proposition 209.

— —

In most cases it's true, as Tip O'Neill once said, that all politics is local. But where affirmative action is concerned, it's quite the opposite: all politics is national. From the beginning, it was clear that the waves caused by Proposition 209 would lap on distant shores. For the NAACP, ACLU, People for the American Way and other institutional grievance groups of the left, 209 was an electoral antichrist, the doomsday measure that would affect their victim-hood clientele and, therefore, their own power. For partisans of a color-blind society, on the other hand, this ballot initiative was the first time that voters anywhere would finally be able to make their feelings known about racial preferences and the affirmative action bureaucracy that had metastasized during the previous twenty five years. It was clear that while 1996 was a presidential election year, the rest of the country would also be keeping an eye on California this electoral season.

I knew that the opposition would draw enormous support from the nationwide preference lobby, and so, soon after becoming chair of the 209 campaign, I began to try to assemble a national team for our side. Consultant Arnie Steinberg got me a list of people he thought might be sympathetic, and I started cold-calling them. One of the first was Thomas "Dusty" Rhodes, a former investment banker at Goldman Sachs. Dusty was not much interested in polit-ical candidates, but he was keenly interested in political issues. He saw the importance of Proposition 209 right away and started opening doors for me.

One of the people I met through Dusty was Bill Kristol, editor of the *Weekly Standard* and a commentator for ABC-TV. A canny political strategist, Bill boosted my spirits by saying that he believed 209 had the potential to alter the way America went about its racial business. He discussed with me ways to give the initiative a national presence.

Another person Dusty put me in contact with was Eric Breindel. Eric was still young, in his mid-forties, but he had been an important figure in the neoconservative movement for fifteen years, making a name for himself as an eloquent spokesperson against communism and for Israel. For several years, he had been in charge of the editorial page of the *New York Post* before moving upstairs to become a personal assistant to Rupert Murdoch. Eric (who died tragically and prematurely in 1998) was very enthusiastic about 209. After we had chatted for a few minutes, he said, "This could be a defining moment in American politics." He arranged a meeting for me with his boss.

I was a little nervous when I arrived at his office. Given the amount of tabloid gossip that Rupert Murdoch generated, it was hard to know what to expect. But from the moment Eric introduced us I saw that this man bore no resemblance to the cartoon figure of the megalomaniac mogul people read about in supermarket checkout lines. He was cool and concentrated, and I got the impression that he was one of those totally organized men who would be comfortable working anywhere in the world. Indeed, at times it almost seemed as if his office was actually a giant piece of luggage that could be folded up, transported, and then reopened by the silent staffers who attend to him around the clock. As we began to talk, I saw that Murdoch was a good listener, but anxious to locate the bottom line of the discussion. While Eric Breindel was more interested in the philosophical implications of Proposition 209, Murdoch was interested in the politics. What was Pete Wilson's role? Who were the important players in California politics? Which of them were on my side? Whom could I really count on?

At the end of the conversation he looked me up and down. "You have any interest in running for office?" he asked abruptly. I said simply that this initiative filled my plate. I didn't say that I'd seen enough of politics to know that running for office, and, even worse, being elected, took away your freedom.

"Well, I'd be interested in supporting you if you decide to run for office," he said.

I didn't ask Murdoch for a contribution in this first meeting, but the contact ultimately bore fruit a few months later. It was just before the Republican national convention in San Diego, which I was attending as a delegate from California. Pete Wilson, Dusty Rhodes, and I scheduled a lunch with Murdoch at the penthouse apartment he had there. His wife Anna (they've since divorced) was present. She sat at the head of the table, talking about a variety of subjects as we ate. After we finished, Dusty and Pete steered the conversation to politics. It was one of those moments wealthy individuals interested in public policy understand: the fund-raising equivalent of a mating ritual. Rupert sat there pensively, making a steeple of his fingers while I talked about 209 and made an indirect pitch for financial support. I told him that the Republican Party needed to stand for something—fairness, equality under the law, real as opposed to phony diversity. From his impassive features I couldn't tell whether I was getting through.

Murdoch then asked, "Why are you doing this, anyway?"

I thought for a moment and then I told him that while 209 was about fairness, it was also about larger issues: whether the racial divisions in this country were going to widen or close; whether the racial policies we adopted would encourage people to buy into the American Dream or make them stand on the sidelines like suspicious outsiders trying to locate the con. I talked a little about my own life and about the hope I saw in the growing number of interracial marriages producing kids who don't fit into any one of the obnoxious little boxes to be checked on official forms.

"I don't want my grandchildren having to check the boxes," I said. "I don't want these PC census takers forcing them to embrace some kind of artificial identity. They're Americans and they don't need to say anything more about themselves than that."

Rupert gave me a noncommittal look, but Anna, who had been paying close attention but saying little, nodded her head enthusiastically: "One of our daughters is married to an African man. We know the pressures they face. I don't want our grandchildren checking boxes either."

"How much do you want?" Rupert asked abruptly.

I was prepared for any question but this one. "Well," I stammered lamely, "I could sure use whatever you gave me."

Pete shot me a despairing look and tried to bail me out: "Ward is making a personal sacrifice here. He's right on the issue, but he's going to take a lot of hell for getting out in front. He can't do it by himself."

Rupert nodded slightly, giving no sign that he had been moved by the appeal. Then, as if some invisible consensus had been reached that it was time to end the meeting, we all stood up. As we walked out of the suite, Pete and I chatted with Anna. Murdoch held back for a minute, whispering something to Dusty. Then he came forward and shook my hand.

"Well, I admire what you're doing," he said. "Hang in there."

As we went to the elevator, the Murdochs waved one last time and then retreated back into their penthouse.

"He's giving *one*," Dusty said under his breath as the elevator door slid open.

"One? A hundred thousand?" I was overjoyed. "God, I can't believe it!"

"No," Dusty smiled as we began heading down to the ground floor. "*One million.* He's going to give a million to the party in two installments."

I stood there awestruck. The donation was to the party, not to 209, but the party was on record as supporting the initiative. Pete laughed and clapped me on the back: "Looks like you're in the big leagues, my friend."

— —

I knew that raising funds for the California Republican Party from people like Rupert Murdoch was only part of the battle. Getting the party to help 209 in return, by contributing some of the money I'd raised, was likely to be the hardest part.

As it worked out, the people in the state party (with one or two exceptions I'll get to in a moment) were great during the 209 campaign. On a national level, however, it was a different situation. In the two years since their 1994 midterm sweep, the Republicans had gone from being favorites to recapture the White House to underdogs against a shape-shifting Clinton, who, under the guidance of Dick Morris's "triangulations," had co-opted much of their agenda. In disarray and generally unclear about its commitments, the Republican National Committee never quite got a handle on 209 or on the concept behind it. Bob Dole, in particular, had trouble with the issue, although he ultimately tried ineptly to grab its coattails in one of those acts of political desperation that gives opportunism a bad name.

If Dole had actually been the master politician we all thought he was, he would have opposed race preferences simply on pragmatic grounds, even if he couldn't understand the moral imperative. He should have picked a fight with Clinton and said that we had to end that horror show that goes by the name of affirmative action because mending instead of ending it simply prolonged what had become institutionalized injustice. Instead, Dole waffled, which was particularly ironic (and ignominious) given the fact that early in 1995, just before resigning from the Senate to make his run, he had put his name on federal legislation (the Equal Opportunity Act, or Dole-Canady bill) to end preferences at the federal level. Thinking the symbolism would help him with conservatives who voted in primaries, Dole wanted identification with the issue, but he didn't care much one way or another if the legislation passed. Later, as the party's candidate, the new Dole, worried now about offending all the sub-groups who never would have considered voting for him in the first place, tried to distance himself from that other Dole who had briefly opposed preferences.

His handlers were as ambivalent as the candidate was. I was told that Sheila Burke, Dole's chief of staff, worried that taking a stand on preferences would alienate women. Haley Barbour, then RNC chairman, decided that strong support by Dole for 209 "might send the wrong message about diversity."

Dole was all over the place on race and preferences during the presidential campaign. Once or twice he seemed on the verge of understanding the role these issues would play in the American future. (However, his only real endorsement of 209 had been one of those disjointed, laconic statements for which he became infamous during the campaign: "It ought to be based on merit. This is America, and it ought to be based on merit.") But, at other times, he came perilously close to embracing the vapid liberal mantra about "inclusiveness."

My lasting impression of the Republican candidate is from a so-called "movers and shakers" meeting I attended in San Francisco. At one point in the afternoon, a big-time donor and philanthropist named Jerry Hume told Dole that he'd better get on board about 209. Shooting Hume one of his dark looks, Dole growled that he was on board and then lapsed into exasperated silence. His wife, Elizabeth, who had accompanied him to the meeting, immediately spoke up brightly in his behalf. She said that not only was Bob on board, but she was on board too. Moreover, not only were they both on board now, but they had both always been on board. As the get-together was breaking up, Elizabeth walked over to me and, as a way of bolstering her husband and herself and their joint on-boardness, insisted on describing the positions she had taken on race while serving as secretary of the Department of Labor. As she began to reel off "accomplishments," I was taken aback because almost all of them involved diversity, multiculturalism, and affirmative action. I saw that she had absolutely no idea of what 209 was all about. I left the meeting thinking about the famous exit line from *Annie Hall* when Woody Allen extricates himself from a weird conversation with Annie's spooky brother by saying, "Excuse me, I've got to be going. I'm due back on planet Earth."

When Pete Wilson, Bill Bennett, and some other party leaders tried to get me on the program at the Republican convention in San Diego, they met strong resistance. As one insider in the Dole campaign told the governor, "We can't have Connerly, because if we have him, we probably won't get Powell."

It shouldn't have been an either/or. Colin Powell had many things to contribute to the Republican Party, but an original or profound view on race was not among them. Still, when Powell came out against our initiative in late spring of 1996 in a commencement address at Maryland's Bowie State College, I was surprised. The position he adopted contradicted the one he had taken in *My American Journey*. ("Equal rights and equal opportunity mean just that," he had written there. "They do not mean preferential treatment. Preferences, no matter how well intended, ultimately breed resentment among the non-preferred and... demean the achievements that minority Americans win by their own efforts.")

I sent a letter pointing out that for him to now do an about-face and begin parroting the line of Jesse Jackson and his crew was demeaning. I noted that in this speech Powell had stated that he knew what it was to be a second-class citizen. I told him that this was an experience he and I shared, but, I added, "You should have told those students how their country had transformed itself into a nation of people who stood in line last year for hours to get the autograph and purchase the autobiography of an American hero who was *once* a second-class citizen."

Powell responded by return mail. He had watched me testify before Congress on C-Span, he noted tartly, and said that he was well enough informed about 209 to make up his own mind without help from Jesse Jackson or anyone else. He described what had been done in the Army beginning in the seventies, when the rising ranks of black enlisted men demanded an increase in the number of qualified blacks in the officers' corps. Then he threw down the gauntlet: "If no program can be race, ethnicity, or gender conscious, [then] affirmative action has been killed in the text of CCRI. And the reality of life in America today is that race, ethnicity, and gender discrimination are still with us. We have made progress and that progress has come about because of government affirmative action programs and voluntary private sector efforts. The work is far from finished."

I replied immediately: "I am troubled that not once in your letter did you evidence any understanding that there are innocent people being harmed by government-sanctioned discrimination practiced in the name of diversity and affirmative action. Under the current system at the University of California, the son of a black four-star general would receive a preference over the daughter of an Asian dishwasher. You have decided to inject yourself into this public policy discussion, as you have every right to do. However, when you decided to use your stature as a resident of Virginia to influence the outcome of a ballot initiative in California, you assumed an obligation to be accountable for the accuracy and consistency of your views. You've been duped, general."

It wasn't vital that I be invited to speak at the convention, but I passed the word to party leaders through Pete that I would not sit by passively and allow Powell to trash 209. If this happened, I let them know, I would make a public show of walking out of the convention, and I knew that there were other delegates who would follow me. In fact, I was preparing myself for such an outcome when, minutes before Powell was scheduled to appear, Howard Leach, my fellow regent who also served as Republican National Committee finance chairman, buttonholed me and said that he had seen an advance copy of the speech, and it did not disparage CCRI. I knew that Howard had been dispatched on this mission, and, indeed, on a couple of occasions during his appearance, Powell looked down at me and gestured in a conciliatory way.

— —

I really didn't expect much from Dole or Powell. But I did expect something from Jack Kemp, whom I had always greatly admired. Some of my friends disparaged him as a self-taught policy wonk who wasn't really happy unless he was giving a three-hour lecture on the gold standard. But I'd always thought of Jack as someone who cared deeply about the issues and had good instincts.

Early in 1996, long before he was the vice presidential nominee, I tried to engage him on the issue of preferences and thought I was having some success. When he came to California in February to keynote the state Republican convention, he interrupted his speech when he saw me in the audience to say that I was "a man destined to be a hero in his own time." When I spoke with him later in the day, he seemed ready to endorse 209. He told me that we'd talk after he had time to think about it.

We finally made contact a few weeks later, not long before the convention. I asked him for an endorsement. Under his aggressively friendly manner, I could sense some hesitancy.

"Look, Jack," I told him. "It's totally inconsistent to believe in free markets and economic empowerment, as you do, and still believe that some people should get special consideration because of skin color, gender, or some other factor."

Kemp said he was concerned that 209 would become another wedge issue. He brought up Proposition 187, which he had opposed: "There, you had a case of certain people engaging in divisive politics by exploiting illegal immigration."

"Proposition 209 is not the captive of the extreme right wing elements in our party," I assured him. "It is a centrist issue by its very nature and polls have shown that we have majority support in one of the most liberal states in the country. There's not going to be anything in this campaign that will embarrass you or anyone else in our party."

Jack got a chagrined look on his face: "You've got to remember that I'm a bleeding-heart conservative." Then he went on to remind me that he was on the Board of Trustees of Howard University. This position was obviously a source of great pride for him, as were all the black friends he'd made in his days playing pro football. He ended the conversation by asking me to fax him a letter outlining why he should drop his neutrality and come out for 209. Although watching Kemp try to make up his mind was becoming tiresome, I faxed such a letter to him a couple of hours before I got on the plane to go to San Diego.

Despite our failure to come to an agreement, I was euphoric upon arriving there to learn that Jack would be on the ticket. When I saw him at a reception on the night before the convention opened, he gave me a thumbs up and said, "We need to talk."

I took this as a sign that, at last, he was committed to carrying the message. But I was worried that because of his previous ambivalence, his new position would be seen as a flip-flop, and further, that because Kemp hadn't really thought out the issues, he would get skewered by the press when the subject arose. I cornered Congressman Vin Weber, a key Kemp ally, and told him that Jack should think out the issues around 209, with me or someone else in the know, so that he didn't get caught off guard when making his announcement. None of this was done. On the following morning, Jack announced his endorsement of the initiative in the most inept manner possible, acting like someone who had been either brainwashed or blackmailed into making a statement he found distasteful. I half expected him to blink "not really" in morse code with his eyelids as he talked about his new-found enthusiasm for Proposition 209.

As the campaign unfolded, Kemp never had very much positive to say about what we were trying to accomplish. He did, however, indirectly indicate his reservations, as when he blurted out at one campaign stop, "Race is a legitimate issue to take into account in entrance to college."

At first I'd been upbeat about Kemp's post-convention vow to "compete for every vote." But as Dole-Kemp entered the late summer dead zone from which it never escaped, I got the feeling that Jack was resigned to losing and was, perhaps, positioning himself to compete for the black vote in some future election. As he went from Harlem to south central Los Angeles telling black audiences about his "new civil rights agenda," he was just another politician trapped in clichés rather than someone trying to break out of a crippling orthodoxy about race. He could have told black audiences how the condescension of the Democrat party had kept them shackled on the liberal plantation for a generation. He could have told them about the dangers inherent in identity politics and how much blacks stand to lose by playing a game of numbers in a time when their numbers are diminishing relative to those of Hispanics and other minorities. He could have challenged them to end their abject servility to cynical liberals who use them by "feeling their pain." But Kemp did none of these things.

He seemed not to realize that Republicans cannot out-pander the Democrats, who are experts at this game. They will never succeed by trying to up the ante with a black leadership that has made itself into a wholly owned subsidiary of the Democrat party. Instead, they must make a conscious effort to circumvent this establishment and appeal directly to average black people—talking to them as rational individuals, not as robots addicted to welfare, affirmative action, and other tokenist entitlements. Kemp not only didn't do this, he actually talked like the other side, saying at one appearance, for instance, that America is "controlled by white people," an absurd statement that plays into the hands of black demagogues.

The most disturbing moment in the campaign for me came during Kemp's debate with Al Gore. The vice president threw him a fat pitch right down the middle, telling Kemp that he was a good guy at heart who had once supported affirmative action but had now fallen into the hands of "mean-spirited" ideologues and was opposing diversity merely to curry favor with them.

If someone like Pete Wilson or Bill Bennett had been at the plate, moderator Jim Lehrer would still be chasing the ball. But Kemp responded with a feeble, rambling comment about how he really did believe in equal opportunity. Watching the way Gore worked Kemp over that night (after himself being worked over by Dan Quayle four years earlier), I began to realize that the defeat of the Dole-Kemp ticket might not mean the end of Western civilization after all.

NINE

OUR MEDIA CONSULTANT, Arnie Steinberg, had a "mole" inside the anti-209 campaign—a highly placed Democrat who was sympathetic to our cause and kept us informed about what was going on. From this individual we learned that the mainstream Democrat activists were inclined to take a hands'-off position on the initiative, regarding it as a volatile issue that could possibly hurt the president's reelection campaign. With this mole acting as a go-between, we reached a tacit understanding with these party regulars: the Clintonites would not try to overwhelm us by pouring huge sums into our opponents' war chest, and, in return, we would not use their man's flabby support for preferences to campaign against him. Surprisingly, this informal compact held until the last days of the campaign.

Most people on our side assumed that with the Democrat regulars on the sidelines because of their concern for the president's reelection, the civil rights left would control the campaign against us, and that race- and guilt-baiting would be the order of the day. In fact, there was plenty of both. But the leadership of the other side decided at the outset that exclusively emphasizing race would be a losing proposition, something Arnie had confirmed in his own focus groups. Gender, however, was thought to be more promising. (The president himself had said, during one of his many campaign visits to the Hollywood entertainment community, "You know, the only way to run a campaign on this issue is to put a woman's face on it.") And so, by late spring, women had become the focus of the anti-209 campaign. The liberal pundits were so anxious to beat us that they ignored the racist implication: in California politics, a woman's face is more appealing than a black face.

A campaign run by soccer moms talking empathetically about the kinder, gentler aspects of affirmative action might have been quite formidable. But fortunately for us, feminist hardliners from NOW and the Fund for a Feminist Majority jumped into the driver's seat of the opposition. These were people who didn't speak soccer mom, and their strategy had nothing subtle or soothing about it. From the outset, they made it clear that they intended to whip up hysteria among women by claiming that 209 was a form of gendercide.

They concentrated their attack on Clause C of the initiative, which allowed for "bona fide qualifications of sex which are reasonably necessary to the normal operation of public employment, public education, or public contracting." Pushing legalisms past the breaking point, the feminists claimed that this innocuous phrase would do away with everything from maternity leave to girls' sports programs. (One of their TV ads showed a woman being systematically stripped of her working, athletic, and leisure apparel, leaving her virtually naked, which seemed to me a strange softcore porn image for feminists to produce.) In fact, Clause C would do none of these things, as has been proven by the lack of a sexist apocalypse following its passage. It was inserted into 209 because there were times when gender blindness was simply not good social policy. When a female inmate must be strip searched, for instance, should not a female corrections officer be given the job?

The majority of California women never bought the feminists' conspiracy theory that 209 was a plot by Angry White Males to strip them of their workplace roles and return them, denuded of power, to the kitchen and the nursery. In fact, a majority of white women, at least, knew exactly where their interests were: with their fathers, brothers, husbands, and sons, who were suffering real discrimination because of preferences. This is why, at the end of the day, 58 percent of them ultimately voted for 209.

However much the opposition to 209 tried to put a smiley face on its positions—whether by emphasizing gender and downplaying race, or in other tactical decisions—there always remained deep divisions within the campaign: women versus ethnics, hardliners versus compromisers, even North versus South. Anti-209 forces in the Bay Area, for instance, seeing at the onset of this struggle that their side would inevitably lose on the merits of the issue, wanted a campaign based on subterfuge instead of all-out war. They designed a competing measure called the Equal Opportunity Initiative, which would have tricked the voters by "outlawing" quotas, which of course were already banned by federal court decisions. The idea was to qualify this measure for the November 1996 ballot, where it would run alongside 209 and, if it got more votes, take precedence as state law. But nobody on the other side ever really got serious about signatures, and so the measure wilted on the vine. And, in any case, the more militant anti-209 forces in the southern part of the state were spoiling for a fight and so the charade proposed by the north didn't appeal to them.

As the months passed, the anti-209 campaign came more and more to resemble a movement of the sixties. It had the moral preening characteristic of the radical sects of that era, and it also featured the constant internal warfare of ever smaller factions over issues of dogma. By mid-summer, as we continued to hold a commanding lead in the polls, the tensions in the other camp boiled over in a conflict over whether it should line up behind the "moderate," mend-it-don't-end-it views of Clinton and agree that affirmative action was a flawed but still necessary social policy that could be improved, or to intensify the attack on 209 as "racist" and "sexist" in violent language more characteristic of the PC university classroom than the political arena. After the dust settled, a group comprised largely of civil rights professionals taking the former view split off to form the Campaign to Defeat Proposition 209, while NOW and the Fund for the Feminist Majority and other harder-line groups formed the Stop Proposition 209 Campaign. Each of these two groups did its own fundraising, and, in effect, ran its own show until the end of the campaign.

The campaign against 209 not only lacked inner coherence, but also a consistent "face" with whom the public could identify. Eleanor Smeal and other feminists and the civil rights professionals—especially state senator Dianne Watson and Jesse Jackson—took their turn auditioning for this role, with Willie Brown functioning as an ongoing understudy. These talking heads tried to speak in a politic manner, but this only suggested that they were unconnected to the body of the anti-209 campaign, which was radical at its heart.

My only disappointment, in fact, is that during the course of the election we were unable to reveal the radical nature of our opposition. We probably should have been more aggressive in pointing out that while there had once been a liberal center and a radical fringe in cultural issues such as race, there was now a radical center and a liberal fringe. But we probably would have had a tough time getting this message across. The media culture doesn't want to inquire too closely into "progressive" politics, possibly because so many working journalists are so heavily invested in these ideas. The media are not, and probably never will be, intellectually ambidextrous. They assiduously promote the notion that there is a right wing filled with "mean-spirited" zealotry and intolerance. But the other side of the political coin is never characterized as a left wing pursuing the sinister objectives that have been at the core of its project for most of the twentieth century. No, it is viewed merely as a collection of well-meaning liberals filled with compassion for the downtrodden.

There was little investigative journalism done on the anti-209 forces. But the effort to get to the presumably insidious bottom of our campaign was ongoing. Journalists sympathetic to the opposition did "profiles" of me that appeared to dig up "news" the other side could use. ("Well, it was in the *Sacramento Bee*, [or *Los Angeles Times* or *San Francisco Chronicle*]," they would say when using this material in some debate.)

What were the primary charges? First, that I was a black hypocrite who had benefited from affirmative action myself. And, second, that I was distorting my past when I talked of the factors that had shaped my life and philosophy because I had never really been poor and my outlook had been molded by a malicious individual, my grandmother, who was a black-hating bigot.

The first accusation was easily refuted: I had never received a preference in getting into college, getting my first job, setting up a business, or getting contracts for Connerly & Associates, and I defy anyone to prove the contrary. The second charge was more painful for me because it slandered my grandmother's memory and because it came from inside my family. The story originated with a white very liberal Sacramento journalist who interviewed my cousin Betty, daughter of my Aunt Hazel, and felt that he had scored a coup when he got her to unload on me as a black man raised to be white. But Betty had a private agenda she didn't declare, and the journalist didn't bother to try to discover. Months earlier, she had asked me to get her husband (a one-time director of the Department of welfare under Jerry Brown and the first affirmative action officer of Sacramento County) a contract with the Lottery Commission. When I refused, she asked me to get her son a job in the Wilson administration. When I refused again, she asked me at least to help get her appointed to the state Economic Development Department. I refused her a third time, making it clear that I just didn't do patronage. This set the stage for her contribution to the phony expose about my past—and Mom's—that was reprinted by papers around the state and regarded with disgust by most of my other relatives.

I didn't complain very strenuously about these lies and distortions at the time, and I'm not complaining about them now. I had taken on a highly visible role in an important campaign and expected to take my share of hits. But it is also true that the nature of the attack on my personal life—that I had taken affirmative action money; that I was a self-hating black who had distorted his past; that I was a race traitor who was sleeping with the enemy; etc.— had consequences. It wasn't much of a step from accusing me of coming from a family of anti-black bigots, for instance, to showing me in a KKK hood, as the *Oakland Tribune* did in a cartoon whose caption was "Connerly and Co.—Ethnic Cleansers"; or to calling me "strange fruit," in Jesse Jackson's phrase, or "Uncle Tom" or "Oreo" or, in the ugliest formulation I experienced during the campaign, "a lawn jockey for the ruling class."

This last insult came from a white man, by the way, and although overtly racist, received no censure from blacks in the anti-

My grandfather Eli Soniea was an ambitious man with a feel for business. He was also a no-nonsense type who didn't like anyone, especially his own kin, putting on airs.

My mother Grace was a beautiful woman with a full exotic face.

Above: My mother and my stepfather William Parker and I were—briefly—a family.

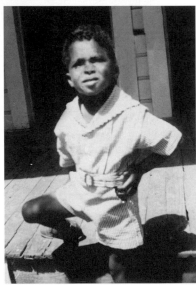

Right: My early years were spent in the heart of Dixie. I didn't know I that I was the great-grandson of a woman who had been born into slavery.

Top: My Aunt Bertha's quiet strength helped fill a hole in my life. My Uncle James taught me what it was to be a *mane*. They were my second parents.

Having grown up family-enriched—this is my Uncle Arthur—I know for a fact that the clichés about black family "pathology" are dead wrong.

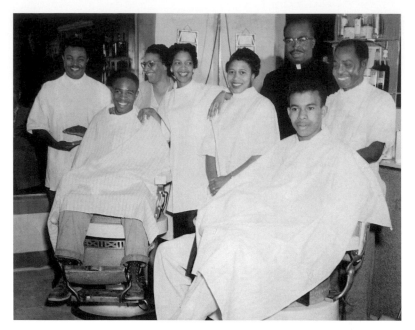

My barber, Cecil York, was a conservative man who believed strongly in black self reliance. Standing behind me is our pastor, Reverend C.M. Cummings, who married Ilene and me. The second woman on my right is my cousin Ora.

As a teenager, I was convinced that I would make my way in the world through hard work. It is a shame that such a belief is not more in fashion among young black people today.

Mary Grace Soniea (Mom) sits next to her mother, Lula Orton Smith, and my Aunt Yvonne and Uncle Arthur. Lula Smith was an Irish woman who married my Indian great-grandfather on the maternal side.

Mom was a forceful woman with a bronze complexion and freckled skin. She was my link between a damaged past and an unknown future.

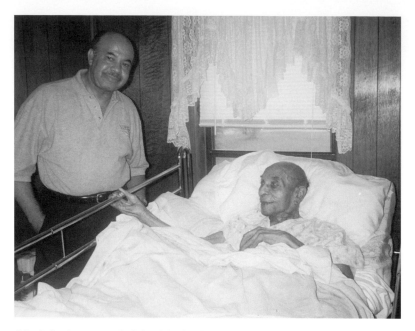

My father's unintended deathbed gift to me was the revelation that it is not the life we're given, but the life we make of the life we're given that counts.

Ilene and I had our share of photo ops with Pete Wilson and his wife Gayle. Despite the abuse he has taken, I know Pete to be a witty and deeply intelligent man. Californians will look back on his governorship as a good time for the state.

Just before the University of California Regents voted to outlaw race preferences, Jesse Jackson called me, among other things, "strange fruit." It was strange to me that he would use this term, a reference to the pendant bodies of black people who had been lynched. Photo ©1997 Richard Ellis for *Meet the Press*.

Bill Clinton and I were both from the South, from broken homes, and both of us had been saved by powerful maternal figures. But we were far apart, not because we came from different races, but because of our different views on race.

John Carlson and I with our band of brothers in Seattle during the fight to pass I-200. I will always think of this one as the "good fight" because of the odds we faced.

209 movement. These liberal blacks rarely condemn such garbage when it is heaped on their conservative brethren. Rather, they hand out the rhetorical equivalent of hunting licenses to their white "progressive" allies to go after blacks like me (who are, of course, black "only on the outside"). Normally morbidly fearful of committing the slightest gaffe when talking to "people of color," these liberal whites attack black conservatives with racist gusto while their liberal black enablers stand back and watch with amusement. Clarence Thomas was right in his charges about a "high-tech lynching." What he didn't say—and perhaps didn't have to—was that while the executioners were white, they had been given the rope by their black comrades.

It is true that words don't break bones, as Mom used to tell me. But they make sticks and stones easier to use. Words can dehumanize, and someone who's been dehumanized is easier to assault. (Is that not the lesson of "nigger," after all?) When the 209 campaign began, I was inclined to laugh off the attacks against me. But then, one afternoon when I had just finished giving a speech to the Commonwealth Club in San Francisco, I was walking down Market Street to my car when a young black male with the disoriented look of a street person passed, did a double take, and then turned and followed me. He began to yell that I had betrayed my race. As I turned to face him he came close with a demented look in his eyes. "See this," he kept tugging incongruously at the lettering of his sweat shirt, which bore the logo of the Yale Law School. "If you win, I would never be able to go to this college." As this spectacle was unfolding, it occurred to me that if words were blunt instruments, my skull would have been crushed.

As the 209 campaign went on, I learned to remind myself when I got up every morning that there were a lot of people out there who simply didn't want me to have a good day. There were anonymous telephone calls to my office in the middle of the day in which a voice said, "better watch your back" and then clicked down the receiver; graffiti scrawled on the side of our office saying, "Big mistake, asshole"; windows shot out by pellet guns or slingshot ball bearings; cars full of young blacks staking me out from across the street and following from a distance as I drove off.

At almost every campaign stop I made there was organized heckling whose racist overtones created an inflammatory atmosphere that could easily have exploded. As the one who opens the mail in our office, Ilene got to see the worst of the hate first. Some of the obscene letters that arrived at the regents' office were forwarded to us with a warning about how ugly they were. Ilene routinely turned this mail over to the California State Police for investigation.

I doubt that any other contemporary black person with the exception of Clarence Thomas has ever faced the kind of abuse that I took in 1996. And, as in the case of Thomas, it continues. In the summer of 1999, in fact, the most disgusting print attack yet appeared in a cartoon by Aaron McGruder called "The Boondocks," distributed by Universal Press Syndicate. The first panel shows "future voice of Black America Huey Freeman diligently working on his first book." This book is called *Ward Connerly Should Be Beaten by Raekwon the Chef with a Spiked Bat.* Then the cartoonist asks of his character, Huey, "Can he broaden the scope of his work without corrupting its cultural integrity and unyielding radical tone?" And in the last panel Huey Freeman has a new title for his work: *Ward Connerly is a Boot-Licking Uncle Tom: A Critical Look at Black Neoconservatives.* And McGruder ends by saying, "Way to go Huey! Everyone knows what a boot-licking Uncle Tom is."

I've grown used to this obscene and threatening abuse. But at the beginning of the 209 campaign, it was still a new experience. I remember almost snapping during one campaign stop. I was being picketed and heckled by a group of aging sixties-era characters calling themselves Angry White Males for Affirmative Action. After I finished, one of them suddenly lunged at me yelling, "Your kind is hurtful to people of color!" I shoved him back and clenched my fist to smack him. But then I stopped myself because I knew that however satisfying it would have been to punch him out, the confrontation would have dominated the news about Proposition 209 for days, drawing everyone's eyes from the prize. I'm not a good enough person to turn the other cheek, but I'm smart enough not to let my opponents provoke me into destroying my own cause.

— —

In the course of the 209 campaign, I came to have a lot of respect for Arnie Steinberg. He understood and believed in our issue, and he was very astute about the pitfalls we were likely to face. When Tom Wood and Glynn Custred first hired him as media consultant, he did a detailed playbook for the campaign, one section of which was devoted to how to handle potentially dangerous situations we might face. Early in the campaign, for instance, Arnie told me that when I met with female supporters, there should always be someone else in the room. He also cautioned me that if by some accident I ever found myself in the vicinity of someone like Jesse Helms, I should be sure to stay away from him in the presence of cameras. Arnie also predicted that if the opposition got desperate, it might try to associate Proposition 209 with a figure like David Duke. In this, he was truly prophetic. But neither Arnie nor anyone else could have predicted the way this gambit would play out.

It all started when Cal State Northridge invited David Duke to address the affirmative action issue on its campus. We were stunned. An important state university bringing a stone-cold racist out to California and paying him a $4,000 speaker's fee to boot?

This mind-boggling maneuver was the brainchild of Vladimir Cerna, an immigrant from El Salvador who had become the school's student body president. (He was the subject of all sorts of strange rumors, one of the most interesting of which alleged that he was related to Lenin Cerna, another Salvadoran who once headed the Sandinistas' secret police.) Cerna later said that he got the idea of bringing Duke to California when he saw him one afternoon on Jerry Springer's freak show. He was pleased with himself for getting the inspiration. A couple of years or so after the 209 campaign, in fact, Vladimir was in the audience when I gave a speech. When I finished, he came up to me and introduced himself, and asked to have his picture taken with me. While we were posing for the photographer, he laughed about the invitation to Duke and asked me to admit that it was diabolically clever of him to have thought it up.

Cerna and the other students tried to get me to come to the Northridge campus to be part of a "debate" with Duke. What they had in mind was more of a show trial. Once I was there, they secretly planned to pair me with Duke and put us up against Willie Brown and a black activist from southern California named Joe Hicks. I discovered the plot when they inadvertently sent me the invitation that was supposed to go to Brown, in which they detailed the plan. I immediately told Cerna and the other organizers that I would not appear on the same platform with Duke, and one of our staff called Blenda Wilson, president of Cal State Northridge, to protest the use of student funds for such an event.

Deprived of my presence, Willie Brown bowed out, and the students had to settle for a debate between Duke and Joe Hicks (whom I have come to repect). I fired off a letter denouncing the invitation to Duke and protesting his presence in California, and I asked the anti-209 campaign to do the same. But a woman named

Pat Ewing, at that point their campaign manager, refused. The other side wanted Duke on the scene. It was both bizarre but somehow appropriate: partisans of affirmative action sponsoring the most notorious racist in the country.

The day of the debate was positively surreal. As Duke and Hicks prepared to square off in the Northridge auditorium, some radicals from Berkeley calling themselves the Coalition to Defend Affirmative Action by Any Means Necessary were raising hell outside. This group, which looked and acted as though it had been rioting somewhere in time warp in the years since 1969, went on a rampage through the campus and fought with police officers mounted on horseback. Television carried images of pepper spray wafting through Northridge's groves of academe, as violent demonstrators were subdued and carted off to jail.

The other side thought it was creating a stark epiphany of the racism at the heart of Proposition 209. But the people of California were confused, and rightly so. Whose side was Duke on? Was he in league with those who opposed this civil rights initiative? Were the rioters for or against racial equality?

Having failed previously with more benign schemes—such as their call for young "idealists" from all over the country to come west for a "California Summer Project" (an almost laughable effort to echo the Mississippi Summer of 1963)—our opponents actually believed that Duke was the answer. Pat Ewing, in fact, predicted that his appearance would be a "defining moment." It was, but in ways she hadn't foreseen. A number of questions were raised about the anti-209 forces that were never answered. Chief among them was this: were preferences so precious that they justified making a devil's compact with America's arch-racist?

There were many moments in the campaign that were not fun. But the one event that still stands out in my mind occurred one weekend when I was out of town and northern California was inundated by a rainstorm of Biblical proportions. I called home and Ilene told me that she had spent all day Sunday trying to deal with the water that had flooded the bottom floor of our office. Being a thousand miles away raising money for our cause while my wife was on her hands and knees with mops and towels didn't make me feel very good.

But there were several moments I still savor. Perhaps the tastiest was the decision of the *Daily Californian*, the student newspaper on the Berkeley campus, to endorse Proposition 209. The argument of the editorial was intelligent: "Race and gender preferences now do more harm than good…. The goal of affirmative action, to redress centuries of shameful discrimination against blacks, Latinos, other minorities and women, is praiseworthy. But the ends of social policy do not justify the means." But the courage of the editors impressed me even more than their rhetoric. They had taken their stand in the face of the institutionalized leftism of the Berkeley campus and knew there would be consequences. And indeed, the morning that this issue of the *Daily Cal* appeared, more than 20,000 copies were immediately stolen from paper racks and destroyed, and efforts were made to intimidate the editors. I was surprised and thankful that this was the extent of the reaction against these young journalists and that the reprisals went no farther than they did.

By mid-October, I felt that 209 was in a good position. All along the opposition had predicted that our support would evaporate once the voters understood our various subterfuges. They cited polls that they claimed showed that the public really supported affirmative action, and had been confused by our "devious semantics" in talking about *preferences* and that we had large support only because of the way we had deceitfully defined the issue. I answered this charge wherever I went by saying that it was the other side that hid behind semantic ambiguity. "Affirmative action" was undefined and undefinable. In the years since its advent under Lyndon Johnson, it had gone from being a process that tried to make sure that excluded minorities had affirmative access to state-supported programs, to a draconian system of quotas and set-asides—in a word, a system of preferences.

I pointed out that these affirmative action addicts seemed to believe that Americans felt about color and ethnic origin the way Marxists continue to insist that workers feel about class. But if this were true, as more than one observer pointed out, only the 27 percent of Californians who were white males would have voted for the initiative. It wasn't hard to convince the voters that affirmative action was all about forcing people to check boxes and socially engineering them into categories. Its own advocates couldn't even define what affirmative action was, which is why they resorted to inane metaphors like "leveling the playing field," never admitting, of course, that they reserved for themselves the role of groundskeeper who says when the field is level, who's allowed to play, and, more to the point, what the game is.

All this wrangling over definitions didn't hurt us. In fact, it probably helped because it put the concept of "preferences" squarely in the public view for the first time. With a couple of weeks to go, we were holding steady in the polls and ready to finish off with a modest media campaign, which consisted of three quite effective commercials Arnie Steinberg had filmed, all of which ended with the tag line, "Yes on Proposition 209! Bring Us Together." I was featured in one of them, sitting with children of all races and backgrounds and talking about how we were all part of the American Dream. In another, Gail Heriot, a professor at the

University of San Diego law school, was shown interrupting the class she was teaching to respond to a question about "diversity" from one of the students. The third, and perhaps most effective of the ads, featured a young woman named Janice Camarena Ingraham, the white widow of an Hispanic man and mother of two small children. Janice had been kicked out of a vocational retraining class in a California junior college she desperately needed because she was the wrong color. Janice was perfectly authentic, almost in tears as she talked to the camera, a classic victim of "reverse discrimination."

The money to run these ads, I hoped, would come from the California Republican Party. I didn't regard this possible aid as a donation, however, since I had raised every cent and then some myself. But at the crucial moment, when Steinberg was about to finalize the media buy, I got a call from John Herrington, former secretary of the Department of Energy under Ronald Reagan and, at this point, head of the Republican state party.

"Well, Ward, we've got to cut off your line of credit," Herrington said breezily.

I was incredulous: if anyone was living on credit, it was the party, which had benefited handsomely from my fund-raising efforts.

When I started to protest, Herrington tried to cool me out: "Don't worry, your ship is going to come in."

An image flitted through my mind of a speck on the horizon that might or might not be a ship, but if so, it was probably receding further into the distance rather than on its way to shore.

"Look, John," I tried to control my voice, "we're ready to launch our TV ads and we need the money now."

"TV ads?" Herrington asked, as if just reminded of something he otherwise might have forgotten. "Oh, don't worry about that. The California Republican Party has ads ready to go. We'll put lots of money into them. You're going to love them."

Something wasn't right. I liked Herrington, but I also knew that he was angling to go back to Washington—in another cabinet post if Dole won or at least to succeed Haley Barbour as national party chairman if Dole lost. I knew he was serving many masters in the 1996 campaign, and I knew that none of them gave a damn about Proposition 209.

A video cassette from the CRP arrived at my office by Federal Express the next morning. With a feeling of dread, I opened it and shoved it into the VCR. As it began to play, I saw a nightmare advertisement showing Martin Luther King giving his "I Have a Dream" speech while in the background a voice droned, "Job quotas and preferences are wrong. Proposition 209 opposes quotas and preferential treatment. But Bill Clinton opposes Proposition 209 just like he opposed Proposition 187." It was a naked act of opportunism in which the sinking Dole campaign tried desperately to hoist itself up onto the deck of 209.

As I soon discovered, the ad had been put together by Sal Russo, a Sacramento media consultant who, ironically enough, was a pal of Jack Kemp's. It committed every possible political sin: linking Propositions 209 and 187; dragging in Clinton and inviting retribution from his people; and, worst of all, cynically summoning up the ghost of Martin Luther King. It was well known that King's family was fiercely protective of his words, anxious to be paid for use of his speech and image, and notoriously litigious. In this case, they would be on the other side of the political issue and, therefore, doubly angry at what they would no doubt regard as a misuse of his memory.

I had wrestled almost since the beginning of the campaign with the question of Martin Luther King. His 1963 speech was a great moment in our history precisely because it summoned America in majestic terms to live up to one of its founding principles—that is, to strive for fairness, equity and colorblindness, and by doing this to *create equal.* Judging people by the content of their character rather than the color of their skin—the most memorable idea in King's speech—was at the very core of Proposition 209. But while it was in some sense fitting to claim Martin Luther King as the patron saint of the fight against preferences, I also knew that he had been a political person as well as a moral figure who had adapted to circumstances of his time. Specifically, King had always been sensitive to pressure by the black left—in the early sixties, by the SNCC workers who launched the Freedom Rides and dared him to come with them; and in the mid-sixties, by the Black Panthers and other radical sects that derided him and his nonviolent philosophy. I knew too that at the end of his life King had been moving toward what would become affirmative action (although he wanted government programs that would apply ecumenically to all poor people, not just those of a certain color), and if he had lived he might well have wilted under pressure from the preference cartel and evolved a position similar to Jesse Jackson's. If this had been the case, I finally concluded, I would still have revered him for the moral vision he had articulated in the past, but opposed him for how he had compromised that vision in the present.

After rewinding the tape of the commercial and watching it again with a sick feeling, I called Pete Wilson: "I've got to show you something. I'm coming over."

When I arrived at the governor's residence, I first showed him the ads Arnie Steinberg had shot.

"Wow, those are great!" Pete said.

"Yeah, well enjoy them now," I said bitterly, "because you'll never see them on the air."

Then I told him how Herrington and Haley Barbour had given

money that I had raised, presuming that some of it would be donated to 209, to Sal Russo to take over the media campaign. As I talked, I pushed the cassette I'd received that morning into the VCR.

"Damn, that's awful," Pete shook his head angrily after watching the Dole-Kemp ad featuring King.

"Right," I said. "And it's going to bring Coretta Scott King, the NAACP, and everyone else out of the woodwork. They'll all be coming down on us like a ton of bricks."

"You're right," Pete said with a sour look on his face. "This could take 209 down."

I sat there for a minute not knowing what to think. Things were so confused at the top of the party, and the major players were cutting each other up with so many conflicting agendas that I couldn't be sure that Pete himself hadn't been involved in this behind-the-scenes maneuver.

"Did you know Haley Barbour was going to do this?" I finally asked him.

"No," he answered without hesitation. "I'm out of the loop on this whole campaign. You know that. Barbour hates me. The whole Dole-Kemp gang is pissed off at me."

This was true. They hadn't forgotten that Pete had formed an alliance with New Jersey Governor Christie Todd Whitman at the convention in an attempt to open up the discussion on abortion and other social issues. Dole-Kemp got even by minimizing Pete's role in San Diego and then humiliated him further by selecting Attorney General Dan Lungren to run their California campaign. For weeks, they allowed Pete to twist slowly in the wind.

While I sat there trying to figure out where I—and 209—now stood, Pete got Ken Khachigian on the phone. Khachigian had been a central figure in Republican state politics since Reagan's governorship and, in 1996, he functioned as a meeting point for state Republicans and the Republican National Committee. From listening to Pete's end of the conversation, I could tell that Khachigian knew what had happened with the ads and that he wasn't offering any hope that an appeal could succeed.

"Those bastards!" Pete slammed down the receiver. "It's a done deal!"

I went back home and called Arnie Steinberg to break the news. He was livid. I told him that we still had a little money in the bank and could do some radio or perhaps even a small television buy. But he was so angry that he could hardly reply. It was easy to see why. His ads, which were admired by everyone who'd seen them, were being replaced by hack work from an outsider who didn't care about what we were fighting for, but who would now be picking up a six-figure check for making the media buy.

Over the next few days, Arnie engaged in an escalating fax war with the Republican National Committee. Sensing that this had the potential to get out of hand and do 209 even more damage, I told him to cool it. But he kept up the fight. Finally it became such a problem that I told him that I was going to have to fire him if he didn't leave the matter alone. Arnie couldn't let it rest, although he understood my position. We had an amiable parting of the ways, and he continued to contribute ideas to the campaign until election day.

Everything I feared about the King ads came true. The King family blasted the use of his image and words and blasted Proposition 209 as a blasphemy on his memory. As a result of the debate occasioned by the ads, according to a new set of polls, we had slipped from a 20 point lead to a 5 point lead in a matter of days.

I waited for an opportunity to air my feelings of betrayal. Then, in a speech to supporters in San Francisco, I took a little detour: "Let me take a moment to comment on the ads about Proposition 209 that are now running on television. I want to say that I dissociate myself absolutely and completely from those ads." I went on to condemn the Republican Party for parachuting into this issue at the last minute when we had been in the trenches so long. "And so I want it known," I concluded, "that if Proposition 209 loses, I'll hold John Herrington personally responsible."*

There was a flurry of calls from Republican higher-ups after these words became public, all of them assuring me that I'd misunderstood what had happened. I wasn't convinced.

I'd been involved in politics for years, but never before had things seemed so byzantine. The California Republican Party, the Republican National Committee, Dole-Kemp and the 209 campaign were all theoretically on the same side, but each organization had its own interests and was using any means at hand—however devious—to further them.

Being part of this situation was like being trapped in a hall of mirrors. Everyone had a distorted image. No one was what he seemed. All the main players were trying to manipulate everyone else secretly to advance their causes. My only hope was that someone in the middle of these machinations would recognize the transcendent importance of what we were trying to accomplish and stop the others from sinking us.

The Dole-Kemp people might well have taken Proposition 209 down with them if the other side hadn't inadvertently thrown us a

---

* Although I was very critical of him at the time, Herrington was truly caught in an impossible situation. As chairman of the state Republican Party, he had to work as facilitator for the national ticket. I knew that in his heart John wanted 209 to succeed, and he honestly believed that these terrible ads would help.

life raft. Jesse Jackson and others had been mau-mauing the Democratic National Committee for weeks for being AWOL. What's the matter with you people, Jackson apparently kept asking, don't you believe in or stand for anything? Connie Rice, West Coast representative of the NAACP, was even blunter. "I asked them if they were selling us down the river," she said angrily after sitting through a meeting with Democratic National Committee bigwigs. "I should have asked how far." Reacting to this pressure (and released from our tacit truce by the King ads), the Clintonites finally dispatched George Stephanopolous to make a speech or two in Hollywood and raise enough money so that the anti-209 campaign could do some ads of its own.

Media consultant Bob Shrum got the job. He was already in California to make sure that the ball didn't take a bad bounce for Clinton's presidential campaign at the end of the game. But Shrum's well-known mean streak—which had been perfected during thankless years spent trying to clean up Teddy Kennedy's public image—made it difficult for him to play defense. He took on the job of designing an ad campaign against us with his usual unprincipled gusto.

After seeing what Shrum had put together, one of the anti-209 spokesmen announced to the press that their campaign had "designed a nuclear bomb." The only trouble was that they dropped it behind their own lines. Shrum's ad was, if anything, even worse than Sal Russo's and possibly the only thing that could have neutralized the impact the King controversy was having on our campaign. What Shrum produced was a nasty farrago of images featuring David Duke, KKK, burning crosses and a confusing message. The narration was lurid: "He's not another guy in a business suit. He's David Duke, former head of the Ku Klux Klan, and he's come to California to support Proposition 209."

Highly respected *Los Angeles Times* political reporter George Skelton was quoted as saying the Duke spot was "so slimy" that it made the usual negative ads look normal by comparison. It was also a loser. It confused and alarmed people and made those who might have been wavering think that they had to vote for 209, which was after all the *California Civil Rights Initiative,* to stop the Klan. Shrum's ad halted our slide in the polls. Its paranoia turned off all audiences, ironically enough, except for blacks, who are, unfortunately, particularly vulnerable to such lurid messages. (In fact, some astute political observers thought that this was Shrum's deep purpose—to make sure blacks turned out in large numbers to vote for Clinton, even if the ad turned off people who might have voted against 209.)

A few months after the election I was on an episode of *Firing Line* with Shrum. Sitting in the green room before taping began, I asked him about the ad. "We didn't have much money," he shrugged, "and had to get the biggest bang we could for the buck." As he spoke, his voice and manner conveyed a quintessence of nihilism, and I had the image in my mind of Saddam Hussein mindlessly lobbing Scuds at Tel Aviv long after it was clear that he had lost the Gulf War.

I had one more moment of concern in the final hours of the campaign. The American people have always been cautious about changing the way we do our racial business. ("Jeez, Dr. King, can't you just be a little more gradual in your approach?" was a frequent plea in the early sixties.) And so, I worried that people might regard Proposition 209 as too abrupt a departure from the status quo, even if they suspected that the status quo was morally corrupt. Indeed, if the opposition had worked this theme, instead of obsessing on David Duke, perhaps things would have tightened even more. But they didn't, and by November 1 we were coasting. The last Field poll taken a couple of days before the election showed us winning by five points. But when I mentioned it to Pete, he said, "Don't sweat it. Mervin Field is a liberal Democrat, everyone knows that. If he says five, it's closer to ten."

As it worked out, ten was almost exactly our margin of victory.

Election night I was at the Radisson Hotel in Sacramento watching the returns on television. The state police had picked up rumors of possible trouble and warned me to stay in my room. But when it became clear that we had won, I insisted on going to the ballroom where 209 workers and supporters had gathered.

I spoke especially to black people who were not much in evidence at the Radisson but might, I thought, be watching on television:

"I believe that in the past we have been saying to young black kids, 'If at first you don't succeed, redefine success.' And we tell them that their failure is the result of culturally biased exams, the lack of role models, and other aspects of a 'racist society.' Our kids have come to believe that they cannot survive in a world without special consideration. Their competitive spirit has been weakened by this dependency on affirmative action. We owe it to them to better prepare them for the rigors of the competitive world. And we owe it to all that is good about America not to let them sink into the debilitating mentality of believing that our nation is racist at its core."

TEN

At some point during the 209 campaign, I stopped being a private citizen who was temporarily involved in politics and, instead, became a public figure associated with a certain cause. This was a strange experience. Part of me was still the poor boy from the wrong side of Del Paso Heights who was gratified—and, frankly, somewhat surprised—to be taken seriously on a matter of national importance. Yet the process of becoming recognizable and identifiable is somewhat threatening—a sort of psychological amputation that robs you of your complexity and leaves you one-dimensional. It was and *was-not* me—that new self I watched being interviewed and commented upon in the newspaper; and the *was-not* part was bothersome. I resented the fact that because people know where you stand on one issue—in my case race preferences—they feel they can clone your position on all other questions from abortion to gay rights. This tendency made me feel, perversely, like taking positions that were against the grain just to defy these expectations, although I've always resisted such impulses.

I raised some of these thoughts with Dusty Rhodes when he called shortly after the election. And when, in the course of the conversation, he asked what came next, my first response was that nothing came next; I was simply glad not to have presided over a loss that would have killed the anti-preference movement and humiliated me personally, and I didn't feel like pushing my luck.

"But you're identified with the issue now," Dusty said. "There's nobody else who can push it."

"That's a problem," I answered.

"You need to stay involved," Dusty pressed.

"I need to get involved with the things I was involved with before all this started," I replied.

I wasn't playing hard to get. Ilene had been very upset by the verbal violence that had marked the campaign and showed signs of becoming permanent now that we had won. The specter of a John Hinckley figure walking around somewhere out there with affirmative action as a cause to die for had been a scary one for all of us since the first days of the struggle at the Board of Regents. We were afraid that if I continued to be a voodoo doll for the preference establishment, sooner or later someone would stick a real pin into me.

Ilene also worried that Connerly & Associates would suffer if the fight against preferences became my day job. In this, I agreed with her. There had been times during the 209 campaign when our firm lost business simply because I was too busy with politics. In other cases, we lost out with local governments that are an important part of our client base either because these elective bodies were put off by my notoriety or because they wanted to punish us for my position on affirmative action. I sometimes had a picture in my mind of those old 1950s cartoons in which dollar bills with wings were shown flying away from their improvident owners.

But Dusty brushed these qualms aside.

"You've got to stay visible," he repeated. "At this point, that's the only way of keeping the issue visible. If this thing stops at the Oregon and Nevada border, it will be a failure. We've got to keep insisting that this is a national issue that happens to have begun, like so many other things that go national, in California."

He was right, of course. Once you embark on a cause like the one we'd undertaken, you have to keep advancing, if only to protect the ground you've already won. Already, a few days after our victory, I was reading articles in the national press that attributed our victory to California kookiness and claimed that no other state in the country would have passed such a measure. Dusty and I talked a while longer and decided to take the next step by forming the American Civil Rights Coalition and the American Civil Rights Institute, nonprofit organizations that would take the fight against preferences national and, if possible, make sure that it remained a front-burner issue.

— —

I'd gotten a number of invitations to speak out of the state during the 209 campaign but had put them aside for lack of time. Now I put them together into a little speaking tour that would give me a sense of where we stood with the rest of the country.

Along the way I met with a few key individuals I wanted on our side. One of them was Steve Forbes. I met him at the *Forbes Magazine* headquarters. As we sat down in his surprisingly modest conference room, he wore that look of nearsighted empathy I had always assumed was just his public face. Steve hadn't made a big issue of affirmative action in his unsuccessful run for the 1996 Republican presidential nomination, and he didn't say much now as I made my pitch. But I could tell from the occasional nod and smile that he was interested. After I finished, he asked some acute, cut-to-the-chase type questions that showed exactly how closely he had been listening. As I was leaving, he handed me one of his "free-market packages" containing a tie with the word "capitalism" repeated in tiny letters, an umbrella of the same design, some copies of *Forbes*, and literature about the genius of our economic system. He said that he believed preferences were a crucial issue.

Some of the groups I talked to over the next couple of weeks were comprised of conservatives and libertarians who, until recently, had been tongue-tied on issues involving race. I had always assumed that their silence was part of a guilty conscience over the doubts they'd had about sitting out the civil rights movement. There was some of this, but it was also true that they simply lacked a vocabulary to discuss race, which had never really been a "conservative" issue. They had embraced color blindness somewhat tardily, but they now believed passionately, if somewhat pessimistically, in this principle. While they thought they were on the correct side of the argument, however, they weren't sure they'd earned the right to speak out. And in any case, they thought that the anti-preference movement—like welfare reform, school choice, social security reform, and other issues—would probably languish in the think tanks for a generation before ever actually affecting public policy. Their pessimism had been dispelled overnight by Proposition 209. They were euphoric over what we had accomplished in California and what it could portend for the rest of the country, although I was something of a curiosity to them: the black businessman who had slain the dragon.

I appreciated the standing ovations these conservatives gave me, and I counted many of them as close allies and friends, but I was also aware that if I had been saying the same things before the same audiences thirty-five years earlier, I would have gotten a far different reception.

But I didn't want to go around the country preaching only to the choir. I also wanted to challenge the people who reflexively hated me and what I believed, thinking, too naïvely as it worked out, that I might be able to change their minds. So I made a point of accepting invitations to speak at several universities, and this, as Monty Python used to say, was something completely different.

Having appeared on campuses in California, I thought I knew the worst that would happen to me—sullen and inattentive audiences, a few of whose members would grudgingly admit that, perhaps, I had a point while most of the others would give me the evil eye the whole time I spoke. But I learned that at home I had been protected somewhat by my status as a UC regent. Now, as I traveled to a variety of campuses, I often didn't get a hearing at all as protestors drowned me out before I could get out a single sentence. But it wasn't the hostility of the radical students that surprised me, or even the fact that the kids in the audience who tried to support my position were intimidated into silence. Far more bothersome was the complicity of the administrators who were always present as representatives of the colleges when I spoke and who always stood by impassively as intellectual thugs drowned me out. To them, the university was a place that enforced right-thinking, not a marketplace of ideas. To them, free speech was less important than correct speech, and I was someone who deserved to be shut up because they didn't like what I said. Every time this happened to me, I thought about how outraged these administrators would have been if students disrupted an appearance by someone like Angela Davis because of her long record of supporting Stalinist causes or someone like Mumia Abu Jamal because he was convicted of murdering a cop.

Perhaps the worst experience I had was at Emory University in Atlanta. I guess I still believed in the myth of Southern gentility because I was taken aback, upon entering the auditorium there, to be confronted by a mob. The leadership there was composed of a handful of black kids with the belligerent looks and stabbing hand motions of gangsta rappers. As they incited the crowd, I could hardly hear myself being introduced. When I tried to speak, the crowd stood and screamed. I stood there as if in a wind tunnel, focusing on a seventy-something white guy in a back row. Looking like an antique hippie, he kept yelling insults at me—the kindest was "Go back to California, you Oreo, we don't need your kind here"—and then immediately turned around to get affirmation from the brothers seated nearby.

As I stood there silently facing the crowd, I wondered what I had done to warrant this. Speaking out for equality under the law in language that had been perfected by the civil rights movement? Proposing that we are far more, each of us, than our skin color, another idea that had grown up right here in Atlanta four decades earlier?

There were a few security guards present, but they stood lack-adaisically in the back of the auditorium where they couldn't have done anything if there had been a physical confrontation, which seemed to me a real possibility. I saw two Emory administrators in the front row with their arms folded, smirking at me as I tried to be heard.

After a few minutes, I finally walked off the stage. I stood in the wings for a moment, shaking with rage as I gathered my things and got ready to leave. But then I decided that I wouldn't let them run me off and went back out. I yelled into the microphone that I would dispense with the speech I had prepared and answer what-ever questions they wanted to ask. This seemed to mollify them somewhat. Anxious for a piece of me, the radicals quickly lined up at the microphone.

"Why does a Negro like you do the bidding of white people?" one yelled above the din of hoots. Another said, "Why does an

Uncle Tom like you come to Atlanta, home of Dr. Martin Luther King, and spit on his grave?" And so it went. They gave it to me and I gave it back. Finally, in an almost comic denouement, the two administrators who had sat silently while the crowd prevented me from speaking rose to speak too. The questions they asked were couched in the aggressive decorousness of the faculty lounge, but they were meant to show the student radicals that they were on their side and were rewarded by predictable applause. I had to restrain myself from calling these two what they were: intellectual degenerates. To cap everything off, I later heard that these administrators had gone to the president of Emory the next day to explain that the mob scene in the auditorium had occurred because I had "provoked" the students, a lie that he apparently believed until others intervened and convinced him to write me an apology.

I'll admit that this experience shook me. But it was probably also good in that it let me know that I should either get battle-hardened or stay home. I took the first alternative and got better at handling these situations. A year or so after my non-speech at Emory, for instance, I walked into a similar situation at the University of Wisconsin. The crowd there was, if anything, more organized, following their leader—an intense black student who seemed very much aware of the television news cameras covering the event. His followers all had yellow cards, presumably an allusion to my selling out of black people, and when the leader waved his, the rest of them waved theirs too. When he stood and yelled at me, they did too. When he started a chant they immediately took it up. It was like a PC version of Simon Says.

This time, I didn't even try to give a speech. As the crowd began to jeer and boo, I put a hand up and spoke into the microphone: "There are TV cameras here. If your objective is to have the lead story of the news tonight be that you prevented me from speaking, you can have that. But if you want to have a give and take, we can have that too. Here's my deal. You promise to be civil [here I looked directly at the ring leader] and I'll take you on one at a time, no holds barred."

I could tell that the idea of a *mano a mano* flattered him and his followers in the audience because it seemed to affirm their power over the situation. They all looked around and nodded at each other while I took off my jacket and rolled up my shirt sleeves. For the next hour we went at it hammer and tongs until the questions were over.

I thanked the crowd for coming and got a grudging round of applause. As I was preparing to leave, the young black man who'd led the crowd came up to the stage and offered to shake my hand.

"I still don't like your position," he said, "but you're a man, I'll give you that."

This made me recall my Uncle James talking about the importance of being a *mane*. "That's all I ever wanted," I told the student.

I have learned a lot from speaking at college campuses, much of it disheartening. However, I still feel hopeful. Invariably, after the radicals have their little drama at these events and people are filing out, a handful of black students will stall until they're almost alone and then come up to talk. One of the things they always say, although in different ways, is that they were sick of the stereotyping that comes along with preferences, and sick too of their elders coercing them into supporting affirmative action with messages like, "Our generation fought for you to have this," or "Our racist society owes this to you." After these conversations, I always found myself wondering if all this seemingly fanatical support for affirmative action on college campuses is really only skin deep.

— —

As it became clear to us that California hadn't been a fluke, we began to consider where to fight the next battle. Under different conditions, it would not have been a question because Congress would have passed and the president might even have signed federal legislation outlawing preferences. (Bill Clinton is a politician who has shown an unerring instinct for scrambling toward the center, after all.) But that possibility had been foreclosed a couple of years earlier when the Dole-Canady bill died a lingering death. In 1997, Congressman Charles Canady was still pushing for a federal law similar in language to 209, but getting no traction. "Whenever I bring up preferences, even in Republican caucuses," he told me, "everyone looks the other way. They don't have the stomach for the fight."*

So, we made plans to go state by state. The first chunk had come out of the Berlin Wall of preferences, but the rest of that decadent edifice was apparently going to have to be brought down piece by piece.

A couple of times during the California campaign, I noticed a large, heavy-set man sitting near the front row nodding his head enthusiastically while I spoke. (Actually I noticed his tie before I noticed him: a flamboyant, patriotic arrangement of stars and stripes.) When we were finally introduced, I discovered he was Scott Smith, a state assemblyman from the Tacoma area. For Scott, affirmative action was not so much a program as a punishment that had affected him personally. He and his wife had once applied for the same job. She was (the two of them agreed) slightly less qualified, but got the offer while Scott was passed over. After this happened, they both realized that they had just experienced a process

* I also learned that the Republican caucus had decided to defer to J.C. Watts on this issue. As I mentioned earlier, J.C. says that he's opposed to ending preferences until "the playing field is level."

that was unfair as well as irrational. After being elected to the Washington state legislature, Smith repeatedly—and always unsuccessfully—introduced legislation to ban preferences based on race, gender, and ethnicity. Until the California campaign he thought that he would always be a lone voice crying out in the wilderness. Now he wanted the 209 franchise in Washington.

I ran into Scott again in Seattle in the spring of 1997 when I gave a speech at the Washington Institute for Policy Studies. He approached me after I had finished and said, "We're ready to go." I did a double take and asked him what he meant. He said that he and a Washington businessman named Tim Eyman had designed a referendum based almost word for word on the California Civil Rights Initiative and would soon be gathering signatures. I was surprised and pleased. It was a good sign that the campaign had been designed by a pair of individuals connected to both the political and the business communities. It was an even better sign that they weren't asking for anything from me but advice.

That summer Smith and Eyman seemed well advanced in the signature-gathering campaign when I saw them at a caucus of Republican legislators at a lodgelike convention center in a heavily forested area outside of Seattle. I gave an off-the-cuff speech about why I had gotten involved in the movement to abolish preferences and why I thought such a movement was in the best traditions not only of this country but of the Republican Party. When I ended, they were all on their feet and pledged strong support for the effort Smith had undertaken. The enthusiasm was such that I had a strong sense that Washington would be the next state to act on preferences and that the people in this room had the power to make it happen.

About this time, however, events were unfolding in Texas that would up the ante.

Texas had been pivotally involved in the issues around affirmative action since 1995, when a landmark legal decision handed down by the Fifth U.S. Court of Appeals ruled in favor of Cheryl Hopwood, a white woman who had sued the University of Texas Law School after being passed over for admission in favor of black and Hispanic students with lower test scores and undergraduate grades. This decision made all universities within the three-state jurisdiction of the Fifth Circuit an affirmative action–free zone.

However, like most major cities and counties, Texas jurisdictions had, over the years, adopted set-aside programs in employment and contracting that were immune to the *Hopwood* decision. Begun in 1984, Houston's program had expanded by 1995 to include "goals." For example, seventeen percent of city construction, eleven percent of purchasing, and twenty-four percent of professional services were to be carried out by minority-owned businesses. Some Houstonians believed that this was a quota system going by another name and decided to do something about it.

Their leader was Ed Blum, a broker with Paine Weber who in his spare time chaired an organization called Campaign for a Color-blind America. This group made its mark by attacking the racial gerrymandering of Congressional districts, an effort that helped bring the issue before the Supreme Court. Now, in the spring of 1997, it began to gather signatures for a ballot measure based on Proposition 209 that would change the way Houston did its racial business.

Blum called me right after the election in California to introduce himself and ask for advice on how to proceed. In the months since then, we had several long conversations and I'd come to like and respect Ed and his wife, Lark. His path to the anti-preference movement was as improbable as my own. Ed had grown up in a committed left-wing family (he calls himself "a pink diaper baby") where politics was always a dinner-table subject. He probably would have reflexively followed the liberal party line on affirmative action if his father had not enlisted in the army during World War II and, because he spoke Yiddish, become a translator working with concentration camp survivors. The senior Blum's experiences in Europe made everyone in his family extremely sensitive to issues involving state-supported discrimination. In the sixties, Ed had been active in the civil rights movement and believed that eliminating preferences in the nineies was an extension of that effort.

Like 209, Measure A, as the referendum Ed and his group crafted was called, said that the city "shall not discriminate against or grant preferential treatment to" racial and ethnic groups. But the Houston power structure, fiercely protective of its status quota, didn't want its citizens to vote on a measure containing this language, which clearly would have passed. Outgoing mayor Bob Lanier convinced the city council to exercise the right it was given under the city charter to change the wording of the measure before it went on the ballot. Despite the strong protests of Blum's group, Lanier and his allies manhandled the language so that instead of forbidding discrimination for and against, Measure A "ended use of affirmative action for women and minorities."

This was more than a minor semantic change. The issue was immediately transformed from a specific one involving forbidding injustice to a vague one appearing to take a right away from the downtrodden. Campaign for a Color-blind America was put into the surreal position of having to try to pass a measure it hadn't designed. Ed filed suit, but his action couldn't be heard until after the election.

The campaign in Houston was more compact than the one in California, in terms of time, and also a good deal nastier. And one of the victims was Ed Blum himself. Playing for keeps, Mayor Lanier twisted the arms of companies doing business with the city to make them take a position opposing Measure A. One of the arms he twisted hardest was Paine Weber CEO David Marston. Complaining about Ed Blum's activism, Lanier pointed out to Marston that Houston let out contracts worth tens of millions to underwrite bonds. The mayor didn't have to say the obvious: it would be a shame if Paine Weber didn't get a share of this business. It wasn't long after that Marston informed his employees in Houston that they would no longer be allowed to speak out on controversial issues.

The edict was obviously aimed at only one person, and it hit the fan for Ed Blum soon after. When he wrote an op-ed piece for *Investors' Business Daily* criticizing race quotas in federal highway contracts, he got a stiff reprimand from his superiors. Blum told them he had written similar pieces before for the *Wall Street Journal* and other publications and that such a workplace gag order trampled on his free speech rights. But the higher ups at Paine Weber kept turning up the pressure on Blum until this highly respected and productive fifteen-year employee was finally forced out of his job. Afterwards, Paine Weber issued a statement claiming that Ed had not cooperated when asked to refrain from publishing articles "reflecting negatively" on the firm's reputation and leading to loss of business.

I watched with a feeling of helplessness as Ed got trashed. There wasn't much that could be done about Measure A either. Although Al Gore had weighed in to oppose the initiative, for instance, "our side" refused to acknowledge its importance. Texas Governor George W. Bush flatly refused to take a position on it.

The position into which Ed and the others in his group had been forced was an impossible one: trying to pass a measure whose antagonistic language had been forced on them by their enemies. In addition to being allowed to choose the semantic battleground, the Houston power structure also had most of the firepower. The large sum of money it raised to fight Measure A allowed them to wage a ferocious media campaign whose essential dishonesty was summed up by a radio ad that began with the sound of sirens and gunfire and then went to a voice speaking portentously: "First *they* tried to stop us with bullets. Now *they* try to stop us with ballots."

I went to Houston several times to speak in behalf of Measure A. Whenever I held a news conference, the media sent their minority reporters, people whose questions made it clear exactly where they stood on the issue. Whenever I made a public appearance the city's minority employees showed up and stood in the back of the room glowering with their arms crossed over their chests, looking like members of Louis Farrakhan's praetorian guard, the Fruit of Islam.

At one point, I sent Arnie Steinberg down to Houston to see if he thought there was anything to be done. He came back with a depressing message: Measure A was going down and there was nothing we could do about it, so we should cut our losses. I didn't doubt him, but I decided that the American Civil Rights Coalition would continue to support Ed Blum and his group until election day.

I wasn't surprised at the outcome: defeat by a margin of fifty-four to forty-six percent. But I was a little taken aback by the extravagance of the victory dance done by the other side. And I'm not just referring to Lanier and his cronies in Houston. The *New York Times* put Measure A's loss on the front page and tried to portray it as a defining moment in the history of affirmative action. ("Houston's voters put the brake on a national movement that has often seemed to have the momentum of an unstoppable freight train.") The *Seattle Times*, which was already getting ready to help finish us off in the next battle in Washington, smirked about the defeat on its editorial page under the headline, "Thank you, Houston!"

Six months after the Houston election, District Judge Sharolyn Wood, acting on Ed Blum's suit, threw out the election and ordered a new vote, ruling that the city had used misleading language ("affirmative action") in changing the wording of Measure A.* The *New York Times* buried Judge Wood's decision on page thirteen of the last edition of the Sunday paper, giving it a scant six sentences. None of the papers in Washington carried a single story about the reversal. As we were discovering, there was some news about preferences that was not fit to print.

* On July 1, 1999, the Texas State Supreme Court upheld Wood's decision, which had been appealed by the city of Houston. Ed Blum was vindicated at last.

ELEVEN

DEMORALIZED BY THE OUTCOME of 209 in California, the preference lobby was now, a scant nine months later, in a cocky mood. It was convinced that our movement had been cut off in Houston, and now they were going to kill it in Washington. When I heard that one of them had said that this election was going to be "the Gettysburg of affirmative action," I thought to myself, Okay, if that's the case, we're going to be the Union army at the end of this thing, freeing people who've been forced to live on the liberal plantation for far too long.

The only problem was that the group put together by Scott Smith and Tim Eyman was having a hard time getting signatures. Until you actually try to do it, qualifying an initiative sounds easy—sort of like Mickey Rooney in those old MGM movies suddenly standing up and saying to his young friends, "Gee, kids, let's put on a play!" You think that you'll print up the petitions and send out a core of dedicated volunteers who will then convince people to sign up. Pretty soon there'll be an election, and you'll win because of the justice of your cause, and everything will be better overnight.

In fact, getting an initiative on the ballot is very tough. It takes money, organization, and sheer dogged commitment. Smith and Eyman had been at it through the spring and summer of 1997 when they finally called me in October to say that the effort was flagging. My first reaction was, Why tell me, I live in California? But I couldn't wash my hands of it. Because of the setback we'd suffered in Houston, a defeat in Washington would be fatal for the anti-preference movement.

With the deadline looming, we needed someone with name recognition and strong managerial skills to take over the signature-gathering campaign. Everyone I talked to told me that the best, and perhaps the only, candidate was John Carlson, a man who was well known around the state, understood the issue, and had the executive ability to bring this issue home.

Still in his thirties, John was one of the most popular media personalities in Washington. In fact, he had helped change the nature of talk radio in the Seattle area. In 1993, when he left television to work at KVI, Seattle was so politically correct that it was the last major city in America to pick up Rush Limbaugh's number-one nationally ranked program. John, who had lived most of his life in the Seattle area, believed that Washington state's new image as a trendy, high-tech latte-land committed to "progressive" ideas was only skin deep. At the mike from three to six p.m. during the coveted drive-time slot, he began raising conservative issues on his program and immediately found a listenership hungry for these ideas.

John convinced KVI management to hire Michael Medved and other talk show hosts with similar ideas. What they sent out over their airwaves helped change the political environment in Washington. In the historic elections of 1994, the composition of the state's congressional delegation, previously eight to one in favor of Democrats, changed to seven to two in favor of Republicans.

John was no right-wing zealot. He was a moderate, politically and personally, and so sober and statesmanlike that he led two previous statewide initiative drives for two issues he championed on the air: the nation's first three-strikes law and a measure mandating "hard time for hard crime." Both of these initiatives raised John's profile, increasing his clout and causing him to be mentioned as a possible future candidate for state office. In terms of the preference issue, what impressed me particularly about John was that he was calm, well informed, and not angry—key qualities for any white male who steps into this minefield of racial demagoguery.

Because his wife was about to have their second child, John was initially wary of becoming involved. But he said that he'd at least find out from Smith and Eyman exactly where the signature-gathering campaign stood. They told him that because so many volunteers were involved, they weren't sure precisely how many signatures they'd gotten during their seven-month effort, but they estimated that there were about 50,000. This was less than a third of the 180,000 needed, and there were only three months to go until the January 1 deadline, but at least it was a running start. John decided to accept the challenge and told me to count him in. Although he never said so, he probably had many second thoughts later on about having made a decision that so profoundly changed his life.

The first thing he did after taking on the chairman's job was try to bring the somewhat scattered operation into focus. He discovered right away that the supposed 50,000 signatures actually amounted to less than 13,000.

In an alarmed telephone call in mid-October, he told me the bad news. After a long silence, he asked, "Do you think we should put the initiative off until the next election?"

I thought for a moment about how such a decision would play in the media.

"If we postpone it, they'll think we've folded our tent," I said. "And they'll be right. There'll be this big sucking sound, which will be the rest of the momentum going right out of our movement."

John hesitated for a moment and then replied, "You're right, we've got to go for it." As he said of this pivotal moment in a later conversation with a journalist: "Ward and I decided to chuck common sense and lower our heads and charge up San Juan Hill."

— —

It was a replay of what had happened two years earlier in California. Smith and Eyman had done their best on a shoestring, but they had never established an effective fund-raising operation, and so the cupboard John and I inherited was financially bare. With our tight deadline, we would have to rely on a professional signature-gathering operation, and that would have heavy costs. I told John that I would match whatever he raised.

Over the next few weeks, John raised $120,000 and I got $150,000, some of it coming from Steve Forbes, who still remembered the talk he and I had had in his office. We put together a mailer and some radio spots urging people to sign our petitions and used the rest of our funds to hire a professional signature gathering outfit.

Proposition 209 may have taken the preference crowd somewhat by surprise in California, but they were lying in wait for us in Washington. Although the state prides itself on being more genteel than its large southern neighbor, the political atmosphere we encountered was far rougher than it had been in California. Our volunteer signature gatherers were often subjected to threats and harassment in public places. (In an incident in Seattle's liberal Capitol Hill neighborhood, one of these volunteers, a middle-aged black man, hauled off and smacked a white lefty in the mouth after being taunted by him for several minutes as an Uncle Tom.) Even the pros, who were used to rough treatment, had a hard time.

The signature-gathering company John hired contracted with another firm to bring in what are called "horses" from other states. Predominantly blacks and Hispanics, these "horses" are paid up to $20 an hour. They are usually smooth and effective and get the job done, but a handful of those brought into Washington had no training or experience, and were intimidated by the self-proclaimed "truth squads" the other side sent to shadow them and harass people who were considering signing their petitions. When they were laid off, they demanded payment anyway. The signature-gathering firm refused. Some of them complained to our opposition, which planted a front-page story in the *New York Times* about how we were "abusing" black workers.

Despite setbacks like this, we continued to work around the clock, and shortly after New Year's Day 1998, we met our deadline with 280,000 signatures, 100,000 more than we were actually required to file and a record for an initiative sent to the Washington legislature. We were now the I-200 campaign.

At this point, we had a tactical decision to make. According to the Washington state constitution, our initiative could now become law by a simple majority vote of both houses of the legislature. Since there was a Republican majority with a leadership that had committed itself very strongly to the cause when I spoke at their retreat the previous summer, I knew that this was a vote we could win if we pressed them. But if we took this route, Washington law also allowed the other side three months in which to gather only 90,000 signatures to place a referendum on the ballot allowing voters in effect to veto the legislative action. John Carlson thought this was too great a risk, and I agreed with him.

We had to pass I-200 by going directly to the people. When our decision was made public, you could almost hear the collective sigh of relief coming from lawmakers who would now not have to stand up and be counted.

— —

At about this time, John first began to feel pressure from his employer. KVI management had allowed him to chair two previous initiatives, and the station's general manager had okayed his involvement in the I-200 campaign as well. John even announced that he was accepting the chairmanship on the air. But KVI had recently been acquired by Seattle-based Fisher Broadcasting, and Fisher, unbeknownst to John, had decided to oppose I-200. The corporation was not happy to learn that one of its most visible employees was crusading for its passage. Suddenly, John was told to talk less about the initiative on the air, then was told to stop talking about it altogether. John resisted management's orders, pointing out that he not only welcomed opposing views, but gave them priority over other callers. He was a little nervous after the conversation because his contract was coming up for renewal. But he still felt that there would be no problem because his audience was large and loyal and his ads were solid. Besides, KVI constantly ran a station announcement assuring listeners that the views of the hosts "are not restricted in any way."

On Martin Luther King's birthday things began to come apart. By mid-morning, there were dozens of pickets on the streets in front of the KVI headquarters carrying signs with messages like, "KVI, Karlson, KKK." The rally had been organized with the help of a prominent black journalist who wrote a column stating his interest to "drive this Nazi [John] off the air." The demonstration was a lacerating experience for John, who had always been a strong supporter of civil rights. Next, in what was now clearly a concerted campaign, a local Mercedes-Benz dealership that had been one of John's staunchest advertisers pulled its spots after being pressured by black state legislators. The same people who organized the MLK demonstrations were invited by John on his radio show and responded by thrusting into his hand an axe handle they called the "Lester Maddox Award." (The former segregationist Georgia governor had used an axe handle to intimidate blacks seeking to patronize his "whites only" restaurant.) Soon after, John got an ax of another kind when Fisher, without advance notice, refused to renew his contract.

It was a front page story for the Seattle media, and for weeks the switchboards of KVI were clogged by people protesting John's absence. The station's ratings fell, taking revenue down with them. (Ratings still haven't recovered.) A Fisher executive eventually asked John to lunch to discuss a return to the station. But the offer was conditional upon his relinquishing the chairmanship of I-200. John refused, even though he was walking away from a six-figure income.

The preference lobby constantly talks about "victims." But they are nameless and faceless and don't exist except as theoretical speculations. But there are people, real people, who have suffered as a result of the role they've played in speaking out against preferences, and John Carlson is one of them. He joins others who've been made to pay for their convictions: Ed Blum in Houston; Pam Lewis, vice-chair of Yes on 209, who was forced out of her law firm because of her stand; and Michael McLaughlin, who was forced out of his firm in Massachusetts after launching the suit that resulted in a court decision holding that famed Boston Latin School had been guilty of discrimination against his daughter and other high-achieving white students.

━ ━

In California, we may have snuck up on the opposition. But in Washington, the liberal power structure—a network of elected officials, media, and corporations—was locked and loaded and ready for war. At the head of this juggernaut was popular Governor Gary Locke, a shrewd, ambitious politician, who was very much aware that his celebrity came from his status as the first Asian American to be elected governor in a mainland state. In the course of the campaign, I became convinced that Locke actually believes in preferences and wasn't just seizing on the issue to boost his image as a model of the new multiculturalist politician. But I also think that he saw a unique political opportunity: if he beat us, he'd become an instant national hero to liberals and a sensation in the Democratic Party.

But Locke was also cautious. He refused to debate John Carlson or anyone else. Neither would Ron Sims, King County executive and the most powerful black politician in the state. Nor would Norm Rice, the genial two-term mayor of Seattle. Their reluctance to engage in a direct dialogue suggested that they realized how weak their case for preferences was.

The Clintonites were fully behind Locke and the No on I-200 campaign. They believed that there was an opportunity not just to make a show of solidarity with their victim-group constituents, but actually to win an election with national implications. So the administration sent Al Gore to Washington (three times) to preach the virtues of mend-it-don't-end-it, and to wave the bloody shirt with charges that racism had reappeared in the anti-preference movement. In his appearances, Gore was very much the figure I remembered from our White House meeting the previous winter—hard-edged and humorless, a hatchet-faced true believer. He railed against us as if we were church burners. ("The winds of hate are blowing in Washington.") He tried to make black people believe that an insidious white offensive had been launched against them. As the vice president demagogued his way through a succession of appearances up and down the state, I found myself thinking, God help the racial situation in America if this man ever gets to the Oval Office!

Along with the national Democrat Party, the civil rights professionals also showed up in Washington to testify that I-200 was the twilight's last gleaming. Along with the ubiquitous Jesse Jackson, who had become a sort of one-man Rent-a-Demonstration in behalf of affirmative action, Julian Bond, new head of the NAACP, flew out repeatedly to say that through him black people were "declaring war" against us. And Colin Powell, in town for one of his $60,000 speeches, sideswiped us as "diabolical."

All of this was played up with mind-numbing propaganda by the *Seattle Times*. In an act of yellow journalism reminiscent of some of the worst outrages of William Randolph Hearst (although this was the only resemblance he bore to America's first great press lord), *Times* publisher Frank Blethen, heir to the Blethen Family Newspaper company, committed himself early in the campaign to personally defeating us. Some said Blethen fancied himself as the latter-day equivalent of Ralph McGill, the crusading publisher of the *Atlanta Constitution* in the 1950s, who found himself in constant danger for bravely speaking out against segregation. The only problem was that Blethen was so blinded by conceit that he couldn't see that he was supporting, not attacking, discrimination; and unlike McGill, who faced death threats, Blethen faced no jeopardy at all. Indeed, he was toasted at several banquets sponsored by "progressive" organizations and pro-preference groups.

Blethen was the epitome of the modern PC executive, so anxious to seem à la mode that he mandated a "diversity tree" instead of a Christmas tree for the lobby of the *Times'* building during the holidays. A company memo ordered that a black Santa be available to black children at the employees' Christmas party because white Santas involved "too great a paradigm shift" for these youngsters.

In addition to publishing free of charge some $275,000 worth of ads against us, the *Times* was so biased in its news coverage of I-200 that it embarrassed even some of the liberal reporters on the paper's staff who were otherwise no friends of ours. One of the most egregious examples came in an editorial page feature entitled "Affirmative Action Tug of War." Beside an illustration showing a black hand pulling against a white one, there were two columns, purporting to be a pro and con; but, in fact, both pieces were written by *Times* editors opposed to I-200, and it showed.

We heard that throughout the campaign Blethen wandered around the halls of the *Times* like a cheerleader saying, "*We* can beat this thing." It was a strange mantra for someone who is supposed to be a keeper of the fire of journalistic objectivity. The publisher's actions were diminishing the stature of his own newspaper.

— —

But the most significant obstacle we faced in the Washington campaign was not the media or even the political personalities who attacked us, but the corporate world, which Governor Locke had adroitly mobilized against us. Boeing, Weyerhauser, Starbucks, Costco, Microsoft, and Eddie Bauer all made huge donations to the No on I-200 campaign. (Boeing alone gave $80,000.) The fundraising was spearheaded by Bill Gates' father, Bill Gates, Sr., a regent of the University of Washington whose famous name seemed to suggest that the whole of the high-tech world was solemnly shaking its head at us. The donations were, for the most part, orchestrated with great fanfare. Some of the contributions were secret, however, and we didn't find out about them until later, as in the case of Fisher Broadcasting, which gave a silent $6,000 to the campaign against us after firing John Carlson.

Some saw this corporate activism simply as an attempt to curry favor with the governor's office. I felt it was more subtle than that. In the last few years, while criticism of affirmative action was focused on public institutions, "diversity" was taking root virtually unnoticed in the world of private industry, the last place one would expect to see it.

Creating a color- and gender-coded hiring and promotion policy may have begun as a defensive strategy on the part of corporations seeking to get protection from lawsuits and from the intrusion of government bean counters scouring the workplace for racial and ethnic disparities. But this movement has since taken on a life of its own, insinuating itself into the corporate "mission." It is altruism on the cheap, functioning in the corporate world somewhat like wearing the appropriately colored ribbon on Academy Awards night. From what I've been able to tell, most of the companies that brag about how diverse they are do very little to improve the lousy public schools inflicted on black kids, say, or to provide for college scholarships for poor students whatever their color—two areas where they could actually improve individual lives. Instead, they hide behind the fig leaf of diversity and, when asked what they've done to make the world a better place, answer by saying, in effect, "We gave at the office."

Boeing, the flagship corporation in the state, was probably the most militant of our opponents, going so far as to assign its chief lobbyist to work exclusively on the I-200 issue. Boeing's politically correct CEO Phil Condit (who once compared the Rodney King beating to the Tiananmen Square Massacre in China) contacted subcontractors and other companies standing in the vast shadow of the aircraft giant and got them on board too. Everywhere we turned in the campaign, it seemed, we saw Boeing's footprints. It was like dealing with a branch of government. After having to endure the company's sanctimonious moral brow-beating throughout the campaign, it was particularly satisfying, a couple of months after the election, to see a report in the *Los Angeles Times* that Boeing had just agreed to pay $15 million to settle two class action lawsuits by black employees alleging discrimination in the workplace. Even better, leading up to the settlement, Condit was forced to endure an appearance with Jesse Jackson in which the reverend said, among other things, that this agreement would "even the playing field." This helped me understand what that mysterious phrase "what goes around, comes around" meant.

Throughout the spring and early summer of 1998, as I-200 began to edge into the national consciousness, and each passing day brought yet more opposition from the establishment, I was afraid that we would be simply beaten down and marginalized in the eyes of the public. From John Carlson's reports I could tell that our volunteers were beginning to feel woozy—like a boxer who was taking too many unanswered punches. I felt I had to do something.

I noticed that one of the corporations lining up against us was U.S. Bank. As it happened, the American Civil Rights Coalition had a fairly large account in the bank's Sacramento branch. I immediately closed it and issued a press release explaining that we did not want to do business with an organization that supported racial discrimination. The next day, a Sunday afternoon, I flew to Seattle and, with John Carlson and some others, including some courageous college kids of all backgrounds supporting our cause, picketed U.S. Bank's headquarters there. We carried placards reading, "Why Does U.S. Bank Support Preferences?" and "U.S. Bank Banks on Quotas." We sent a letter of protest to the Chamber of Commerce and put an ad in the Seattle papers.

The following week, when I was back in Sacramento, I got a call from a U.S. Bank executive. He let me know that his superiors had gotten the message and asked me to back off. He admitted sheepishly that most of the company's Washington employees were probably in favor of I-200 and that they would have been outraged to learn that the bank had used funds they had contributed to the corporation's political action committee to bash us. This executive promised that U.S. Bank would not participate further in the No on I-200 campaign. After this episode, in fact, no other major corporation came out against us.

I was also involved in another aspect of the 1998 election as finance chairman of the California Republican Party, a job I had reluctantly taken to help Dan Lungren's campaign for governor. I was sad to see Pete Wilson leave office. He had done a good job and had stood fast against a lot of unfair publicity. He was embattled most of his time in Sacramento and portrayed by Democrats as nothing more than a cynical manipulator of wedge issues. In fact, he had been a first-rate governor, inheriting a state that had been an economic basket case and leaving it a powerhouse. Pete's departure would leave a huge hole and, because of the coming census and statewide redistricting, whoever filled it would determine the shape of California politics for the next decade.

The issue was fairly simple for me. I liked Dan Lungren and thought that while he might not be the greatest campaigner in the world, he would make a good governor. Gray Davis had taken some cheap shots at me to ingratiate himself with the civil rights professionals. Moreover, I had seen him operate on the Board of Regents as an *ex officio* member when he was lieutenant governor, and found him to be one of those politicians who is always licking a finger and holding it up to see which way the truth is blowing; someone always working behind the scenes for whatever scrap of personal advantage it could yield him. I would modify my view of him somewhat after he was elected, but during the campaign he seemed so completely beholden to the teachers' and public employees' unions that he was virtually a blank tablet on which they would write their needs and requirements if he became governor.

I believed that Davis could be beaten. But as it turned out, Dan Lungren was not the person to do it. It was not a matter of money; the funds were there. The campaign, however, was inept. For example, even though every pollster made it clear that education was the buzzword of 1998, Dan focused on crime, and became the political equivalent of the general who fights the last war. Many of his supporters urged him to hit hard on issues like the way the educational status quo condemns black and minority children to violent, illiterate public schools and to a self-fulfilling prophecy of failure. Instead, he introduced himself to the voters with a speech about his Catholicism that made him look like a religious zealot. He did the Davis forces' work for them by giving the impression that he would do away with state support for family planning and other such programs. Even Dan's natural constituents were nervous. My own daughter, Tracy, said to me at one point, "You know, Dad, I like Mr. Lungren, but I'm not too keen on some of the things he's been saying."

Dan was so busy explaining and justifying himself throughout the campaign that Gray Davis got a free ride. It was a textbook case on how to lose an election, which was unfortunate because Dan is a decent man who would have been a good governor.

— —

Late in the summer of 1998, just when Initiative 200 was beginning to heat up, Jennifer Nelson, who had been executive director of the

American Civil Rights Institute since Dusty Rhodes and I founded it, took a maternity leave. Jennifer had been working with me since the early days of the 209 campaign, and her departure was a tremendous setback. Worse news was to come. In the two weeks following her departure, three other ACRI employees also left the organization, one for personal reasons and the other two for new jobs.

The ACRI had become pivotal in the fight against preferences, the organizational vehicle that gave the movement focus. Although I was deeply involved in the Washington initiative, I knew that it would be a catastrophe if the organization went down. I tried in my free moments to find new people who could make the organization go, but I had little luck and at one point actually considered closing ACRI. But then one afternoon when I was at Cal Expo, a Sacramento facility that shows horse races and conducts betting by satellite, I began talking to a young woman named Robyn Miller who worked there part time. I had seen her there occasionally but never talked much. (Horses, more than betting, are one of my passions.) Now, she told me that she had just gotten her degree in business administration and was mulling over several job opportunities.

She had taken a number of courses dealing with management. As she described her experience, I decided on a whim to hire her to do an analysis of the internal operations of ACRI. This decision turned out to be providential. Robyn immediately saw how to revive the organization and make it function more smoothly. She designed and produced a long-planned newsletter that would help in fund-raising, and, more importantly, suggested that instead of hiring a new executive director to replace Jennifer Nelson, we reallocate the duties of this position to other employees so that responsibilities could be shared more broadly.

Robyn recruited a young woman named Caroline Kreling, who would become the ACRI director of administration and bring competence and organization to our operations. As a result of another of Robyn's recommendations, I created the position of director of federal and state affairs and hired Kevin Nguyen, an articulate and politically sophisticated young man I'd gotten to know in connection with my work as regent and who had been an aide to state senator Quentin Kopp.

After a few months, Robyn Miller finished her work and went on to pursue longer range career objectives. But as a result of her efforts, ACRI found two wonderful employees who rejuvenated the organization so that it could continue the fight against preferences.

— —

We certainly needed all the help we could get at this point in the Washington campaign. The battle over I-200 had become exactly the sort of climactic struggle that pundits had been predicting it would be. The other side was throwing everything it had at us: all its political muscle and all its best arguments as well.

One intellectual line of attack arose out of developments at the University of California. Late in the spring, as the I-200 campaign began heating up, statistics were released for UC's incoming class for fall 1998, the first year under the new color-blind regime established by the regents. Banner headlines in papers all over the country announced an "admissions disaster." Black enrollment was down 57 percent at Berkeley and 40 percent at UCLA, while the decline for Hispanics on these campuses was, respectively, 40 percent and 33 percent. The *New York Times* wrote that the University "was closing its doors to black and Hispanic students at an alarming rate." The anti–I-200 campaign charged that this was a preview of things to come: we had "resegregated" the University of

California and would do the same thing in Washington if we won. Did the voters want Jim Crow to make a comeback?

I had known for a long time that this news about admissions was coming. (In a sense I even looked forward to it because it confirmed our charge that the UC administration had been engaged in a coverup for the past several years when it denied that race and ethnicity were significant factors in the admissions process.) I also knew that behind the scare headlines there was a different reality, and I tried to describe it to the voters of Washington.

First, not a single qualified black or Hispanic student had been denied the opportunity to get an education in keeping with his ability or ambition at the University of California. And while it was true that the numbers were down at Berkeley and UCLA, on other UC campuses minority enrollment had actually increased. (At UC Riverside, for instance, there were 34 percent more blacks and 43 percent more Hispanics.) Clearly, the students were redistributing themselves within the UC system according to their competitive status, a development Thomas Sowell had predicted in his work on race and education many years earlier.

Secondly, there had been an increase in the enrollment of high-achieving Asian students; and when they were factored into admissions figures, the decline of minorities, while large at Berkeley and UCLA, was actually relatively minor overall. But the partisans of preferences, still playing semantic games, now talked of "non-Asian minorities" to maintain their claims of there being a crisis of "resegregation." UCLA law professor Eugene Volokh was the first to identify this Orwellian maneuver for what it was, and he wrote a clever and biting essay about it called "How the Asians Became White."

But the intellectual main event of the I-200 campaign was the publication of *The Shape of the River* by Derek Bok and William

Bowen, former presidents, respectively, of Harvard and Princeton. The book is based on an analysis of a large data base called "College and Beyond" compiled by the Mellon Foundation (which is currently led by Bowen). Taken from a couple of dozen elite universities and colleges (Yale, Bryn Mawr, Stanford, the University of Michigan, etc.), the data measured several thousand black students' initial academic qualifications, their achievement as undergraduates, and, most importantly, their postgraduate experience. After examining this material, the authors concluded that as a result of affirmative action, these students graduated at high rates, despite lower entering qualifications. They also entered professional schools and professions in greater numbers and experienced more satisfaction in their working lives.

Bok and Bowen saw the social implications of the data as starkly obvious. They argued that affirmative action, particularly when provided by elite schools, has had the long-range effect of building a black middle class and reducing income inequities between black and white; it has also created racial amity and made whites more comfortable with black students. "It was not irresponsible to oppose affirmative action … when the consequences of this policy were still uncertain," they wrote with a triumphant flourish. "But it would be wrong for the nation to prohibit that policy now when comprehensive statistics and analysis have apparently demonstrated its value."

The Shape of the River was greeted with hosannas by the liberal intellectual establishment whose defenses of affirmative action had grown increasingly feeble over the previous few years. The *New York Times* not only gave the book a glowing review, but took the relatively rare step of printing a lengthy excerpt from it in the news section. When Derek Bok went to Washington to share his enthusiasm for "racially sensitive" admissions policies with university officials, he was greeted like the intellectual cavalry that had arrived just in the nick of time.

My "knower" made me a little more skeptical. The black success stories Bok and Bowen boasted about were people who, for the most part, had received preferences at every step of the way: getting into college, then into graduate or professional school, then into a job, and then promotions within that job. No wonder they felt optimistic! Moreover, the notion that these beneficiaries of preferences formed the backbone of the black middle class struck me as simply absurd. The black middle class had been created not by affirmative action, but by the end of discrimination, the advent of equal opportunity, and simple hard work.

Most questionable of all, as far as I was concerned, was Bok and Bowen's assertion that affirmative action built deep bonds among racial and ethnic groups. I had heard this line before from my friend, UC Berkeley Chancellor Robert Berdahl, who engaged in melodramatic public handwringing about how killing preferences had "morally diminished" his campus and stunted the ethical growth of white students who would no longer have as many black faces in their classes. But from everything I had seen, while affirmative action may have made administrators feel good about themselves, it had created only discord among students, forcing them to identify as part of groups engaged in a zero-sum game. It was, in fact, a wellspring of racial tension and intellectual separatism, deforming the curriculum as well as the social life of the campus.

After the initial publicity blitz in favor of *The Shape of the River*, other scholars began to weigh in with doubts about the book's research and conclusions. Bok and Bowen's claim that it is "Yale or jail for young blacks," as Abigail Thernstrom aptly put it, was as questionable as their suggestion that those who "only" got into schools like Sacramento State or Howard might as well count their lives a failure. Analyzing the same data as Bok and Bowen, Abigail her husband Stephen, a respected scholarly team, pointed out that the graduation rates by black students given preferences by these elite universities might be higher than expected, but so were the drop-out rates—three times those of whites and Asians at the same institutions—and that failing to consider this fact was like considering black employment figures, say, without also considering black unemployment.

In a separate piece of research, Stephan Thernstrom questioned the rosy picture painted by Bok and Bowen about affirmative action and minority attendance of professional schools. He noted that 43 percent of blacks admitted to law school through affirmative action either failed to graduate or to pass the bar. And more than half those black students admitted to medical school as a result of preferences failed a crucial examination administered by the National Board of Medical Examiners, while those blacks admitted on their merits failed at about the same rate as white students, 12 percent.

And later on Robert Samuelson delivered the *coup de grâce* to Bok-Bowen when he reported in *Newsweek* on a study by Alan Krueger, an economist at Princeton, and Stacy Berg Dale, a researcher at the Andew Mellon Foundation. Examining the salary histories of students from thirty-four colleges—some of them elite and others lower-ranked schools—Krueger and Dale found that while graduation from an elite school may help somewhat early in a career, it was ultimately the individual qualities of the students, rather than where they attended college, that determined their economic potential. (As Samuelson put it in summarizing the results of the study, "Graduates of these [elite] schools mostly do well. But they do well because they're talented. Had they chosen colleges with lesser nameplates, they would on average have done just as well.") By dispelling the notion that elite institutions automatically confer lifetime earnings premiums on their graduates, this study destroyed Bok and Bowen's central assumption: that "affirmative action" in our best colleges is necessary for the success of the black middle class and is therefore vital to our national well-being.

Rather than turning a corner in the intellectual debate on affirmative action, it seemed to me that *The Shape of the River* had merely done a better job than prior apologists in creating what Joseph Conrad once scornfully referred to as "the sentimental lie."

Liberals are the true disciples of Machiavelli in our political culture. They are so sure of the holy nature of their ends that they can resort to the most outrageous means and still feel on the side of the just. Julian Bond, for instance, came to Washington during the I-200 campaign and made inflammatory speeches to black audiences. He claimed that the measure would eliminate school lunches for needy children, something he certainly must have known not to be true. And the League of Women Voters, although presumably a nonpartisan organization, allowed its name to be used on an anti–I-200 mailer that ludicrously claimed that the initiative would end equal pay for equal work for women.

As in California two years earlier, this last issue—the women issue—began to hurt us as the campaign went into its final stages. For the first few months, the polls never changed much: 60 percent to 40 percent in our favor, despite all the opposition's firepower and the $1.7 million it was spending to defeat us. But on October 24, with a little over a week to go, our lead had shrunk to 38 percent to 37 percent, with a huge number of undecideds. Our opponents smelled blood.

In thinking about how to defuse the gender issue, I focused on

Congresswoman Jennifer Dunn, a rising star in the Washington delegation. She had a long-standing policy of staying neutral on state initiatives, but by a stroke of luck, I was asked to appear at a fund-raiser for the Dome Club, a group of Dunn's well-heeled key supporters. After speaking generally about the California gubernatorial campaign and other matters, I took a chance and began to talk about the importance of I-200 and why I was devoting so much of my life to the fight against preferences. I could tell that the people at the event were galvanized by what I was saying, and so I slipped in a few words about how important it would be to get the support of someone like the Congresswoman in this battle. As I said this, Dunn gave me a sly smile as if to indicate that she knew I'd smoked her out. A few days later, she gave me an open letter to the people of Washington, in which she said that as a single mother involved in women's issues she found the other side's statements on the gender implications of I-200 to be irresponsible. She went on to say that she herself was going to vote for the measure. Her support was significant.

As part of the campaign, the issue of women and preferences was just another political game of parry and thrust. But at a deeper level, it actually did raise important issues. Liberals typically assume that by merely mentioning the subject of gender they put the anti-preference movement at a tremendous disadvantage. But, in fact, they are opening Pandora's box, and one of the facts that escapes from it is that women are as likely to be victimized as benefited by affirmative action.

This was not a hard case to make, since it was women who were bringing some of the high profile suits against colleges and universities for discrimination. Sharon Taxman, for instance, filed a suit in which she sought restitution from her employer, the Piscataway, New Jersey school board. Facing budget problems, the board had laid her off, although it had retained a black teacher hired the same day as Taxman and doing the same job.* The discrimination faced by Cheryl Hopwood at the University of Texas Law School led to a decision that changed the way states in the Fifth Circuit did their racial business. In the 209 campaign in California, the figure symbolizing the injustice of preferences had been Janice Camarena Ingraham, a poor woman who had married a Hispanic and who couldn't get into a vocational skills program because she herself was white. In Washington, another version of this story was played out even more poignantly in the experiences of a woman named Katuria Smith.

Katuria grew up in rural Washington and was raised by a single mother in a low-income household. She worked hard through high school and qualified to go to a four-year college, but couldn't because of a lack of money. She worked after school detailing cars, stocking auto parts, and doing janitorial work. This enabled her to go to a community college. After three years there, she was finally able to transfer to the University of Washington, where she eventually graduated with honors. Then, she applied to the UW law school. Although she had a 3.65 grade point average and had

---

* The case seemed headed for the U.S. Supreme Court, but Taxman was bought off at the last moment for $500,000 by black leaders fearful of a definitive decision on affirmative action. This has become part of a pattern. In the *Boston Latin* case of 1998, civil rights professionals begged the city school board not to appeal a federal court decision killing quotas at Boston's most prestigious public school. Explaining why he had agreed, the Boston superintendent of schools said, "The whole country would have had to live with the decision." In San Francisco, meanwhile, they helped strong-arm school district officials into settling out of court a suit brought by Asian parents against the quota system at prestigious Lowell High School, again avoiding a precedent. Faced with these courtroom trends, the proponents of preferences must know that their game is up. But they continue to fight a desperate rear-guard action that makes them the heirs of George Wallace and all the others who stood in those doorways of the past, protecting a corrupt and outmoded way of life. "Preferences today!" these bitter-enders are saying by their actions. "Preferences tomorrow! Preferences forever!"

scored in the 94th percentile of the Law School Admissions Test, she was turned town. Meanwhile, four of the fifteen black applicants accepted had lower test scores and grade point averages.

After her case was publicized by columnist Nat Hentoff, an old-fashioned liberal with an old-fashioned belief in civil rights and civil liberties, Katuria became something of a symbol in Washington, particularly after a dean at the law school, according to Hentoff, said that Ms. Smith would have been admitted if she had been black. (The dean's office later denied, not particularly convincingly, that such a statement had been made.) The University of Washington tried to hide behind the ghost of the *Bakke* decision by claiming that race was only "one of many factors" at the law school. But Katuria Smith's experience proved once again that when race enters the picture, it inevitably becomes, in effect, the only factor.

Katuria appeared in a series of radio and television ads we did at the end of the campaign. She was very appealing—an attractive and intense individual with whom other women could identify. They could also identify with the simple question our ad posed after telling her story: Is this fair? Katuria's experience and what it said about how preferences kill individual dreams helped reverse the tide that had been moving against us in Washington and kept women from falling for the other side's misleading attempt to make them think that the anti-preference movement was also anti-woman. The No on 200 people later admitted that the Smith ads, particularly the television spots, had been the *coup de grâce* of the campaign.

As I got up on election morning, I knew I should probably stay in California to support Dan Lungren as he went down to his fore-doomed defeat. But my heart was with Katuria, John Carlson, Mary Radcliffe, and all the others who'd fought what to me was not just a good fight, but one of the best fights I'd ever been involved in. So, I got on a plane and headed to Seattle.

By the time we landed, butterflies were beginning to take wing in the pit of my stomach. News reports of exit polls on early voters confirmed that Lungren was going to get buried and Congressional Republicans nationwide were getting creamed. As far as I-200 was concerned, the last numbers I'd seen looked good for us, but we'd been forced to stop our tracking polls a week before because of a lack of money. Now, many of Washington's most respected political commentators were saying that the momentum was with the other side and that the race was, therefore, a toss-up. They said that we could get smothered by the electoral landslide building in the East. Given all these omens, I asked myself why I felt so good. The only answer I could come up with was that, win or lose, we'd given a good account of ourselves, and this ordeal was now about over.

I spent the afternoon in my hotel room doing radio interviews with stations around the country that saw I-200 as a local contest with national implications. By early evening our group was beginning to gather at the Doubletree Hotel in Belleview. We watched the Democrat tide roll west. At eight o'clock, polls finally closed. As early results appeared, we looked for a pattern. Other ballot issues in Washington that the media thought to be ideologically compatible with ours, such as a measure to ban "partial birth" abortions, were clearly losing. Those presumed to be incompatible, such as an initiative to increase the minimum wage, were clearly passing. In addition, Washington Republicans were losing three-quarters of their Congressional seats and losing control of both houses of the state legislature.

Television commentators were "calling" races right and left, but curiously, although I-200 was leading by a large margin in scattered returns, they kept saying that our contest was "much too close to call."

By nine o'clock, with close to 20 percent of all precincts counted, we were leading by a margin of 61 to 39 percent, but the race was still considered "a toss-up" by the media. I agreed to be interviewed by a Seattle television station, and while on camera I asked the reporter why his analysts weren't calling I-200. He mumbled something about how the results were at variance with exit polls. I joked that it was more likely that the professional pundits were in denial, although it was certainly possible that the voters interviewed earlier as they emerged from polling places had fibbed when asked how they'd marked their ballot on I-200, for fear of appearing politically incorrect.

As the evening wore on, our lead held. The opposition didn't concede, and neither did the television stations. Perhaps they didn't want to admit defeat before people on the East Coast had switched off their sets and gone to sleep. Just before ten o'clock, John told the packed ballroom, "The media won't call it, but I will. The election is over and I-200 has passed!" Before introducing me, he added, "You just helped move the entire country forward!"

The protocol of victory celebrations demands that one be gracious and high-minded, but as the television cameras rolled, I couldn't help sending one last dart Frank Blethen's way. "The *Seattle Times* ought to rethink its position on this," I said, "and ask itself about the dangers of crossing the line between reporting and advocacy."

Our victory—by a final margin of 58.3 percent to 41.7 percent—was the news they didn't want to announce or print. The next morning, in its election wrap-up, the *New York Times*, which had stationed three reporters in Washington during the I-200 campaign and had written about it regularly for weeks, especially when the news was bad for us, buried its story on our victory within an omnibus piece about how initiatives had fared nationwide.

We knew that we had made history, even if there were those who wanted to pretend that nothing had happened. After the last champagne cork was popped and our supporters had dispersed, I did a little reckoning. The $1.7 million spent by the No on 200 forces (not counting the over $275,000 in ads from the *Times*) was almost three times what we spent. Each vote we got cost us 60 cents; each vote they got cost them $2.50.

I could imagine Jesse Jackson, Al Gore, and all the others who had put everything else on the line to defeat us now shaking their heads and trying to figure out how the people of Washington could have allowed themselves to be duped into passing this initiative. In his post mortem the next day, Governor Gary Locke took exactly such an approach. Trying to deconstruct the basic numbers—I-200 had been supported by 80 percent of Republicans, 62 percent of independents, and 41 percent of Democrats; by 51 percent of women and 54 percent of union households—the governor said that the voters had been "confused" by the language of the initiative. As I listened to him, I thought to myself, What contempt they have for the people's intelligence!

Just one day later there was a crow-eating article—in the *Seattle Times*, of all places—indicating that the people were not confused at all. In lengthy interviews with pollsters, they indicated that they knew exactly what they had voted for: fairness and equality. When a reporter from the *San Francisco Chronicle* asked me for my reaction to the passage of I-200, I said it was simple: "Two down, forty-eight to go."

TWELVE

AFTER THE I-200 VICTORY, there was considerable specula-
tion in the press about, as one journalist put it, "where they will
strike next." *Washington Post* eminence David Broder wrote a long
speculative piece about how the national tide now seemed defini-
tively to have turned against affirmative action. Broder's article
picked out Michigan and Florida as fertile ground for initiatives
similar to Proposition 209 and predicted that either might be the
next battleground. I had the same thought.

Michigan strikes me as a state whose no-nonsense voters have
made it clear that they are skeptical about race-based solutions to
social problems, particularly in the wake of a class action lawsuit
filed against the University of Michigan in 1997 by students denied
admission there because they were white. But I thought that
Florida was an even better place for the next round in what was
beginning to look like a rolling national referendum on preferences. Florida has unique demographics, with its large Cuban-
American presence. More importantly, it is a state with a strong
Republican presence. Some people close to me hinted that I ought
to forget Florida for precisely this reason. But it seemed hypocrit-

ical to give a pass to my own party, which was all too willing to cheer me on when the target was liberal strongholds like California, but less forthright when it came to rooting out the preference regimes in its own backyard.

The other reason for focusing on Florida was that a dialogue about preferences had already gained some momentum there. In the spring of 1997, when the smoke was still clearing from the battle over the California Civil Rights Initiative, a man named John Barry had crafted a Florida version of the measure and tried to raise money and gather signatures to get it before the state's voters. The Democrat-controlled state government appointed a Constitutional Review Commission that began to talk of a competing ballot measure that would make affirmative action official state policy and embed its mandatory provisions in the Florida constitution.

Because of political inexperience and other factors, Barry made little headway with his proposed initiative, and as a result, the Constitutional Review Commission eventually lost interest too. But the question of preferences had been put into public view in Florida. In mid-1999, I was contacted by Allen Douglas and Bill Stroop of the Associated General Contractors, a group that was particularly interested in the issue, and asked to help them revive the prospect of an initiative. I agreed to check things out.

I had been to Florida to talk briefly with Barry a year or so earlier, but my first substantial visit to the state came in October 1998, when I debated *Chicago Tribune* columnist Clarence Page in front of a blue-ribbon audience in Orlando. I began by chivvying Clarence: "We must be doing something right because two years ago, after Proposition 209, Mr. Page said I'd had my fifteen minutes of fame." Then I waved a clipping of his old column, along with a more recent one in which Page had said reluctantly that

although he hated to admit it, I was probably right about preferences coming to an end. Page gave a good-natured "I surrender"
gesture, and we went on to have a civilized discussion of when,
rather than whether, to end affirmative action. Much of the audience, composed of CEOs of local companies, architects, builders,
and even some affirmative action compliance officers from local
government, was enthusiastic about bringing the issue to the voters. As one of the contractors said to me at the conclusion of the
event, "It's time to drive a stake through the heart of affirmative
action in Florida once and for all."

The other factor that made Florida interesting to me was the new
governor, Jeb Bush. I had high hopes for Jeb, who was part of an
extraordinary brother act with Texas governor George W. Bush,
and, given George W.'s presidential possibilities, also potentially
part of a political dynasty with a reach unequaled since the Adams
family emerged at our nation's founding. After their sweeping vic-
tories in Florida and Texas in the face of the 1998 national
Democrat landslide, the Bush boys' potential for binding up the
Republican Party's self-inflicted wounds made them seem like sav-
iors. I agreed with others who believed that their joint venture in
"compassionate conservatism" had the potential—if it managed to
make the transition from a slogan to a philosophy—to bring the
Republican Party out of the wilderness where it had gotten lost in
its frantic pursuit of Bill Clinton.

Nevertheless, my first dealings with George W. had been disap-
pointing. Our initial contact, an indirect one, happened when I got
a call from Don Evans, chairman of the University of Texas Board
of Regents. Evans noted that both the Universitiy of Texas and of
California were at a disadvantage in attracting good minority students because they couldn't use preferences, while private schools,

and many other state universities and colleges could. For this reason, he said, there had been some talk among his board members about appealing the *Hopwood* case to the Supreme Court in the hopes of getting a decision that would make it into a binding national precedent. He wondered how I would react to such a move.

I said that even though it was always possible that *Hopwood* would be struck down in such an appeal, I'd be in favor of rolling the dice. As we talked further, Evans told me that he was a close friend of Governor George W. Bush, who was then beginning his campaign for reelection in Texas, and asked me what I thought of him. I said that I liked much of what I'd seen and heard of the governor, but had been disappointed that he was at that point missing in action in the campaign to end preferences in Houston. Evans replied, somewhat implausibly, "Oh, George doesn't involve himself in 'local issues.'"

I heard nothing more from Texas until early in 1999, after the I-200 victory in Washington. That spring, my friend and ally from Houston, Ed Blum, asked me to come to Austin to endorse an antipreference bill he planned to introduce in the Texas state legislature. Several people suggested that I talk to Karl Rove, the governor's chief aide, strategist, and mystery man, about a face-to-face meeting between me and the governor in which I would "brief" Bush about preferences. After getting nowhere in setting up this meeting with Rove, my staff suggested that I contact Don Evans again. I told him of our objective and our frustration. A few days later, continuing to act as go-between, Evans called back to say that I'd soon be getting an invitation to visit G.W. while I was in Texas. Then a message came from someone on Bush's personal staff saying that a meeting time was being set. After that, silence.

At about this time, the media began calling our office in

Sacramento to ask if Bush was avoiding me. My response was that he wasn't: a meeting would be held. But the journalists knew more than I did. I soon got another call from Evans, who said that Rove didn't want a meeting between me and Bush after all because of the possibility of "demonstrations" if I was seen going into the governor's office.

I was still trying to figure out the meaning of all this byzantine maneuvering a few days later when I flew to Austin. As I was getting out of a van in front of the capitol building for a meeting with legislators, I practically ran into George W. He was standing on the steps of the capitol a few feet away from me in a classic political posture: cooing over a baby cradled in his arms. Seeing me, he quickly handed the infant back to its parents and came down to greet me.

"Ward, buddy!" he put his hands on my shoulders, "It's good to see you!"

Then he walked me inside the capitol building making small talk as he looked to see who was watching us.

"We need to talk," he said. "I've got to get you down here for dinner. Just the two of us."

I asked if I should call his office to arrange it. He said he'd clear the way and then headed off for an appointment.

The next day one of my assistants in Sacramento once again called Karl Rove to make the date. The message was taken, but there was no call back, and after a few days, the *National Review* ran a story (which it did not get from me) asking if I'd been snubbed. When he saw an advance copy of the magazine, Rove called apologetically to say that Bush hadn't been able to schedule a meeting because the legislature was still in session. But he said that the governor was coming to California in June and wanted me to travel with him up and down the state.

The visit approached, but there was still no contact. I bought a table for Bush's fund-raising speech in San Francisco. When he saw me in the receiving line, Bush grabbed my shoulder and blurted out, "Did you see I'm talking about need-based affirmative action now rather than race-based?"

I told him I was glad to hear it, shook his hand and moved on.

Later in the evening, *Washington Post* writer Dan Balz ran into me coming out of the men's room. He asked me what I thought about Bush. Trying to be diplomatic, I told him that I liked much of what he had to say.

"Does that mean you'd endorse him?" Balz asked.

I thought for a minute and said, "I suppose so."

The next day my endorsement was all over the newspapers. George W. Bush was on his way back to Texas without having had the dialogue about preferences I thought we were going to have.

That dialogue still hasn't taken place. Bush has not exactly dodged the issue of preferences; he just has not confronted it directly and gives evidence of hoping that he is nimble enough to keep it from catching up to him. His evasive technique was on display in California when he said, "I support the spirit of no quotas, no preferences." But this "spirit" did not include Proposition 209, the state law whose principles he pointedly declined to endorse when asked about it at a news conference. As columnist John Leo observed, this was like saying you were for the spirit of fair housing and then refusing to endorse fair housing laws.

The calculated ambiguity of George W.'s remarks—particularly the way he drags the red herring of already illegal "quotas" across his statements on affirmative action—is so well calibrated that the liberal *New York Times* has praised him for his "moderate" opinions on the issue, while the conservative *Washington Times* also feels that he is saying the right things. But as I've watched him do the Texas two-step on preferences, my fear is that George W. may be talking out of both sides of his mouth because he simply doesn't want anyone to be able to read his lips.

— —

In early 1999, as we began to focus on an initiative in Florida, I was hopeful that things would go well with Jeb, who, unlike his brother, had the freedom that comes with not running for president. I first met Jeb Bush during his gubernatorial campaign when he came to California for a fund-raiser set up by Pete Wilson. He was obviously very smart, solid on the issues and confident as only one who was his mother's favorite—so the rumors went—could be. When we talked about the issue of race-based affirmative action, I got the feeling that Jeb was on board. At one point during the California visit he told me, "You're a brave man, Ward. What you're doing is very important. I'm opposed to quotas and set-asides."

Bush's words didn't have the tinny ring of just another politician on a charm offensive. In fact, I felt so certain that Jeb would be supportive of a 209-like initiative in Florida that I disagreed with Tyler Bridges, a columnist for the *Miami Herald*, when he said while interviewing me in February 1999 that the new governor was conflicted about the preference issue.

"No," I said, "I'm pretty sure that you're wrong about that. I talked to him in California and I think he's on our side."

Bridges then went to Bush and told him of our conversation. Bush said that, indeed, he did oppose putting an anti-preference measure on the ballot in Florida. I was so taken aback when I heard this that I immediately called the governor's office in Tallahassee for a meeting.

Jeb received me with the grace that all the Bushes possess in such abundance. But I could see from the outset of our conversation that I represented a complication that neither he nor his brother needed or wanted at this point in their family's political life. He listened to me intently while I made my case. Then he stood up from his desk and said he wanted to show me something. Putting a hand on my arm he guided me to one of the walls of his office that was filled with personal memorabilia and photos.

"I know how strongly you feel about this issue, and I respect you for it," he said, putting a finger on a framed snapshot taken of him in the middle of a group of black kids, "but I'm committed to helping *them*."

The pious tone made it hard for me to keep from rolling my eyes and saying, *Come on!*

"So am I, Governor," I replied. "But we don't help them by keeping them walled up inside the ghetto of racial politics. And we don't help them by presuming that they're inferior. If you really believe in these kids, you've got to act as if you think they can make it on their own without relying on a whole structure of discrimination that hurts others. I would hope that's not a point of disagreement between us."

Bush gave a noncommittal shrug.

I decided to get it over with: "Let's not play games, Governor. There are people in Florida who think it's time to run an initiative like what we did in California and Washington here. They've asked for my help and I'm going to give it to them. I hope we'll have your support."

Bush's response was equally candid: "Look, I'm trying to put together a coalition in this state that will approve my school voucher proposal and other ideas like tort reform, and I can't do it if I get dragged into something divisive like an initiative on affirmative action."

I told him that throughout American history the price of attaining equality had always been divisiveness.

"You're a fighter," the governor flashed a mirthless smile that told me our conversation was coming to an end. "And, I'm a lover. I just don't want to go to war on this issue."

"I don't want war either," I said, "but this is an issue that to me goes to the very heart of what it is to be an American citizen."

As I walked out of the governor's office, a group of news reporters were waiting for me. They quizzed me about the meeting and asked what I'd told Bush and what he'd said in return. I tried to be diplomatic. I told them that the meeting was instructive, although the governor had made no commitment to me. I made a particular effort not to box Bush into a corner, but I noticed that a member of the governor's staff had followed me out the door and was listening in on the interview with a concerned look on his face.

The next morning, there was a story on the front page of the *Miami Herald*. In addition to a truncated version of my conversation with Bush given out by his press representative, there was some rather strong language on the part of Jeb, reaffirming his view that I wanted to go to "war" over the issue of preferences, while he was a "lover." I was flabbergasted by the way Bush had portrayed me as some kind of wild man who was hell-bent on stirring things up in his state.

Trying to piece together what had happened, I made a few calls and discovered that some of Florida's black state legislators, who had known of our meeting, called Bush soon after I left and told him that if he didn't publicly distance himself from me, the honeymoon with them that had been in effect since his inauguration would come to an abrupt end. When he told the *Herald* that I "wanted war," Bush was sending them a signal that the honeymoon was still on. After the story appeared, the Speaker of the Florida state assembly and the president of the senate, both Republicans, each cancelled appointments with me as a result of pressure from the black caucus and probably from Jeb as well.

Some people accuse the Bushes of being "soft." This is obviously not my experience. The president was, after all, a first baseman, and his sons haven't gotten where they are without knowing how to play hardball too. It was clear to me after this first dust-up that in going ahead with an anti-preferences initiative in Florida I would be colliding with Jeb and that he would probably do everything he could to beat me. And, indeed, in the months after that first meeting, as we began the long process of getting a measure on the ballot, he gave me a lesson in how you play the political game when you're playing for keeps. He alternated between fierce opposition and vague overtures; between outright condemnation of the measure we were designing and hints that we might have some common objectives; between implying that it might make sense to abolish preferences in contracting and being doubly adamant about retaining them in education; between implying that he might be ready for a rapprochement and having his operatives blackball us from even having a booth at the state Republican convention. Throughout this game of parry and thrust, he gave no indication that he understands that justice delayed is justice denied.

After a talk at the Manhattan Institute in the summer of 1999, Jeb was asked by philanthropist Heather Higgins why he was so ambivalent about what should be such a clear-cut matter for someone who says he is a conservative. He repeated his position that he didn't want Florida to become a "battleground" between "divisive" forces. Then he launched into a minor tirade against "mudslinging demagogues" that led Higgins and others to conclude that he was referring to me.

I'll admit that this bothered me. I've tried as hard as I can since my first days as a regent to be calm in my demeanor and civil in my discourse. I know that politics is an art and that you can't get everything you want exactly when you want it. Yet, I understand too, as the old saying goes, that in some instances you have to break eggs if you care enough about the omelet you're making. You don't end preferences by waiting for a politician—or a family of them—to decide that the time is right to end them.

Every time he had the opportunity, Jeb tried to stigmatize me as a "carpetbagger" out to destroy Florida's tranquility. Yet some of his sign language was contradictory. In mid-1999, for instance, Al Cardenas, head of the Florida Republican Party, who knows my friend and former UC regent Tirso del Junco from the world of Cuban-American politics, called him to ask if he would broker discussions between the Florida Republicans and me. Nothing came of this overture, but there were other indications that the governor, despite his attacks on me, wanted to maintain an open line of communication.

In the summer of 1999, Allen Douglas and Bill Stroop, with my assistance, formed an organization to begin gathering signatures for the Florida Civil Rights Initiative. As it became clear that our campaign was succeeding, there were indications that the governor was plotting some kind of dramatic move to head off our effort * On November 1, results of an ambitious state poll on affirmative action conducted jointly by the *St. Petersburg Times* and the *Miami*

---

* According to Florida law, the first step was to get roughly 43,000 signatures, which would allow the state supreme court to rule on the constitutionality of the measure. The next step was to gather over 430,000 signatures to get it on the ballot. The process was made somewhat more difficult by the fact that as a result of Florida's "single-subject" rule, we had to qualify four measures before the Court—one about preferences in education, one about preferences in hiring, and another about preferences in contracting as well as our principal, "omnibus" measure containing all these elements—in case the judges decided that the latter did not comprise a "single subject."

Herald were released. The front-page stories in papers around the state were astounding, even to optimists on our side. Sixty percent of Floridians supported our initiative, 26 percent opposed it, and 14 percent were undecided. When the undecideds were apportioned according to which way they were leaning, our support was over 70 percent, including 50 percent of Hispanics and 42 percent of blacks.

Even more significant were the responses to two questions pollsters also asked voters to choose between. One said: "I support affirmative action because I believe it insures fairness and equality for all Floridians, and because race and gender should be considered in government hiring and college admissions, in order to help eliminate discrimination against racial minorities and women." The other said: "I oppose affirmative action because I believe that government hiring and college admissions should not be influenced by a person's race or gender. A person's ability is the only issue that should matter."

Just 19 percent of those questioned supported the first statement, while 75 percent supported the second one. What this meant was that the chief argument used against our movement since 1995—that we were employing deceitful language by substituting the loaded term "preferences" for "affirmative action," which Americans were said to support—-had collapsed. People in Florida, at least, recognized that affirmative action was preferences.

This poll must have caused panic in the governor's office because two days later Jeb Bush announced his "One Florida Initiative." Billed as a way of "transcending" affirmative action while still "embracing diversity," this executive order dealt with the issue of preferences in higher education by opening up Florida's public universities to the top 20 percent of the graduating class of the state's high schools, regardless of test scores. It also asserted that "quotas" in state contracting would end.

The initial reaction around the state was euphoric, as some political commentators claimed that the governor had finally found a way to resolve the seemingly eternal conflict between individual and group rights. Yet after the dust had settled, doubts began to surface. Some educators worried about the inequity involved in treating the top 20 percent of graduates of poor schools better than the second 20 percent of graduates of schools with higher standards—students who might well be seen as more highly qualified for college if testing were still allowed. Businesspeople were skeptical about a provision hidden in the One Florida plan that called for the appointment of a large number of purchasing agents, under the immediate control of the governor rather than of civil service, and their performance would be evaluated by the number of minority contracts they let. "Race consciousness," under this provision, would substitute for racial preferences.

If Jeb thought he would be regarded as a savior by minority spokespeople addicted to affirmative action, he was sadly mistaken. The civil rights professionals with whom he had tried to prolong a political honeymoon soon denounced him. Representative Corinne Brown, the radical black congresswoman from Florida who had called me "a freak of nature," spoke for all the others when she said that Bush was "trying to take away our piece of the pie," and then issued an ominous threat: "His brother is running, and we're going to deal with his brother."

My reaction to Jeb's announcement was that it was a bold plan, but also a somewhat desperate one undertaken primarily to disarm our effort. It was also a naïve plan in its underestimation of the civil rights professionals' commitment to maintaining affirmative action "by any means necessary." (And in fact these individuals, backed up by some university administrators around the state, began to claim almost immediately that the Bush plan would actually result in *fewer* blacks in Florida colleges than before!) The idea that basic fairness in government doesn't inhere in the people, but is something that can be "given" by a political figure is disturbing because it means that this right can be taken away just as capriciously. (Executive orders and judicial decrees, after all, helped create the mess we're in today.) I was also bothered by the fact that the governor exempted county and city government from his decree about quotas in contracting. (He said that he didn't want to "micromanage" them, but the net effect would be to leave close to 80 percent of Florida's preference programs in tact.) And although he found a way to diminish the effect of race in college admissions, race-based scholarships would still exist. In other words, race would still be central to Jeb Bush's vision of what government is all about.

Despite the hostility of black activists and legislators and the One Florida plan's own internal contradictions, the governor seemed confident that his announcement would succeed at least in killing our initiative. Shortly after Bush's announcement, in fact, Daryl Jones, a black state senator whom Bush had recently named to head a state task force on equity in education, gave a speech to a pro–affirmative action group in which he said, "Connerly will save face, declare victory, and fold his tent." Of course, this was not the case. (In fact, it was Jones who folded his tent after a few days of trying to defend the governor in the black community, resigning from the education task force and eating crow as he denounced the One Florida plan for killing affirmative action.)

It is possible that the Florida Supreme Court, generally considered one of the most liberal and activist high courts in the country, will find some way to claim that our ballot measures do not meet the state's "single subject" rule for initiatives. But if we qualify the Florida Civil Rights Initiative for the ballot, we will win in the 2000 election. And if, by some legal quirk, we don't qualify in 2000, we will use the Florida Supreme Court decision to design a "bullet proof" initiative for 2002. In either case, one of the ironies will be that by admitting that affirmative action needs to be "transcended," Jeb Bush will have helped us make our case. Having admitted that race preferences exist in Florida and that they have destructive consequences, the governor will find it difficult to tell the citizens of his state why they shouldn't support a proposal that gets rid of them once and for all.

—   —

I am sad to have been forced into this conflict with Jeb because I agree with him and George W. on the importance of "compassionate conservatism." Most liberal attempts to portray Republicans as "mean-spirited" over the past few years have been bogus, although it is also true that some conservatives have tended to draw lines in the sand on a host of issues that are far from being black and white and, as a consequence, have sometimes appeared smug and morally simplistic. But in contrast to the damage done by liberalism over the past generation, conservatives have certainly been "compassionate" in their efforts to limit government's intrusion into individual lives and to create policies that promote personal responsibility and autonomy.

It is conservatives, after all, who provided the moral vision to reform a welfare system that resulted in forty-five-year-old great grandmothers living in the same home with thirty-year-old grandmothers, fifteen-year-old mothers, and yet another generation of babies for whom the only father of record was the government. It is conservatives who worked to free poor children, most of whom are black, from a public education system that condemns them to school days of violence and ignorance and chronic underachievement. It is also conservatives who labored in churches and community organizations to reestablish those compassionate personal connections that de Toqueville rightly said defined America, connections that have become so frayed and broken in the last thirty years that we have become a nation of suspicious strangers.

And, I would also say without hesitation that conservatives have been compassionate as well in the effort to end race preferences—compassionate not only to the people disadvantaged by these measures but also to those who are their alleged beneficiaries.

The compassion I'm talking about has no relationship to the condescending paternalism of liberalism. Call it "tough compassion" if you will—the kind of social policy that may not make everyone happy in the short term, but will be justified by long range benefits. Getting the government out of the racial discrimination business is the perfect example of such tough compassion. It is true, for instance, that instead of attending UC Berkeley some minority students may have to attend another of the university's campuses or a good state college, and that some minority contractors may miss out on bids because they are not truly competitive or because they are merely fronting for unprincipled whites trying to work the system. But when the message is delivered that government will do everything in its power to promote diversity, *except* engage in discrimination, individuals of all races will dig deeper into themselves to find a source of personal power. Tough compassion on the issue of preferences will restore faith in the essential fairness of our institutions and end the Darwinian struggle between racial groups that has made events such as college admissions and contract bidding a brutal and degrading competition.

Ending race-based affirmative action is a conservative principle because preferences are unfair and against the spirit of the

Constitution. But ending them because of the collateral damage they cause—fostering dependency and demeaning authentic individual achievements based on merit—is *compassionate* conservatism. So is the commitment to finding fair and constitutional ways of improving the competitiveness of black and other minority children so that they can be admitted to universities on their own steam. Finding ways to bring them up to speed rather than taking others out of the race is, I believe, what Martin Luther King, Jr. had in mind when he said that all he wanted was for black people to be brought to the same starting line as everyone else.

If principles such as these are not at the heart of the call to "not leave anyone behind," a phrase frequently used by George W., then such a slogan is not compassionate conservatism at all; it is Clintonesque double talk on a par with "mend it, don't end it." I applaud the humanitarian sentiment expressed in this idea of "not leaving anyone behind," but I strongly object to starting people ahead too, and most of all I object to making the task that lies ahead for black people into a racial version of the Special Olympics.

In talking about these issues over the past year, I have, of course, received calls from friends who are desperate to have Republicans capture the White House in 2000. They plead with me to cut my fellow Republicans some slack. Accommodate Jeb for now while he consolidates his hold on Florida politics, they say. Assume that George W. will be sympathetic to your cause if he becomes president, they say. Assume too that you will have a voice in policy later if you play ball now.

We've come too far to give in to this sort of compromise. I know that change happens gradually in a democracy, and this is one of the primary strengths of our system. But the fight against preferences has also taught me that individuals and parties must stand for something fundamental or the whole enterprise of politics becomes a cynical charade, an endless series of tactical decisions and spin doctors' "triangulations." We've had enough of that during the past few years. Race, in all its social forms, is a heavy weight on the American spirit. The time has come to leave it behind.

— —

This fight I've gotten involved in has at times been an exhausting one. It has taken me away from my family to the degree that I sometimes feel that I'm communicating with Ilene and my kids and grandkids by semaphore from afar. It has taken me away from the business she and I built which is, next to my family, the accomplishment of which I'm most proud. There are times when I have felt that I was simply not cut out for public life—that I'm too thin-skinned and impatient, too fearful of rejection and too stubborn and unable to compromise.

Even worse, there have been times over the past few years when I felt that despite all the frenzied effort, I was not making a dent in the problem. (In one such gloomy mood, I considered titling this book *Nowhere Fast*). There have been times as well when I was disoriented by having to listen to people use a term like "African American" as if it had anything to do with national origin, and to hear people talking about a nineteenth century term like "race" as if it could have scientific validity in twenty-first century social policy. And there have been times when I have been disturbed to see liberals particularly, including many mainstream Democrats, turn up the volume of racial politics and insist with increasing shrillness that race matters at the very moment when we should be *consciously* saying that we should be *less conscious* about race. The notion that we cannot learn unless taught by someone who "looks like" us, or that we cannot succeed in medical school unless surrounded by a critical mass of "our people," is morally imbecilic. It is the wind which, once sown, will cause a terrible whirlwind for generations to come.

Still, despite all of these difficulties, I have gained something profound from this undertaking. My fight against race preferences has sharpened my appreciation for the principles that are at the core of the American experiment. I feel more fully a citizen now—more a part of this nation—than ever before in my life. I sometimes remember the frantic search for utopia that characterized some members of the radical movement of the sixties, a search that led them on a twisting path to exotic Third World dictatorships and corrupt authoritarian systems. The irony was that utopia was right under their feet all along—a limited and incomplete utopia to be sure, and one still trying to live up to its own principles, but as close as we are likely to get to that ideal in this imperfect world.

Looking back on my initial conversation in 1994 with Jerry and Ellen Cook, I realize that it set me off on a journey that, in the course of a few short years, has covered a lot of territory. When this journey began, the systematic and bureaucratized inequality erroneously referred to as affirmative action was entrenched not only in the University of California, but in institutions at every level of state government. To question it was to be dismissed as quixotic, and to actually challenge it was to risk being stigmatized as a racist. The stronghold of affirmative action, which we have succeeded in renaming for what it is—a system of race preferences—seemed impregnable those few short years ago. We didn't know then that it was actually a house of cards waiting for a gust of wind to blow it down. That wind, which I know is the wind of freedom, is blowing strongly now—in the electoral and legal arenas, and most of all in the court of public opinion.

State-sponsored discrimination is now prohibited in California and Washington and will soon be tested in Florida and other states. However well disguised it once was as "diversity building" and "inclusion," this affirmative racism has been unmasked for what it is.

I believe that one day soon we as a nation will shake our heads incredulously and wonder how we ever allowed this malignant structure to arise in the heart of our wonderful country in the first place. What was it that ever made us think that by encouraging government to disadvantage some we would liberate others? How could we have ever believed that the recipients of such condescending help would actually profit from it and not internalize the message it conveyed about their inferiority and incompetence? How did we ever convince ourselves that such a policy was consistent with the promise at the heart of American life? Why were we blind to the fact that rather than binding up our racial wounds it made them deeper, uglier, and more likely to become septic? How did we ever forget that *creating equal* was the unfinished business we inherited from the Founding Fathers?

The reign of terror presided over by affirmative action officers will soon be a thing of the past, and those thick manuals of affirmative action rules, guidelines, and timetables are headed for the ash heap of history, where they belong. Affirmative action has become an idea whose time has gone.

We have succeeded in our effort because the American people, with their sound common sense, are aware that the government has no place in the discrimination business. In almost every poll, by large majorities, they support the end of preferences. On the other side, of course, the bitter-enders insist that Americans of this opinion are compromised by unconscious racism and too easily swayed by demagogic figures like myself. They try to gin up a doomsday scenario of "resegregation" when the facts suggest that ending race-based affirmative action has been a fundamental liberation.

Consider recent developments at the University of California.

When the regents first made their historic decision, proponents of preferences claimed that the sky would fall. And, indeed, in the first year that the new, color-blind rules took effect, there was a drop in black and Latino admissions. Those of us who had seen the system up close counseled patience and said that this was exactly the sort of shaking out that might be expected of a system that had become a maze of double standards. We were proven right in the spring of 1999, when black and Latino enrollment in the UC system took a dramatic jump upward, with only twenty-seven fewer minority students being admitted systemwide than in 1997, the last year of the old regime.

At Berkeley, for instance, scene of the greatest unrest after preferences were banned, admission of black students was up by 16 percent (from 95 to 116) and of Hispanics by 21 percent (262 to 321) over 1998. Overall, there were slightly fewer blacks admitted to the entire University of California in 1999 than in 1997, but more Asian American students (15,415 to 13,649) and more Hispanics (5,753 to 5,622). Even the *Los Angeles Times*, one of my harshest critics, was forced to admit that "the minority students considered 'underrepresented'—black, Latino and American Indians—are not being squeezed out of the system in the post–affirmative action era."

There is a huge added dividend in this development. For the first time in twenty-five years, those minority students now entering the University of California in increasing numbers can hold their heads high and say, *We are here not because of your "help," but because we belong here; we were admitted on our merits.*

The revolution occurring at the University of California has shaken the administration out of its outmoded orthodoxies about race and ethnicity. Looking back at what now must be regarded as an ancient régime of preferences, UC Irvine Chancellor Ralph

Ciccerone recently said, "I think it was coming close to leading us to a quota system." Administrators are also beginning to acknowledge—unfortunately, for the most part in private—what should have been obvious all along: that in a quarter century of affirmative action (as *Time* magazine columnist Jack E. White recently wrote) achievement levels between blacks and whites had not narrowed but actually widened, proof not that there is something wrong with black kids but something wrong with the way we are educating them.

What caused this turnaround at the university? It's simple. Administrators who had spent decades trying to get "diversity" on the cheap did what they should have done years earlier. They undertook a massive program of "outreach" initiatives aimed at creating a competitive pool of minority students. The program stretched not only into high schools around California, but into junior highs and even elementary schools to create a competitive pool of minority students. And they did this for one reason: written into my resolution to end preferences at UC there was also a mandate to begin an outreach task force. After a period of stalling while waiting to see if the protests against the regents' decision would cause us to rescind it, all aspects of the university community have joined together to form partnerships with K-12 schools in California to help underperforming kids—and the results have been amazing.

One significant success story is at El Cerrito High School, a few miles away from UC Berkeley. Although El Cerrito High is 43 percent black, very few black students had traditionally enrolled in advanced math courses. In 1995, for instance, just twelve black students took those classes. But by 1998, there were thirty-nine, thanks to an after-school math tutorial program led by black UC students.

At Hoover Elementary School in Oakland, twenty minority first-grade students outscored second-graders in fourteen of sixteen categories on a standardized reading comprehension test. Why? Because these first-graders received tutorial assistance for a year from UC Berkeley students in reading and science. At Washington Elementary School in Richmond, a similar volunteer outreach effort helped to increase from 30 percent to 72 percent the number of first-graders scoring above the 50th percentile in standardized math tests.

What can we achieve with projects like these? Not long ago I saw a model outreach program in Los Angeles that may provide an answer. It is called the Neighborhood Academic Initiative and it was begun several years ago by Dr. James Fleming in partnership with the University of Southern California, which provides space and part of the funding for the program. The program recruits seventh-grade inner-city students bound for Manual Arts High School (only 25 percent of whose students perform at grade level). These students—all of them selected because they are "average" and otherwise would have little chance of attending college—are bused to the USC campus every day at 7:30 in the morning. They work on English and math with tutors until 9:30, when they are bused back to their home schools to take up their regular schoolwork.

Each student in the Neighborhood Academic Initiative has an academic counselor who helps with schoolwork and with personal and family problems standing in the way of success. The students' parents must attend a Family Development Institute meeting twice a month where they learn about parenting, family planning, and how to create a learning environment within the home. (As a result of these meetings, many of the parents have developed a newfound regard for learning and have themselves gone back to get a high school diploma).

If a child stays in the Neighborhood Academic Initiative throughout high school and gets decent grades and SAT scores, USC picks up the tab for a full scholarship for four years. If a student wants to go to another private college and is admitted, he or she receives financial assistance and is guaranteed a scholarship for two years of graduate study later on at USC.

Of the 140 kids to graduate so far from this unique program, only fifteen have not enrolled in college somewhere. Of the rest, twenty-nine are in junior colleges; sixty-one have taken advantage of USC's offer; another fourteen are at state colleges in California; seven are studying at one of the campuses of the University of California; and eight are in private colleges and universities including Yale, Cornell, and the University of Michigan.

All of these outreach programs involve immense effort. They make headway against the grain of liberal opinion, which, as it loses the battle on preferences, desperately turns its fire on standardized tests in a last ditch effort to cast doubt on the concept of merit and preserve what it calls "diversity." But the dedicated people who work in outreach programs such as those I've mentioned above, programs that *believe* in young people and their ability to overcome obstacles as they try to reach their full potential, have all seen a central truth: in our social world, "big" solutions often do more harm than good; we save people one life at a time. And they know that when the students they've helped arrive at Berkeley, USC, and all the other schools where they'll be admitted in the years to come, they will enter campus with full citizenship as individuals who have earned their way. And that will make all the difference in their world.

— —

I still hear every day that this debate over preferences has been divisive for America. Yes, it has allowed some racist voices, like those of David Duke, to be heard. But, it has also swept away the intimidating silence that previously shrouded this issue, a silence that was far worse than the present robust and occasionally rowdy dialogue. On the whole, this debate has in fact been good for our country. It has broken down the dangerous symbiosis between white guilt and black shame that Shelby Steele has described so well, a symbiosis in which white liberals get to feel moral by "saving" blacks, and blacks are affirmed in their righteous victimhood and given the sense that they are actually "owed" the handouts they receive from white liberalism. Now, the subject of preferences— and of this corrupt bargain between white liberals and their black allies—is no longer a taboo subject. And once it can be discussed freely, the end is near because discrimination is one of those pathologies—whatever its source or rationale—that can only thrive in the dark.

The debate about race preferences has changed our country. But the main change I've seen is in blacks themselves. I still get the killing looks—cold hard stares of contempt and hatred. But it is not as universal as it once was. Now the looks are sometimes questioning as well, indicating a curiosity and a willingness to talk further.

Not long ago, I was on Chris Rock's television show. To me, Rock is one of the funniest men alive and, certainly, one of the most gifted. I was wary about going into the ring with him and letting him cut me up with his sharp wit, and, as it worked out, he did get in some good hits. But I could tell he was not a party-liner on the issue of race preferences when he began hilarious riffs about why there should be affirmative action for people who were bald or short.

After the show, we shook hands and walked off the set. As Rock headed to his dressing room, he called back to me, "Well, you're half right, man."

"Which half?" I asked.

"The half which says that we should not lower standards for anybody," Rock answered. "People perform at the level that is expected of them. I believe I have to be twice as funny as Leno and Letterman just to be equal. That is not fair, but it keeps me on my toes."

To be even half right in the eyes of someone as sharp as Chris Rock feels good to me. And I have received more of this in recent days. I was boarding a plane recently when a black flight attendant recognized me and made eye contact. In the past, this has always meant trouble, and I steeled myself for an acidic comment or a cold shoulder. How could I sell out my people? she would probably ask. How could I be such a traitor? Wasn't I aware of how much blacks had *suffered?*

I was surprised, after we reached cruising altitude, when she came to my seat, bent down and whispered: "Know what? I agree with you."

A few moments later, after beverages were served, she returned, knelt beside me, and started a conversation. "I don't need someone telling me what they're going to do for me," she said after saying she had supported Proposition 209. "I'm comfortable with who I am, and I feel I can make it on my own."

Our talk went on in this vein for several minutes. Then, as someone rang the call button, she stood and patted me on the arm lightly and walked off, saying, "Don't let them get you down."

＊　＊

As I write these final pages, my daughter Tracy has just given birth to her first child, Katherine Brooke. Standing in the delivery room this morning holding this new addition to our family, I felt a rush of emotions. When I held my new granddaughter, the tiny hand grasping my brown fingers was white as snow, yet she was blood of my blood, life of my life—living proof that the categories that are supposed to separate us in this world are an illusion.

I wondered what kind of a life she would have; what she would feel about her background; what kind of pressures she would feel to declare herself as a member of one group or another; and which of the silly little boxes she would be required to check. But by the time she comes of age, God willing, perhaps all that will be a thing of the past.

As I looked at this wonderful baby, I felt a surge of hope and optimism. I had the thought that perhaps all of us, whatever our color, may yet get to that promised land Martin Luther King talked about. We'll certainly know it when we've arrived, because then we'll finally be able to get under each other's skin and see each other face to face at last.

APPENDIX

Text of the California Civil Rights Initiative,
Proposition 209, on the November 1996 ballot, passed by
54 percent of California voters

(a) The state shall not discriminate against, or grant preferential treatment to, any individual or group on the basis of race, sex, color, ethnicity, or national origin in the operation of public employment, public education, or public contracting.

(b) This section shall apply only to action taken after the section's effective date.

(c) Nothing in this section shall be interpreted as prohibiting bona fide qualifications based on sex which are reasonably necessary to the normal operation of public employment, public education, or public contracting.

(d) Nothing in this section shall be interpreted as invalidating any court order or consent decree which is in force as of the effective date of this section.

(e) Nothing in this section shall be interpreted as prohibiting action which must be taken to establish or maintain eligibility for any federal program, where ineligibility would result in a loss of federal funds to the state.

(f) For the purposes of this section, "state" shall include, but not necessarily be limited to, the state itself, any city, county, city and county, public university system, including the University of California, community college district, school district, special district, or any other political subdivision or governmental instrumentality of or within the state.

(g) The remedies available for violations of this section shall be the same, regardless of the injured party's race, sex, color, ethnicity, or national origin, as are otherwise available for violations of then-existing California antidiscrimination law.

(h) This section shall be self-executing. If any part or parts of this section are found to be in conflict with federal law or the United State Constitution, the section shall be implemented to the maximum extent that federal law and the United States Constitution permit. Any provision held invalid shall be severable from the remaining portions of this section.

AUTHOR'S NOTE

When you have lived a life chock full of rich experiences—and you have lived it "your way"—you find that when the day comes to settle the score, the fuller the life, the greater the sense of indebtedness to other people. In my own case, I am deeply indebted to many.

My wife Ilene has been the wind beneath my wings. Her moral strength, her efforts to shield our children from the adverse publicity that has surrounded my high profile campaign, and her competence in running our business have enabled me to do what I have done. If I have made a contribution to advance the cause of equal rights in our nation, her contribution is as much as mine.

My children Marc and Tracy have blessed me with their support. The fact does not escape me that their mother deserves most of the credit for this accomplishment.

Dusty Rhodes has been a true friend and partner in leading this equal rights movement, which might have ended at the California border if not for his vision, insight and leadership.

The Lynde and Harry Bradley Foundation made a generous grant that enabled me to write this book. Without that assistance and especially the support of Mike Joyce, this product would probably still be languishing in my word processor.

Throughout my campaign to promote the concept of true equality, I was sometimes criticized for being supported by "conservative" organizations. In fact, there is not one donor who has ever asked me to modify a position or pursue a strategy based on their ideology. I proudly acknowledge our major supporters, because I know from first-hand experience how much they want to do what is best for America—Glenn and Rita Campbell, B.A "Blue" Grassfield, John Uhlmann, Terry and Mary Kohler, Edward Pawlick, Theodore and Vada Stanley, Richard Gilder, William Dunn, Ray Zemon, Bruce Kovner, T.J. Rogers of Cypress Semiconductor, Paul Singer, K. Rupert Murdoch, Tom Stewart, Virginia Gilder, Richard Scaife, The John William Pope Foundation, Charles Stine of the Montgomery Street Foundation, the William H. Donner Foundation, Heather Higgins of the Randolph Foundation, John M. Olin Foundation, Sarah Scaife Foundation, and the Lynde and Harry Bradley Foundation: These individuals and foundations have very different perspectives on specific issues. What they have in common is the desire to make this nation a better place.

I know it hasn't been easy for my staff at Connerly & Associates to come to work and find themselves having to contend with a horde of photographers and journalists on many occasions. Thanks for understanding and being supportive.

My staff at the American Civil Rights Institute—Adrianna Barajas, Matthew Davenport, Caroline Kreling, Robyn Miller, Kevin Nguyen and Royce Van Tassell—binds this whole enterprise together. Their contribution to the "equal rights movement," (as Ed Blum so accurately describes it) has been significant.

I also want to acknowledge my fellow UC Regents—Clair Burgener, Glenn Campbell, Frank Clark, John Davies, Tirso del Junco, Sue Johnson, Meredith Khachigian, Leo Kolligian, Howard Leach, David Lee, Velma Montoya, Stephen Nakashima, Dean Watkins, and Pete Wilson. They have taken much criticism for their courageous stand on July 20, 1995 in voting in favor of SP-1. Although I regret being the source of that discomfort, I never have a moment's doubt that history will judge us kindly for being the first public agency in America to vote in favor of returning our great university to the principle of equal treatment, and, more importantly, for our vigorous pursuit of outreach activities that truly seek to provide equal opportunity to all students.

I have never met Shelby Steele or Thomas Sowell, but their writings were my philosophical compass on the issue of affirmative action long before I entered the battle in 1994. Their work shows that the written word has enormous power to inspire and give focus to black kids who are willing to think "outside the box" and show them that they are not alone in wanting to question the mind-numbing rhetoric they are dosed out every day of their lives.

Peter Collier's insight and talents are to be found on every page of this book. He steered this project and helped identify those events, people and experiences that have helped to shape me. I am in his debt.

Finally, I ask librarians and bookstore owners not to put *Creating Equal* in the African American section, and I thank God for letting me be born and raised in a country where I could have such a rich and fulfilling life.

INDEX